French Westerns

For Mom and Dad

French Westerns

On the Frontier of Film Genre and French Cinema

Timothy Scheie

Edinburgh University Press is one of the leading university presses in the UK. We publish academic books and journals in our selected subject areas across the humanities and social sciences, combining cutting-edge scholarship with high editorial and production values to produce academic works of lasting importance. For more information visit our website: edinburghuniversitypress.com

© Timothy Scheie, 2024, 2025

Grateful acknowledgement is made to the sources listed in the List of Illustrations for permission to reproduce material previously published elsewhere. Every effort has been made to trace the copyright holders, but if any have been inadvertently overlooked, the publisher will be pleased to make the necessary arrangements at the first opportunity.

Edinburgh University Press Ltd
13 Infirmary Street
Edinburgh EH1 1LT

First published in hardback by Edinburgh University Press 2024

Typeset in Arno and Myriad
by Manila Typesetting Company

A CIP record for this book is available from the British Library

ISBN 978 1 3995 2037 9 (hardback)
ISBN 978 1 3995 2038 6 (paperback)
ISBN 978 1 3995 2039 3 (webready PDF)
ISBN 978 1 3995 2040 9 (epub)

The right of Timothy Scheie to be identified as the author of this work has been asserted in accordance with the Copyright, Designs and Patents Act 1988, and the Copyright and Related Rights Regulations 2003 (SI No. 2498).

Contents

List of figures vii
Acknowledgements ix

Introduction 1

PART I FRENCH + WESTERN
1. *Ce genre qui n'en est pas un* 13
2. Imagined (and unimaginable) communities of film 28

PART II THE WILD, WILD *MIDI*
3. The curious geographies of Arizona Bill 41
4. The modernity of tradition and the cinematic Camargue 62
5. The return of the western repressed 80

PART III *CHEZ NOUS* ON THE RANGE
6. Little colony on the prairie 101
7. The language of stars on the francophone frontier 121
8. Cowboy and alien: the Bardot western 137

PART IV THE BAGUETTE WESTERN
9. Spaghetti and camembert 163
10. East meets west(ern) 179

Epilogue	205
Bibliography	214
Filmography	228
Index	233

Figures

3.1	Pre-release advertisement for *The Mong-Fu Tong*. Source: *Moving Picture World*, 13 August 1913.	49
3.2	A cowboy in a car: Hamman prepares to jump in *The Mong-Fu Tong*. The Library of Congress.	51
3.3	A bid to astonish: Bill's leap off the moving train in *The Last Minute*. The Library of Congress.	55
4.1	Riders of the world – and two electric plants. The Library of Congress.	70
5.1	Homage to John Ford.	84
5.2	'Miss Cow-boy' and 'Tom Mix'.	86
5.3	Huguette and Frédé (on the fence) take in the show.	87
5.4	Nowhere to hide: Johnny is pursued through a *noir* Paris.	89
5.5	Johnny sings of a new life under brilliant blue skies.	90
5.6	Johnny returns to Paris on foot.	93
6.1	Fernand's struggle with English.	110
6.2	A francophone future?	116
7.1	Mariano as a singing cowboy.	125
7.2	A Parisian in America.	126
7.3	French speech, English writing.	131
7.4	Antoine and Jack converse.	132
8.1	Bardot in *Viva Maria!*: 'a man's role'.	142
8.2	Moreau and Bardot: the hunters, not the prey.	144
8.3	*Shane*, the 'guiding light'.	145
8.4	The retro-Hollywood bid.	145
8.5	Having a 'lovely time' speaking English.	150
8.6	Bardot as Frenchie King.	151

8.7	The *duel d'actrices*.	154
9.1	Spaghetti-style framing.	170
9.2	The determined widow.	174
9.3	*Pietà*: Maria's dying disclosures.	176
10.1	'I am General Motors!'	191
10.2	Just an image: Cohn-Bendit at the *assemblée générale*.	197

Acknowledgements

Preparing a monograph can seem a solitary endeavour, especially during the confinement of a pandemic, but I was far from alone. I thank all who supported and encouraged me.

Sections of this book expand on previously published material. Chapters 3 and 4 include passages from 'Genre in Transitional Cinema: "Arizona Bill" and the Silent French Western 1912–1914', *French Forum* 36, nos. 2–3 (Spring & Fall 2011). The article 'Chez nous on the Range: Language, Genre and the Vernacular French Western (1956–1961)', which appeared in *Screen* 57, no. 3 (Autumn 2016), is reworked as part of Chapters 6 and 7. Chapter 8 is a revision of 'Cowboy and Alien: the Bardot Western', *Studies in French Cinema* 19, no. 2 (2019).

The Eastman School of Music provided funds for my research activities, and I thank Donna Brink Fox and the Professional Development Committee. A number of institutions opened their archives to me, including the *Cinémathèque française*. Others facilitated the viewing of prints of films that were not otherwise available: the *Centre national du cinéma et de l'image animée* (CNC) in Bois d'Arcy, the Library of Congress's Moving Image Section in Washington and the George Eastman Museum in Rochester (special thanks to Jared Case). The Terra Foundation for American Art, in conjunction with the Institut National de l'Histoire de l'Art, funded travel to Paris to participate in the *journées d'étude*, organised by Emily Burns, on French perspectives on the American West.

The late David Pendleton introduced me to the serious study of westerns. Sue Matheson provided a timely nudge with a request to submit further research to the 'Film and History' conference. Elise Leahy and Dolly Weber invited me to their campuses to speak on French cinema, and Cheryl Krueger was present and encouraging as I wrote the first lines of this book. I thank my colleagues at the Eastman School of Music, a singular community of scholars, artists and teachers. I am grateful for a richness of enduring and sustaining friendships. Finally, I thank Craig Sellers, my primary interlocuter, editor, nurse and husband, for his immeasurable support.

Introduction

In a 1913 letter to the editors of *Le Courrier cinématographique*, cinema pioneer Georges Méliès contests the suggestion, made in a previous issue, that his company's American affiliate is not French. Noting both his French nationality and that of his brother Gaston, who managed the American branch, Méliès proudly observes that the *Maison Méliès* once had the distinction of being one of only two French firms licensed to access the technologies and distribution rights of the Motion Pictures Patent Company (Thomas Edison's 'Trust').[1] After characterising Gaston's operation as 'a French firm planted in America, and making, on site, American subjects', he asserts: 'Being, as you know, one of the oldest founders of our industry, I am absolutely determined to render unto France what is French; to each his pride, no?'[2]

A number of ironies attend Méliès's good-natured bout of pique, not least the fact that the firm he revindicates for France had, in 1913, all but ceased to exist: Gaston and his outfit had left America, and Méliès himself was bankrupt and no longer made films. The evidence he cites to support his claim further undercuts its decisiveness. The firm's prior participation in a multinational trust that regulated finances, technologies and networks of distribution would seem more starkly to show how, from its earliest years, film production has been enmeshed in a global industry that overflows the decisive national frame he is seeking to enforce. Moreover, the Méliès Company previously promoted not the French provenance but the authentic Americanness of *The Redemption of Rawhide* (1911), *The Immortal Alamo* (1911), *The Spring Round-Up* (1911) and at least 70 other western-themed films in which Gaston's outfit specialised.[3] Filming on location at the Star Film Ranch in San Antonio and later in California, with American actors and directors (including Francis Ford, John Ford's brother), Gaston distributed his 'American subjects' under the name 'American Wildwest'[4] and advertised them as the 'real, genuine article' of the American West.[5]

Méliès seems to want it both ways: to produce authentically American 'subjects', which at the time were just becoming known as 'westerns', and to claim them as French films. And why not? The American West is a rich subject with deep roots in French literary and popular culture. French-language evocations of the North American wilderness include canonical works of French literature, among them l'Abbé Prévost's *Manon Lescaut* (1731), whose title character dies in the wilds of the Louisiana territory, and René de Chateaubriand's *Atala* (1801), a Romantic declension of the 'noble savage' invoked by Jean-Jacques Rousseau. A more popular literature draws even closer to narratives, characters and situations that are recognisable as westerns. Gabriel Ferry's *Le Coureur des bois* and Gustave Aimard's many novels set in the North American wilderness contributed to a steady stream of fiction inspired by the enthusiastic reception of James Fenimore Cooper's *Leatherstocking Tales* in France.[6] At the *fin-de-siècle*, two extensive European tours of Buffalo Bill's *Wild West* sparked unprecedented interest in the American West and fuelled the mass production and consumption of dime novels, fascicules and early comic books, many of them based on the life and exploits of Cody himself. In the twentieth century, a taste for the American West has driven the publication of a vast number of titles in *bande dessinée (BD)* albums (akin to comic books and graphic novels), and new western-themed *BD* series continue to be launched in the twenty-first century.

With the advent of cinema, French filmmakers, too, found the narratives, situations and characters of the American West ripe for exploitation. Early silent films made in the Fontainebleau forest and the Camargue region on the Mediterranean coast count among the first westerns made anywhere, and before World War I the Pathé, Méliès and Éclair studios had subsidiaries making western films in the United States. In the sound era, western-themed vehicles featured some of the most visible French stars of their day: Luis Mariano and Jeanne Moreau each made one, Johnny Hallyday and Fernandel starred in at least two (or more, depending on how one counts), and Brigitte Bardot made three. Directors who worked with the western genre include bankable regulars of mainstream cinema Richard Pottier and Christian-Jaque, and also 'art cinema' auteurs Louis Malle and Jean-Luc Godard. There are French co-productions made in the Italian spaghetti western style, and the *bande dessinée* inspired transpositions of its cowboy heroes to the screen in both animated and live-action features, including twenty-first-century versions of the popular *Blueberry* and *Lucky Luke* series with internationally known stars Vincent Cassel and Jean Dujardin in the title roles. The 1970s saw the release of French pornographic films with western themes, and the French parody of American westerns dates from the early silent era. Depending on the criteria for inclusion, 'The French western' may count hundreds of films whose production spans the history of cinema.[7]

Nevertheless, by positioning the western genre as an enunciation of a French cinema, Méliès conjures an unwonted strain of film. Even in 1913, at the only moment in history when French-owned firms were regularly producing western-themed films, a defensive Méliès is compelled to explain and, when necessary, to force the cinematic conjunction of 'French' and 'western'. The Méliès Company's production of westerns was short-lived, but the dissonant note struck by the cinematic meeting of 'French' and 'western' reverberated for far longer. The end of the serial production of western-themed films in France in 1914 only augments the surprise of this coupling. '*French westerns?!*' an incredulous Lucille Ball blurts to Charles Boyer nearly forty years later in a televised episode of *I Love Lucy*, the humour of the line deriving from a lack of purchase so complete that the very notion rings absurd.[8] This sentiment is not exclusively aroused by an American perspective, and over the years it has echoed widely on both sides of the Atlantic in popular and scholarly discourse. The pre-1914 films are here the exception, and the silent production in the Camargue region has drawn serious interest.[9] Elsewhere commentary on 'The French western' is scarce, often disparaging, and rarely more than a list of titles.[10] Individual films may draw attention in press reviews upon their release or in studies of their director or star, but as a group the prevalent treatment has been to overlook them altogether. The present author may attest, from ample experience, that the conjoining of 'French' and 'western' continues to strike interlocuters in both France and America as a surprise, a meaningless or grotesque coupling, or, as in Lucy's case, a joke. Films that have been called both 'French' and 'western' may exist, but one may also comfortably submit, at least for films after 1914, that as a collective designation with recognised meaning and discursive currency 'The French western' does not.

A book that opens with the assertion of its subject's non-existence might seem a fanciful undertaking. However, a central claim of this study will be that the French western, hereafter a term to be understood under erasure even without quotes, becomes a compelling object of study precisely because of the dissonances that volatilise its two constitutive components. The tensions that inhere in this cinematic pairing work to destabilise the integrity of the western genre and of the French cinematic referent, and at times push the logics of both to the threshold of incoherence. However, the discordances that resound at this zone of contact between a national cinema and a film genre do not announce unqualified failure. They also generate possibilities for cinematic practice, lend dimension to a film and at times hone a critical edge that would otherwise be lacking. The present project is therefore not to bring the French western into existence, but to examine what its non-existence reveals and enables.

How to study what does not exist?

The task, as it has been framed above, immediately encounters a basic conundrum: which films and cinematic practices will draw attention? Establishing a critical filmography is fraught enough with confidence that a genre exists, but conventional methods, however provisional, are here foreclosed. Definitions of the western derived from 'classical' Hollywood production risk allowing very few French films, in the extreme none at all. Recourse to empirically observed characteristics is inconclusive: the premise that the genre in question does not cohere, and that this failure constitutes its interest, precludes the identification of core defining traits. Shifting focus to the discursive realm to examine how the genre has previously been enunciated is unreliable when discourse is generally tacit on the subject, explicitly denies the existence of the French western, or traces a footprint that is faint and blurred, 'faux' and hyphenated, or otherwise derivative and insignificant. Representative lists of films that best meet requisite measures of 'Frenchness' and 'westernness' seem foredoomed.

On the other hand, a permissive approach that embraces all concurrent instances of 'Frenchness' and 'westernness' will cover a vast swathe of cinematic practice. The horseback chase in the opening section of Abel Gance's *Napoléon* invokes similar chases in silent western production, Jean Renoir's *Le Crime de Monsieur Lange* sets a fictional western serial in a film whose narrative and style otherwise bear greater affinities to the gangster genre, and films set in South America or colonial settings may share a certain 'syntax' and 'semantics' with westerns. Similar questions are raised by a film's Frenchness: no film, arguably, follows all of the vectors along which the nation may be enunciated in cinema, and a transnational perspective on the institution of cinema may reveal any film to be only conditionally French. If the French western stages the spectacle of the inherent instability and incompleteness of its two constitutive terms, by what criteria could a film with any degree of both be excluded? More restrictive measures for inclusion – fixed bars for what is French enough and western enough – will effectively resolve the tensions that, it is being argued, constitute the interest of the study.

These tensions, and not their resolution, have been allowed to shape the purview of the following sections and chapters. Certain films and practices amplify these dissonances and bring them into relief. A substantial measure of both 'Frenchness' and 'westernness' may augment these discordances, but they also resonate in films that less surely qualify as western or as French. When these dissonances resound with a similar tonality, it is possible to observe commonalities among certain films. This study took form around groups of films that expose like contradictions when evocations of the western encounter others that are registered as French: in filmed landscapes, in cultural and regional traditions, in language use, in stardom, and in relation to a singular moment in French political and cultural history. These groupings, and the questions they raise, became the focus of the book's sections. The commonalities between the films therefore determine the organisation of this study more than strict chronology, and while the first chapter begins with early cinema and the epilogue bears on twenty-first-century production, there is also overlap, at times significant, in the time periods discussed throughout.

This project is therefore not a comprehensive survey of 'The French western' and holds no promise of encyclopaedic inclusivity. Indeed, under its terms such coverage would be impossible, as the field of study has no stable centre or margins. If another author undertook this project, even under similar premises, the filmography would almost certainly look different. Certain omissions may surprise some readers. *Gli specialisti* (*The Specialists*, Sergio Corbucci, 1969) and *Soleil rouge* (*Red Sun*, Terence Young, 1971) have sometimes been called 'baguette' westerns in the Italian spaghetti vein; the terms under which these multinational co-productions may be called 'French' are also contested.[11] There is plenty to say about the Eddie Constantine vehicle *Chien de pique* (*Jack of Spades*, Yves Allégret, 1960), a gangster film set in a western-tinged

Camargue. However, a close examination of other films already exposes the intersections of stardom, western tropes, Camargue filming locations and the post-war French film industry's dialogue with American popular culture; a reading of *Chien de pique* would, in this discussion, have been driven primarily by a bid for coverage. Likewise, the characterisation of the early silent films by the Eclipse studio would in many respects describe their contemporaries produced by the Gaumont company, but it was the Eclipse films that first revealed to me the unstable diegesis of the pre-1914 westerns. Although the choice to focus on them is somewhat personal, it is not arbitrary: the Eclipse films are under-studied relative to their Gaumont contemporaries, and their distribution, marketing and reception in the United States bring a further dimension to the contradictions they harbour. If it was chance that these films 'spoke' to me first, they did so in a compelling manner.

The first section opens with a critical survey, in Chapter 1, of the theoretical and discursive gestures that have historically hampered the emergence of the French western as a recognised category of film. Chapter 2 then aligns this volatility with more recent epistemologies of film genres, national cinemas and transnational cinematic flows. The purpose is to locate the French western's specificity at the destabilising encounter of a genre and a national cinema, and to position this tension as a critical lens for considering the cinema that has been practised at this site of contact.

The remaining chapters, divided thematically into sections, each include the reading of a film or group of films. They begin with three chapters on the production of western-themed films made in the Camargue region of southern France. The first of these studies bears on pre-1914 production. Instead of positioning these films as an early consolidation of the French western, or even of the western more generally (these films have been hailed as the first westerns ever made), I identify the constitutive contradictions that condition their production, distribution and reception. Two surviving films from the 'Arizona Bill' cycle present a discordance between the region's distinct landscape and continuity in the western narrative. In this period between the earliest years of cinema and the integration of the 'classical' narrative film style, the diegetic setting of a fiction film could remain unstable; it is not always clear whether the narrative of these films is unfolding in contemporary (1913–1914) France or on the American frontier decades earlier. This ambiguity may appear primitive by later standards of continuity, but it is also permissive and may be considered an asset in this 'transitional' mode of cinema: the appeal of these films, I submit, lies less in a convincing or decisive rendering of either America or of France than in the surplus attraction the indeterminacy allows. The following chapter traces how the western inflection remains constitutive of the picturesque cinematic Camargue in subsequent decades. Even as this nostalgic setting appears to eliminate the western element that sowed ambiguity in earlier productions, the spectacle of the American West informs the filmed traditions, people and landscapes represented in regional dramas in the 1920s and 1930s. In the post-1945 films examined in the final chapter of this section, explicit evocations of the American West are again invested in the cinematic Camargue. A reading of these films exposes how both western tradition and American-style modernisation return not as an alien element, but as tropes and situations that were, effectively, already at home in filmed representations of this setting.

In the following section, the focus lies on star vehicles that exploit the dissonance between a French performer and a film genre that, historically, has strongly been identified as American. Like film genres, the 'star system' is often associated with studio-era Hollywood, and stardom in France may be considered both derivative of and distinct from its American counterpart. Manipulation of language is a crucial constituent of a star performer's persona and, because it is often lost in translation (dubbing, subtitling), it also divides the global audience's perceptions of a 'star image'. While the conceit of having a French citizen travel to the American West provides the alibi for a star's French speech, it also becomes the agent of ambiguity in displays of both 'Frenchness' and 'westernness'. In Chapter 5, I study how the logic of this ploy stumbles when it meets the tropes, settings and situations of the western, with focus on the registration of race and ethnicity in the speech of Native American characters. In Chapter 6, an examination of post-World War II star vehicles exposes how the exigencies of stardom compete with those of genre, resulting in licence for discordance and the spectacle of a francophone frontier straining under the weight of these inconsistencies. The third chapter of this section is an examination of three films that stage the encounter of Brigitte Bardot, the French language and the western genre. Bardot's blazing stardom had international appeal, and she has been named the emblem of a cosmopolitan, transatlantic film culture. However, these films also reveal how her manipulation of language, both in French and imperfect English, resists organising logic, be it of a French assertion, of the Hollywood western or of a transnational 'Frenchness' that would supersede them. In her westerns, Bardot is at once the face of transnational cooperation and of a failure to translate that is both figurative and literal.

The focus in the final section lies on two nominally French films whose production and reception play out against both the rising popularity of the 'international' western and the events of the May 1968 uprising in France. Robert Hossein's *Cemetery Without Crosses* (*Une corde, un colt*, 1969) is a venture into the Italian spaghetti western style produced with the support and participation of the cycle's leading figure, Sergio Leone. With an established pairing of French stars (Hossein and Michèle Mercier), a French director, predominantly French dialogue, an initial release in France and the evocation of a tragic mode, the film enunciates a French cinematic assertion along plural vectors that distinguish it from other co-productions that have been identified as 'baguette' or 'camembert' westerns. In doing so, it nonetheless fails to speak to the watershed event in French social and cultural history that conditioned the climate of its release. Hossein's film contrasts sharply with an experiment that could easily be called an anti-western, or even anti-cinema. In the Dziga Vertov Group's *Wind from the East* (*Le Vent d'est*, 1969) the western genre, in both its Hollywood and Italian iterations, is presented as the foremost emblem of an irredeemable mode of cinematic representation. However, insofar as the genre this film eviscerates is also positioned as a French enunciation, specifically as a cinematic response to May 1968 issued by participants in the uprising, the western not only acts as the target of the critique but, through its dissonance in a French mode, adds dimension to the critical estrangement of familiar cinematic practices. To conclude this study, an epilogue traces how the western genre's friction with French cinema persists into the twenty-first century to act both as a provocation and a generator of possibilities.

It may be an overdue gesture, at this point, to acknowledge an irony in this project as it is framed. The act of moving the French western out of the shadows, of asserting that it merits attention, of naming it and analysing the representational strategies of a selection of films, may work to bring a 'genre that does not exist' into existence. The focus on certain films may contribute to a discursive sedimentation that, if there be further inquiry, accumulates, builds and possibly hardens into a recognised corpus for which dissonances, tensions and volatility were once the interest. Perhaps. The present emphasis remains on the diversity and discontinuity of this production, and on how it disrupts a coherent integration of 'French' or 'western' that would explain these films. With its oblique and sometimes obtuse eloquence, the French western exposes instability in ideations of national cinema and film genre that have elsewhere been deemed more solid, more grounded, more necessary. The French western has lacked such necessity, and what this lack has allowed is the focus of this study.

Notes

1. 'Deux Maisons Françaises seules sont titulaires des licences Edison: la Maison Pathé et la nôtre, uniquement parce que nous étions établis l'un et l'autre à New York, avant la création des licences, et que, par conséquent, nous avions droit de cité, à cette époque, en Amérique, tout en étant bien français.' ('Only two French firms are holders of the Edison licences: the Pathé firm and ours, solely because we were both established in New York before the creation of the licence, and consequently had full and legitimate rights, at the time, in America, even though we were quite French.') Georges Méliès, letter to the editor, *Le Courrier cinématographique* (10 January 1913): 42. Translations are by the author, unless otherwise noted.
2. 'Une maison française installée en Amérique, et fabricant, sur place, des sujets américains [. . .] Etant, comme vous le savez, un des plus anciens fondateurs de notre industrie, je tiens absolument à rendre à la France ce qui est à la France; chacun a son amour-propre, n'est-ce pas?' Ibid.
3. The three films listed are believed to have been directed by William Haddock.
4. Elizabeth Ezra, *Georges Méliès* (Manchester and New York: Manchester University Press, 2000), 18. Madeleine Malthête-Méliès recounts that Gaston founded 'American Wildwest' as an independent operation, initially unbeknownst to his brother in Paris. Madeleine Malthête-Méliès, *Méliès l'enchanteur* (Paris: Editions Ramsey, 1983), 333.
5. Paul Hammond, *Marvelous Méliès* (London: Gordon Fraser, 1974), 74.
6. Ferry's novel was published in 1853 and later revised for a younger readership. Gustave Aimard (Olivier Gloux) wrote over forty novels, many of them about the American West. Other authors who represent the American West include Paul Duplessis, Louis-Xavier Eyma, Benedict-Henri Révoil and Albert Robida. On this production see Paul Bleton, *Western, France: la place de l'Ouest dans l'imaginaire français* (Paris: Les Belles Lettres, 2002); Mark Wolff, 'Western novels as children's literature in nineteenth-century France', *Mosaic: A Journal for the Interdisciplinary Study of Literature* 34, no. 2 (June 2001): 87–102; and Daryl Lee, 'Robida's Mormons', *Transatlantica* 2 (2017). Available at <http://journals.openedition.org/transatlantica/10869> (accessed 20 February 2021).
7. Jean-François Giré lists over 200 films in his survey of French films with western themes and imagery. See Jean-François Giré, *Il était une fois. . .le western européen: 1901–2008* (Paris: Bazaar & Co., 2008); and the second volume *Il était une fois. . .le western européen volume 2: Les dernières chevauchées du western* (Paris: Bazaar & Co., 2012). Giré's account will be revisited in Chapter 1.
8. 'Lucy Meets Charles Boyer', *I Love Lucy* season 5, episode 19, directed by James V. Kern, written by Jess Oppenheimer et al., aired 5 March 1956.
9. See, in particular, the work of Bernard Bastide, including *Aux sources du cinéma en Camargue: Joë Hamman et Folco de Baroncelli*, Avignon: Palais du Roure, 2018;

Estelle Rouquette and Sam Stourdzé, eds, *Western Camarguais* (Arles: Actes Sud, 2016); and Gergory Mohr, 'The French Camargue Western', in *Crossing Frontiers: Intercultural Perspectives on the Western*, ed. Peter W. Schulze, Thomas Klein and Ivo Ritzer, 87–95 (Marburg: Schüren Verlag, 2015). Some of the early Gaumont westerns films have been released on DVD and are widely accessible. *Le Cinéma premier, volume 2*, directed by Emile Cohl, Jean Durand, Pierre Phillipe et al. (1907–1916, Neuilly-sur-Seine: Gaumont Vidéo, 2009), DVD. The terms under which a regional drama set in the Camargue may be called a western are contested despite explicit invocations of cowboys, lassos and sheriffs. The relation of the cinematic Camargue to the American western will be examined in Chapters 3, 4 and 5.
10. There are rare exceptions. See Chapters 1 and 3.
11. In its DVD re-release, *Gli specialisti* has been marketed under the rubric 'Great Italian Westerns' (*I Grandi Western Italiani*).

I
French + Western

1

Ce genre qui n'en est pas un

Distinctions between film genres and among national cinemas have long been important parameters in the ordering of knowledge about film. Library call numbers, university courses, conference panels and published scholarship have circumscribed national cinemas and film genres as areas of study, and continue to do so even as the presumed stability of both yields to critical pressure.[1] This historical partition of knowledge may seem to favour the study of the French western film, which would find footing in two broad domains of film criticism and theory. However, both fields have proven inhospitable, even hostile, to the study of these films. To understand the pressures that hold the French western under erasure, it is helpful first to examine the discourses that have failed to accommodate this encounter between a national cinema and an emblematic film genre. They include characterisations of film genre, of French cinema and, more recently, of transnational cinematic practices even when they bear directly on the western.

The theorisation of film genre has tended, strongly, to favour American cinema through a primary focus on studio-era Hollywood production. This trend is particularly conspicuous in Anglo-American criticism.[2] In the opening of *Genre and Hollywood*, Steve Neale concedes that 'most of the writing on genre and genres in the cinema has focused on the feature film and Hollywood'.[3] The book's title signals that Neale's study will be no exception, and intentionally so: there are compelling reasons for the close association of film genres with Hollywood. The American film industry thrived on the mass production of 'commercial feature films which, through repetition and variation, tell familiar stories with familiar characters in familiar situations'.[4] Rick Altman, who similarly places focus on Hollywood production in his study of genre, observes how the industrial organisation of the studios promoted strong 'genrification' through marketing, cultivation of star images and managing audience expectations.[5] Films from other sites and modes of production are not necessarily excluded from these discussions: a genre theorist might acknowledge *The Cabinet of Dr Caligari* as a foundational work of horror cinema, the importance of Italian production for the western genre, the prolific production of martial arts films from Hong Kong, or the proto-noirness of French films of the 1930s. However, these films, important as they may be within their genres, do not participate in Hollywood's strong and enduring 'genre system', whose singular scale, mode of production and worldwide commercial success led to the privileging of American feature films in studies of film genre. As late as 2009 a film scholar could observe that 'film genre study was, and for the most part still is, synonymous with Hollywood cinema'.[6]

A primary focus on Hollywood features holds genre markers in other modes of film production, in France as elsewhere, to a touchstone against which they almost inexorably measure deficient, derivative, or of diminished importance. Even as he argues that distinct conventions and patterns exist in French contemporaries to studio-era films, Colin Crisp concedes that 'conventional elements as developed within [French cinema] seldom coalesced into the *recurrent arrays of related conventions* that are necessary for a genre to begin to exist in the minds of filmmakers and spectators'.[7] The French categories contemporaneous to studio-era Hollywood that Crisp identifies (realism, comedy, *film d'atmosphère*) may appear by comparison broad and ill-defined, while others (Military Vaudeville) are meaningless in an Anglo-American context. Responding to the emphasis on Hollywood, Raphaëlle Moine does not contest that unstable markets, geo-political disruptions and the lack of large-scale industrial production in France led to disruptions in production, less homogenous outcomes and less consistency in genre groupings. However, she also observes how the critical lens honed to bring clarity to Hollywood production may distort or blur genre markers when it is trained on other cinemas: 'when critics fail to find a structured system of genres like that of the studios, they too quickly deduce an absence or weakness of a generic regime, when, in fact, it may not be organised to the same logical system'.[8] Genres may exist in French cinema, but they act differently and invite consideration on their own terms.

The western, enduring and prolific, holds pride of place as the *locus classicus* of Hollywood studio production in the theorisation of film genre.

This status is already evident in two early accounts of film genre, one from an Anglo-American perspective and the other French. Both stake out a discursive terrain that has proven averse to westerns made elsewhere, and to French films specifically. These texts have been seminal for the study not only of the western but of film genre more broadly, are widely cited, and will be familiar to some readers.[9] A re-examination of their terms will underscore specifically how they, and much of the commentary in their wake, inhibit the meeting of 'French' and 'western'.

Robert Warshow's 1954 essay 'Movie Chronicle: the Westerner' is hailed as ground-breaking for its serious examination of two genres, gangster films and westerns, that were previously deemed beneath 'intelligent commentary'.[10] Focusing on the figure of the western hero, Warshow traces the genre's organic evolution (its 'natural' development) from its 'unsophisticated' phase to an 'aestheticised' state evident in *Stagecoach* (John Ford, 1939), *Destry Rides Again* (George Marshall, 1939) and *My Darling Clementine* (John Ford, 1946), and even more pronounced in new releases like *High Noon* (Fred Zinnemann, 1952), *The Gunfighter* (Henry King, 1950) and *Shane* (George Stevens, 1953).[11] Thematic and evolutionary accounts of genre development (primitive origins, development, classic phase, decadence) are, as noted below, contested. A more enduring legacy lies in the canon of films that anchors Warshow's characterisations. In subsequent studies, new releases supplement his filmography,[12] but for decades English-language scholarship on the western dwelt assiduously on the same titles Warshow lists. John Cawelti's *Six-Gun Mystique*, one of the earliest scholarly studies of the genre, has a lengthy appendix of 'major and representative westerns', but *High Noon*, *Shane* and John Ford's oeuvre count among the few films cited by name in the analysis.[13] A few years later, in *Sixguns and Society*, Will Wright's data-driven criterion (films that grossed over 4 million dollars in North America) broadens the field of inquiry, but also guarantees the inclusion of these same feature films. Some are singled out for more extensive commentary, while other modes – the silents, the vast 'B' production, nearly all non-Hollywood pictures – are a priori excluded from the data set. Jane Tompkins's and Lee Clark Mitchell's investigations of gender dynamics in westerns place focus on a select swathe of films that includes *High Noon*, *Shane*, and Ford's films.[14] In Richard Slotkin's influential *Gunfighter Nation: The Myth of the Frontier in Twentieth-Century America*, many western films are named but far fewer draw sustained commentary, among them, again, *High Noon*, *Shane*, and Ford's *Stagecoach* and *My Darling Clementine*. The full filmographies of these and other studies vary according to their purviews and purposes, and may be extensive. They also evince how, out of the profusion of western films, the characterisation of the genre has long tended to privilege a nucleus of A-list Hollywood features with top-drawer stars, eminent directors and a good number of Academy Awards between them.

Here, the Italian westerns of Sergio Leone may stand out as evidence that the purview of these studies extends beyond Hollywood to accommodate other modes of production. Despite scorn from some quarters, Leone's films were so popular and profitable they could not be ignored: Leone's *The Good, the Bad and the Ugly* (1966), for example, was the only foreign film to meet Wright's 4-million-dollar threshold.[15] However, Leone's films may also be considered an exception that proves the rule. The immense *Cinecittà* studio rivalled its American counterparts in size and had the resources to produce films on a scale that favoured genres and cycles, or *filone* as this Italian mode of production is known. With American stars (Clint Eastwood, Henry Fonda) and a production facility modelled on Hollywood studios, Leone's films could join the short list of American features that anchor characterisations of the western in a way that a film produced outside such large-scale and centralised production – a western made in France, for example – could not. Furthermore, a small group of Leone's films (the *Dollars* trilogy, *Once Upon a Time in the West*) has become the emblematic expression of the Italian *filone* even though, due to their success and their exponentially increasing budgets, they, too, are exceptional and in many respects unrepresentative of the broader spaghetti corpus.[16]

Relying on a narrow slice of prestige productions to gauge a film genre's typicity no longer goes unchallenged. Noting 'extreme selectivity' in the entrenched canons against which other modes of production appear degraded, devalued or denatured, Barry Langford observes how this 'unrepresentative sample' distorts characterisations of a genre. The western, again, serves as the signal example. Langford suggests that classic films, like those cited by Warshow, 'might well be *less* generically representative' than other modes of production that far outpace, in numbers, Hollywood's A-list features.[17] Silent westerns, the early 'Indian film' genre, 'B' and serial westerns, and singing cowboy pictures count among variations that have recently drawn commentary.[18] There are now numerous accounts of race, gender and sexuality in westerns, both in its classic mode and in revisionist productions that challenge it. Recently, post-westerns, eco-westerns, late westerns and other re-framings of the genre's persistence into the present have drawn the interest of scholars and critics.[19] The 'international' western, too, provides a revealing canvas for presenting styles, audiences and cultural traditions from outside the American national context. Initially the focus lay primarily on the Italian spaghetti production, but there are now also studies of German, Korean, English, Latin American, Australian and other inflections of the genre.[20] Attention to this diverse production provides a more inclusive account of the western, and reveals a range of modalities beyond the mere imitation of American production.[21]

This broadened perspective does not necessarily unseat Hollywood from a central position around which other iterations orbit. If film genres are cinematic hybrids that channel uneven flows of heterogeneous elements, these elements are not necessarily co-equal and the terms of their relation may be more imposed than chosen: Hollywood may remain the original and the centre, the other films the hybrid or the periphery.[22] Even nuanced accounts that allow for agency at local sites of production and reception may continue to reinscribe Hollywood as the universal element, and to mark the 'indigenous practice', however subversive or critical, as the 'parochial eccentricity'.[23] In the case of westerns, the practice of naming a non-American iteration after a national dish (Italian spaghetti westerns, German sauerkraut westerns, Korean kim-chi westerns, etc.) effectively hyphenates a corpus, and the designation may continue to mark it as derivative, niche and (from an American perspective) foreign, loading it with the epistemological baggage this positioning imposes: impure, confused, contaminated, inessential.[24] With no parallel designation for American production (e.g. a 'Hamburger western'), 'the western' *tout court* may continue to harbour the presumption of A-list Hollywood provenance at its centre: an ample portion of John Wayne and John Ford, *High Noon* and *Shane*, Howard Hawks and Sam Peckinpah, against which an international western is positioned as an outlier or outside the field of consideration altogether. Moreover, one may still ask: where are the French films? Even under the expanded inquiry into the diversity of international westerns it remains difficult to locate French western production after 1914.[25] When the terms 'Baguette' and 'Camembert' western are deployed, they rarely designate more than a few titles with some measure of French provenance and a simple recognition, often couched in surprise, that such films exist at all.[26]

The historical emphasis on Hollywood in studies of film genre is not solely the consequence of an Anglo-American point of view.

In an influential theorisation of film genre roughly contemporaneous to Warshow's, André Bazin, the editor of *Cahiers du cinéma*, constrains discourse on the French western film from a French perspective. In the 1950s, the critics and future filmmakers who wrote for the journal – among them François Truffaut, Jean-Luc Godard, Jacques Rivette, Claude Chabrol and Eric Rohmer – championed Hollywood production at a time when other critics dismissed it as formulaic commercial entertainment. Genre films provide fertile ground on which exceptional auteurs (Alfred Hitchcock, Howard Hawks, John Ford, to name the most prominent) could project their distinct and personal mode of expression despite Hollywood's centralised and industrial system of production. However, the critics' admiration generally lay in what the individual director brought to a genre, not in the genre *per se*, and without the singular stamp of the authorial figure a film may be dismissed as cinematic platitude: only a 'great interpreter' enacts gestures that elevate the genre 'like Furtwängler's baton, for example, enriched a Beethoven symphony'.[27] Genre is, effectively, straw that an able auteur transmutes into cinematic gold.[28]

Bazin takes exception with his contributors by asserting that genre itself constitutes the 'genius of the system' in Hollywood production, and reproaches his co-contributors who 'systematically look down on anything in a film that comes from a common fund and which can sometimes be entirely admirable, just as it can be utterly detestable'.[29] He invokes the western as the *ne plus ultra* of film genres for its 'rigorously pure' form based on a recognised set of 'traditional themes and devices' that derive from 'primitive rules' already evident in the films of Thomas Ince, the producer credited with founding the Hollywood studio system in great part through the mass production of westerns.[30] Bazin joins other *Cahiers* critics in admiring the westerns of Nicholas Ray, Samuel Fuller, Howard Hawks, Budd Boetticher and Anthony Mann, but he locates the genre's genius earlier in the studio era: he situates Ford's *Stagecoach*, not a flashy auteurist turn like Ray's *Johnny Guitar*, at the apex of the developmental arc, and bemoans the genre's decadence in overwrought productions by directors who are no longer content to let a western be a western. The classic Hollywood western is, simply put, 'the American cinema par excellence'.[31]

The logic that elevates studio-era Hollywood production to the genre's ideal and quasi-natural state (Bazin invokes the 'organic elements of the genre') advances an inverse inference that westerns made elsewhere will be unnatural and derivative. It is not merely a question of indigenous authenticity: how, for example, French production will distort an experience that only a genuine American sensibility can convey (as director Jacques Tourneur's Hollywood westerns would demonstrate); French films are produced outside the mode of production that confers 'genius' on a western in the first place. In the essay that serves as the preface to Jean-Louis Rieupeyrout's 1953 *Le Western, ou le cinéma américain par excellence*, Bazin, while sensitive to the vitality of the silent French westerns, signals their existence only as proof that the American genre is strong enough to withstand such 'counterfeits, pastiches, or parodies'. The primary target of Bazin's critique remains recent American production, but Rieupeyrout amplifies Bazin's dismissal with a withering repudiation of French westerns specifically. In a subsequent study, he derides the claim of more recent French productions to a 'label ['western'] abusively sought by films that tiresomely imitate Hollywood production, but that belongs to a genre that perishes under other skies'.[32] Calling the French films 'false witness, counter-truths, and enormous lies', he bemoans the 'distressing spectacle' of these 'heavy parodies, admitted or not, of a genre that only belongs to one country'.[33] The French westerns draw attention only to be summarily dispatched as fakes and clumsy jokes beneath further comment.

Bazin and Rieupeyrout set a course for the subsequent reception of French western films among French critics: to disparage, to disavow and, most often, to disregard. In the following decade, Raymond Bellour categorically spurns all European westerns in unambiguous terms: 'This devastating production ... which only stands out for its inanity and dishonesty, must not claim its place in the index of westerns.'[34] It is little surprise that no French westerns figure in his study. Other writers mention French westerns only to exclude them from consideration as unrepresentative derivatives of an American mode of production. Some note the scantiness of the French western corpus or bluntly proclaim its nonexistence after the early silent era: 'to the innumerable deaths of the [First World] War one may add that of the French western'.[35] Many simply omit mention of these films altogether.[36] Others do both: 'rather oddly, France will produce no (or few) cinematographic westerns'.[37] The hesitancy to allow that such films even exist situates them in a zone of indeterminacy where the claim of a French film to the term 'western' is left unprosecuted.

The critical neglect of the French western film may be considered, to a degree, symptomatic of a broader unwillingness to examine genre in French cinema. In his study of genre in 'classic' (1930–1960) French cinema, Crisp, for example, surveys the 'prevailing disregard for genre' among French writers and critics, and the historical indifference to, and at times overt contempt for, genre in French cinema.[38] For subsequent production, the theory and practice of the French New Wave further train the focus of critics and scholars on original films realised by distinctly individual directors. These auteurs may wryly redeploy Hollywood genre conventions, but their films are positioned to contrast with generic familiarity bred by a systematic mode of commercial feature production.[39] Alongside the close association of genre films with Hollywood in Anglo-American criticism, Moine identifies an inverse corollary for the French context: 'the understanding of French cinema propounded by critics and university scholars, who favour auteurs, schools, and movements at the expense of generic groupings, is another cause for this neglect'.[40]

A student of European Cinema is no longer limited to examining the familiar canon of prestige productions by art house auteurs.[41] Star vehicles, genre films and commercial box-office hits – comedies, musicals, courtroom dramas, horror and crime films – have been rescued from marginal obscurity and draw critical attention in their own right. While genre arguably 'remains a poor relation in French criticism',[42] the *série noire*, the musical film, the 'polar' police film, the costume drama, the blockbuster action film and other groupings have now garnered critical attention, and the recovery of more popular and commercial strains of French cinema remains an ongoing project.[43]

Nonetheless, attention to westerns remains scant within this expanded account of a French cinematic imaginary, though they do not elude consideration entirely. Jean-François Giré's two-volume chronicle of the 'Euro-western' stands out for its annotated list of more than 200 French films, and provides an illustrated narrative history of production in France from the early silents through the twenty-first century.[44] This comprehensive survey reveals the scale, diversity and longevity of the French production of western films, and positions them alongside Italian, German and other European productions in the genre. However, recognition does not necessarily entail revindication, and the genre's worthiness as an object of study is, in this characterisation, more quantitative than qualitative. Giré relegates a significant number of the films to the rubric 'fake westerns and curiosities' (*'faux-westerns et curiosités'*), and doses the commentary with disparaging epithets: 'silly' (*'niais'*), 'old-fashioned' (*'démodé'*), 'a dud' (*'un navet'*), 'a tumble down a slope as dangerous as it is slippery with stupidity' (*'dégringolade sur une pente aussi dangereuse que glissante d'imbécilités'*).[45]

Rare praise is couched in backhanded deprecation: Hamman, though admired, is invoked as the hero of a lost golden age of the French western, and Robert Hossein's *Cemetery Without Crosses* (*Une corde, un colt*, 1968), the 'sole western worthy of the name since Hamman' (that is to say, for more than half a century) exhibits 'qualities that were cruelly lacking in most of the previous imitations'.[46] The charge of inauthenticity echoes earlier criticism, and despite the admirable exceptions, Giré concurs with the prevailing conclusion that French westerns, as a group, remain a degraded derivative of Hollywood production: 'The drama in French westerns, stuck between clumsy imitations and plodding parodies, did not figure out how to distance itself from its originary model and find its own identity.'[47] Hollywood remains the standard, the original, against which the French films measure deficient and *faux*.

This conclusion is cautionary for a study of French western films. It may be possible to approach this corpus of overlooked films as a small uncharted island of cinematic practices to be explored and surveyed, and then to emend the maps of the western genre and of French cinema accordingly. The French western, a stone unturned, will finally get its due measure of attention. However, this measure may be duly meagre, and winning a seat at the table does not mean it will be a place of honour. A more inclusive reckoning of the western may land not far from where it started. In Giré's case, greater visibility ultimately confirms that, taken as a whole, these films are indeed cheap knock-offs that constitute a motley and mediocre corpus. The catalogue of the western may be more complete, but the recognition of its French declension redounds to the dismissive characterisations of earlier critics.

Nevertheless, couched in the failure of the French western to 'find its own identity' lies the suggestion that this deficiency is not only a matter of insufficient 'western-ness'. Slavish rehearsal of Hollywood is a common ground for criticism (when these films are mentioned at all), but also lacking is a positive cinematic assertion that will fill the opening left by this shortcoming and distinguish the French films from other expressions of the genre. If the French western does not measure up against Hollywood's mode of production and American frontier narratives, could this deficiency be less a void than an opening through which something else may be affirmed? If we listen to what reverberates in this space, what will we hear?

In a rare scholarly account of post-1914 French westerns, Cécile Sorin reconsiders two of the post-World War II films that Rieupeyrout derided,

Fernand cow-boy (Guy LeFranc, 1956) and *Sérénade au Texas* (Richard Pottier, 1958), as a strategic 'borrowing' of genre conventions that effectively constitutes a defiant French take-down of the American behemoth.[48] Sorin contends that the comedic parody in these films is 'pure spectacle' in a distinctly French mode unfettered by reverence for the western hero or the myth of the frontier found in many of their American contemporaries. An affirmative manifestation of 'the specificities of the French cinema and of French culture' contests both Hollywood's mode of production and the genre's expression of an American national myth, which are tightly aligned in this analysis. This critical gesture moves consideration of the French western beyond measures of its inadequacy: the failure and defeat of American-style westernness in these films is not a deficiency but an assertion of French cinema, of French culture, and of French identity.

This conclusion nonetheless reinscribes a constitutive antagonism between a genre aligned with Hollywood and a rival French cinematic referent: the western is the un-French measure, and the French assertion enacts the genre's defeat. Moreover, characterising the French impulse that prevails over Hollywood's hegemony raises further questions. The 'dynamism of French cinema' and an identity 'which is both geographic and cultural' garner little precision beyond the choice of actors, of language and decor that are 'very French specific', claims complicated by the fact that two of the stars featured in the article, Luis Mariano and Eddie Constantine, were not native French, often played non-French characters, delivered their lines with signature accents and sometimes acted in other languages and for other film industries.[49] The French cinematic affirmation and the prevailing 'French culture' are defined primarily against what they outstrip, namely the western itself: the French element 'rejects', 'deprives', 'strips away', 'belittles', 'undermines', 'neutralises' and 'diminishes' the tropes and narratives of the genre, whose assumed stability in its Hollywood iteration remains similarly unexamined. 'French' and 'western' are again adversaries from separate spheres, circumscribed by mutually exclusive logics that remain secure even as 'French', in this case, takes the upper hand.

There is a different tack. One may recognise the tensions between 'French' and 'western' without subscribing to the premise that the dissonances sounded by this meeting resolve in either a harmonious hybrid or in the triumph of one term over the other. By examining instead how these discordances expose instability in ideations of both 'French' and 'western', the scope of the inquiry broadens beyond the study of a marginal cinematic curiosity. The 'genre that does not exist' offers a revealing lens for considering how film genres and national cinemas act in collusion as provisional and imagined groupings of films, and how the failure to reify the two constitutive terms – 'French' and 'western', an important world cinema and an emblematic film genre – opens a vantage apart from that of groupings that have been accommodated more comfortably within these arenas. Instead of a battleground between established rivals, the French western may be considered a zone of contact where the encounter volatises the two constitutive terms and, in doing so, generates distinct possibilities for cinematic practice.

Notes

1. Susan Hayward casts a critical eye on the studies of national cinemas sitting on the shelves in *French National Cinema*, 2nd edition (London and New York: Routledge, 2005), 1. Hayward's account will be examined more closely in Chapter 2.
2. Tim Bergfelder observes this trend in 'Transnational Genre Hybridity: Between Vernacular Modernism and Postmodern Parody', in *Genre Hybridisation: Global Cinematic Flows*, ed. Ivor Ritzer and Peter W. Schulze (Marburg: Schüren, 2013), 40.
3. Steve Neale, *Genre and Hollywood* (London & New York: Routledge, 2000), 9–10.
4. Barry Keith Grant, 'Introduction', *The Film Genre Reader*, ed. Barry Keith Grant (Austin: University of Texas Press, 1986), ix. Also quoted in Neale, *Genre and Hollywood*, 9.
5. Altman deploys the term 'genrification' a number of times in *Film/Genre* (London: British Film Institute, 1999).
6. Marc Betz, *Beyond the Subtitle: Remapping European Art Cinema* (Minneapolis: University of Minnesota Press, 2009), 218.
7. Colin Crisp, *Genre, Myth, and Convention in the French Cinema, 1929–1939* (Bloomington: Indiana University Press, 2002), xiii.
8. Raphaëlle Moine, *Cinéma Genre*, trans. Alistair Fox and Hilary Radner (Malden, MA and Oxford: Wiley-Blackwell, 2008), 194. In a similar vein, Dimitris Eleftheriotis cites research that exposes how generic classifications based on Hollywood production are 'largely irrelevant' in the context of Hindi popular cinema. He asks: 'Where are the studies of other (non-American) film industries in genre formation?' Dimitris Eleftheriotis, *Popular Cinemas of Europe: Studies of Texts, Contexts and Frameworks* (New York & London: Continuum, 2001), 94.
9. Robert Warshow's 'Movie Chronicle: The Westerner' first appeared in 1954, and André Bazin's 'Evolution du Western' in 1955. These studies have been widely reprinted, and are the first two entries in Jim Kitses and Gregg Rickman, eds, *The Western Reader* (New York: Limelight, 1998).
10. Lee Clark Mitchell dates the beginning of 'intelligent commentary' on the genre to Warshow's essay. Lee Clark Mitchell, *Westerns: Making the Man in Fiction and Film* (Chicago and London: University of Chicago Press, 1996), 11.

11. Warshow mentions other modes of production (serials, singing cowboys, silents) but dismisses them alongside early silent films as 'little that an adult could take seriously'. He concedes: 'I have seen none of their movies'. 'Movie Chronicle', 39.
12. Frequently encountered supplements to Warshow's filmography include *Duel in the Sun* (King Vidor, 1946), *Red River* (Howard Hawks, 1948) and *She Wore a Yellow Ribbon* (John Ford, 1949) from the 1940s; *Hondo* (John Farrow, 1953) and John Ford's *The Searchers* (1956) in the 1950s; *Butch Cassidy and the Sundance Kid* (Richard Lester, 1969), Sergio Leone's *Dollars* Trilogy, and Sam Peckinpah's *Wild Bunch* (1969) in the 1960s; and still later *Dances with Wolves* (Kevin Costner, 1990) and *Unforgiven* (Clint Eastwood, 1992).
13. Cawelti mentions few films specifically, and invokes Ford by name over three times more frequently than all other directors combined. John G. Cawelti, *The Six-Gun Mystique* (Bowling Green, OH: Bowling Green University Popular Press, 1970).
14. See Mitchell, *Westerns*; and Jane Tompkins, *West of Everything* (Oxford: Oxford University Press, 1994).
15. Jim Kitses's study of western auteurs (first published in 1969, expanded and re-issued in 2004) includes a chapter on Leone alongside those devoted to Ford, Budd Boetticher, Anthony Mann, Sam Peckinpah and Clint Eastwood. Jim Kitses, *Horizons West: Directing the Western from John Ford to Clint Eastwood* (London: BFI, 2004).
16. Christopher Frayling singles out these four Leone films as 'the best' of the cycle in contrast to other 'rotgut' production, and he makes their analysis the lynchpin of his study. Christopher Frayling, *Spaghetti Westerns: Cowboys and Europeans from Karl May to Sergio Leone*, revised edition (I. B. Tauris 2006). The situation of French films in relation to the spaghetti cycle will be taken up in Chapters 9 and 10.
17. Barry Langford, *Film Genre: Hollywood and Beyond* (Edinburgh: Edinburgh University Press, 2005), 59.
18. On these other strains of production, see, among other studies, Peter Stanfield, *Horse Opera: The Strange History of the 1930's Singing Cowboy* (University of Illinois Press, 2002); *Back in the Saddle Again: New Essays on the Western*, ed. Edward Buscombe and Roberta Pearson (British Film institute, 1998); and the consideration of silent westerns and 'Indian films' in Andrew Brodie Smith, *Shooting Cowboys and Indians: Silent Western Films, American Culture, and the Birth of Hollywood* (University Press of Colorado, 2003).
19. See, for example, Neil Campbell, *Post-Westerns: Cinema, Region, West* (University of Nebraska Press, 2013); Joseph Heumann and Robin L. Murray, *Gunfight at the Eco-Corral: Western Cinema and the Environment* (University of Oklahoma Press, 2012); and Lee Clark Mitchell, *Late Westerns: The Persistence of a Genre* (Lincoln: University of Nebraska Press, 2018).
20. This body of research includes the essays collected in Cynthia Miller and A. Bowdoin Van Riper, eds, *International Westerns: Re-locating the Frontier* (Lanham, MD: Scarecrow Press, 2014); Austin Fisher, ed., *Spaghetti Westerns at the Crossroads: Studies in Relocation, Transition, and Appropriation* (Edinburgh: Edinburgh University Press, 2016); Rita Kersztesi et al., eds, *The Western in the Global South* (New York and London: Routledge, 2015); and Stephen Teo, *Eastern Westerns* (New York and London: Routledge, 2016).
21. Arguing in favour of a more nuanced account, Chelsea Wessels brings to light practices other than 'a narrow, one-sided relationship with Hollywood': for example, the dimension lent by translation into languages other than Italian or English.

Chelsea Wessels, '"Do I look Mexican?": Translating the Western Beyond National Borders', *Transformations* 24 (2014), online version. Available at <https://www.transformationsjournal.org/wp-content/uploads/2016/12/Wessels_Transformations24.pdf> (accessed 10 July 2022).
22. Ivo Ritzer and Peter W. Schulze, 'Genre Hybridisation: Global Cinematic Flows', in *Genre Hybridisation: Global Cinematic Flows*, ed. Ivor Ritzer and Peter W. Schulze (Marburg: Schüren, 2013), 20.
23. Bergfelder, 'Transnational Genre Hybridity', 41.
24. Bergfelder calls these monikers 'culinary epithets'. Ibid. For a summary of the meanings loaded into the term 'foreign', see Rebecca Saunders, 'Theoretical Dialogue', in *The Concept of the Foreign: An Interdisciplinary Dialogue*, ed. Rebecca Saunders (Lanham, MD: Lexington Books, 2003), 3–67.
25. In the single entry on French westerns in *International Westerns: Re-locating the Frontier*, a nearly exclusive focus on the *bande dessinée* effectively evacuates cinema itself from the discussion. Pierre Lagayette, 'Visions of the West in Lucky Luke Comics: from Cliché to Critique', in Miller and Van Riper, *International Westerns*, 83–103.
26. Marek Paryz mentions, with a note of surprise, two French films: 'Interestingly enough, it is French filmmakers who have tried to re-establish the western as a popular genre in *Blueberry* (Jean Kounen, 2004) and *Bandidas* (Joachim Roenning and Espen Sandburg, co-written and co-produced by Luc Besson, 2006).' The anthology that follows does not contain an analysis of either film. Marek Paryz, 'Introduction', in Paryz and Leo, *The Post-2000 Film Western* (New York: Palgrave Macmillan, 2015), 9–10.
27. Eric Rohmer, 'Redécouvrir l'Amérique', *Cahiers du cinéma* 54 (December 1955): 14.
28. The *Cahiers* critics are careful to dissociate the authorial gesture from the genre markers that another director, if asked to film the same scenario, might clumsily rehearse. Hawks, Lang and Ray were noteworthy for their ability to make outstanding films across genres or, as Claude Chabrol suggests, in spite of the genre: 'The script of *Pushover* is very bad, and that of *Bronco Apache* very unbalanced, but both possess that precious and rare element: an intelligence behind the camera.' ('Le scenario de *Pushover* est très mauvais, et celui de *Bronco Apache* très déséquilibré, mais l'un et l'autre possèdent cet élément précieux et rare: une intelligence derrière la caméra.') Claude Chabrol, 'Petits poisons deviendront grands', *Cahiers du cinéma* 45 (March 1955): 45. Linking the weak scenarios to genre conventions, Chabrol also cites Robert Aldrich's reworking of the 'most deplorable, the most nauseous product of a genre in a state of putrefaction', namely a Mickey Spillane story (*Kiss Me Deadly*); Aldrich, a favoured auteur in the pages of the *Cahiers*, takes 'this threadbare and lackluster fabric and splendidly [reweaves] it into rich patterns of the most enigmatic arabesques'. Claude Chabrol, 'The Evolution of the Thriller' ('Evolution du film policier'), 1955; trans. Liz Heron, in Jim Hillier, ed., *Cahiers du Cinéma, the 1950s: Neo-realism, Hollywood, the New Wave*, Cambridge, MA: Harvard University Press, 1985, 163.
29. André Bazin, 'On the *politique des auteurs*' ('De la politique des auteurs'), 1957, trans. Peter Graham, in Hillier, ed., *Cahiers du cinema* 257.
30. André Bazin, 'Beauty of a Western', trans. Liz Heron, in Hillier, ed., *Cahiers du cinéma* 166.
31. André Bazin, 'The Western: or the American film par excellence', in *What is Cinema?*, 142.

32. '...étiquette abusivement sollicitée par des films péniblement imités de la facture hollywoodienne propre à un genre qui dépérit toujours sous d'autres cieux.' Jean-Louis Rieupeyrout, *La Grande Aventure du western: du Far-West à Hollywood, 1894– 1963* (Paris: Editions du Cerf, 1964), 430–1.
33. '...de faux-témoignages, de contre-vérités, d'énormes mensonges [...] ce navrant spectacle [...] de lourdes parodies, avouées ou non, d'un genre qui n'appartient qu'à un seul pays.' Jean-Louis Rieupeyrout, *La Grande Aventure du western*, 431.
34. 'Cette production dévastatrice [...] qui ne brille que par sa nullité et sa malhonnêteté, se devait de ne pas trouver sa place dans l'index des westerns.' He continues: 'Pour quiconque aime le western, le vrai, son cadre, sa mythologie, son mythe et son incomparable pouvoir d'évocation, il ne peut s'agir ici que de marchandises frelatées, dont l'amateur de westerns doit particulièrement se défier.' ('For whoever loves the western, the true one, its setting, its mythology, its myth and its incomparable evocative power, it can only be a question here of adulterated merchandise of which the lover of westerns must particularly beware.' Raymond Bellour, *Le Western* (Paris: Gallimard collection 10/18, 1966), 352–3.
35. 'Aux morts innombrables de la guerre s'ajoute celle du western français.' Francis Lacassin, *Pour une contre-histoire du cinéma* (Arles: Actes Sud, 1994), 130.
36. See, among others, Georges-Albert Astre and Albert-Patrick Hoarau, *Univers du Western* (Paris: Cinéma Club/Editions Seghers, 1973); Jean-Jacques Dupuis, *Le Western* (Paris: J'ai lu: 1990); William Bourton, *Le Western, conscience du nouveau monde* (Paris: Campion, 2016); and Gérard Camy, ed., *Western: que reste-t-il de nos amours?*, *CinémAction* 86 (1st trimester, 1998).
37. 'Assez curieusement, la France ne produira pas (ou peu) de westerns cinématographiques, contrairement à d'autres pays comme l'Italie et l'Allemagne.' Jean-Louis Leutrat and Suzanne Liandrat-Guigues follow this assertion by listing a few titles, but their qualification as a 'western' has been a priori called into question. Jean-Louis Leutrat and Suzanne Liandrat-Guigues, *Western(s)* (Paris: Klincksieck, 2007), 12.
38. Crisp, *Genre, Myth, and Convention*, 204.
39. Here the diverse meanings of the term 'genre' may blur an important distinction between a genre's defining elements, genre films, and genre as a category. The distinction is salient in New Wave films: to call *Breathless* a 'gangster film' or *Les Demoiselles de Rochefort* (Jacques Demy, 1967) a 'musical' on Hollywood's terms obscures crucial differences: both aesthetically and in means of production, they are positioned outside the commercial demands, stylistic constraints and business model of a genre 'system' designed to mass produce films to fill screens worldwide. Neale proposes the term 'generically marked film' to characterise more precisely a picture that remains distinct from a group of 'generically modelled' films. Neale, *Genre and Hollywood*, 28.
40. Moine, *Cinema Genre*, 194. A quantitative measure reveals the scale of this historical trend within the field. A 2003 survey of both British and French dissertations on French cinema shows that studies of auteur directors have dominated since the inauguration of film studies as a discipline. Godard alone is the focus of nearly 15% of all dissertations. Only a handful of studies emphasise French popular cinema, and even there the focus often remains circumscribed by the oeuvre of an eminent director. 'French cinema studies is often said to be relatively uninterested in genre studies. Although there are a couple of theses on the polar or police thriller, work on comedy is confined to director studies, particularly Tati, as was the case for

completed theses.' Phil Powrie, 'Thirty Years of Doctoral Theses on French Cinema', *Studies in French Cinema* 3, no. 3 (2003): 199–203.
41. Studies of a more commercial European cinema include Richard Dyer and Ginette Vincendeau, eds, *Popular European Cinema* (London and New York: Routledge: 1992); Dimitris Eleftheriotis, *Popular Cinemas of Europe: Studies of Texts, Contexts, and Frameworks* (New York and London: Continuum, 2001); and Bergfelder, *International Adventures*.
42. Moine, *Cinema/Genre*, xiii.
43. See, for example, Gwénaëlle le Gras and Delphine Chedaleux, eds, *Genres et acteurs du cinéma français* (Rennes: Presses universitaires de Rennes, 2012); Sébastien Layerle and Raphaëlle Moine, eds, *Voyez comme on chante*: *Films musicaux et cinéphilies populaires en France (1945–1958)*, *Théorème* 20 (2014); Susan Hayward, *French Costume Drama of the 1950s: Fashioning Politics in Film* (Chicago: University of Chicago Press, 2010); Charlie Michael, *French Blockbusters: Cultural Politics of a Transnational Cinema* (Edinburgh: Edinburgh University Press, 2019); and Phil Powrie and Marie Cadalanu, *The French Film Musical* (London: Bloomsbury, 2020).
44. Giré, *Il était une fois* (volumes 1 and 2). The first volume, initially published in 2002, was revised and republished as a set with a second volume in 2008.
45. The precise criteria for qualification as 'faux', or as 'French', are unspecified.
46. 'qualités qui faisaient cruellement défaut à la plupart des imitations précédentes'. Giré, *Il était une fois*, vol. 2, 718. Hossein's film will be examined in Chapter 9.
47. '[L]e drame du western français, coincé entre les imitations maladroites et les parodies poussives, n'a pas su se démarquer de son modèle d'origine et se trouver une identité particulière', Ibid., 731.
48. Cécile Sorin, 'The Art of Borrowing: French Popular Cinema before the New Wave', *Studies in French Cinema* 4, no. 1 (2004): 53–64. The two films will be examined in Chapters 5 and 6.
49. Ibid., 62. Mariano was born in Spain (Basque country) and emigrated to France as an adolescent; Constantine was American but made most of his acting career in France and Germany.

2

Imagined (and unimaginable) communities of film

Open one of the monographs on a film genre or a national cinema that sit in their separate zones on library shelves, at least one that was written over the last forty years, and you stand a good chance of finding a less monolithic characterisation than the titles often suggest. The a priori coherence of both film genres and national cinemas sits under sustained and mounting critical pressure. While genres and national assertions remain consequential for understanding cinema, a broadening consensus holds them to be constitutively contested. To position the French western film within this dynamic relationship it is useful to trace the lines of these arguments, not to rehearse their scope and nuance (impossible and unnecessary in these few pages) but to expose how the epistemologies of film genres and of national cinemas are not as distinct as they might appear.

The characterisation of narrative, dramatic, literary and artistic genres dates to the ancient Greeks, and over the centuries has proven to be a notoriously fraught endeavour. The definition of genre in film is no exception. When it emerged as an area of scholarly inquiry, the theorisation of film genre often entailed the examination of chosen representative works with the goal of identifying constitutive 'semantic' (lexical, iconographic) and 'syntactic' (structural, narrative) markers.[1] However, the assumption that discrete film genres exist as empirical fact, waiting for their essential traits to be discovered and catalogued, is conspicuously unsafe even for a genre with as apparently strong and distinct features as the western. As early as 1973, Andrew Tudor observed a circularity that plagues definitions of genre grounded in the study of representative films: if by accepted benchmarks of 'westernness' a film like John Ford's *Stagecoach* seems undoubtedly to exemplify the genre, it is hardly surprising, given that these benchmarks were culled from *Stagecoach* and other films like it in the first place.²

The definition of film genres yields time and again to such 'empiricist's dilemmas'.³ A film widely hailed as the 'first western', *The Great Train Robbery* (Edwin S. Porter, 1903), was made before 'the western' was a recognised category of film, and in the context of its initial release would more aptly be called a railroad picture, a chase film or a crime film.⁴ Most westerns, like most Hollywood feature films, could also qualify as melodrama; indeed, in early years they were often called 'western melodramas', and the adjective only later became a stand-alone substantive.⁵ It has been frequently noted that genres are defined by an eclectic array of criteria: horror films by the emotions they incite, westerns by their historical and geographical setting, 'women's films' by the gender of their target audience, *film noir* by a visual style and mood, musicals by a particular mode of music use – the list goes on. Consequently, a film may be placed into different categories in diverse measures by various interests at different times, and for multiple reasons. *Stagecoach*, for example, also presents key elements of a melodrama, a love story, an action/adventure film, and a road film. To name even such a 'classic' definitively a western (or not) demands prior acts of emphasising certain traits, downplaying others, asserting what is and isn't essential, and measuring the relative dosage (the romance between the lead characters is not primary enough to make it a *film d'amour*, the score and the song outside the cantina are insufficient to qualify it as a musical) against representative films from which the generalisable traits derive.

Rick Altman contends that 'genres are not inert categories [. . .] but discursive claims made by real speakers for particular purposes'.⁶ These discursive gestures, moreover, are performed by diverse constituents, follow multiple logics, and answer plural and possibly competing interests. Instead of pinpointing a genre's origin, tracing its development, characterising its classical perfection, and charting its decadence and decline as if this evolutionary arc were an observable natural phenomenon, a different critical task lies in identifying and examining the various acts that 'do' genre, or more precisely, because they are often discursive claims, that 'enunciate' genre.⁷ New questions arise: enunciated by whom? For whom and against what? When and where? And to which ends?

Filmmakers, for example, may rehearse familiar narratives, characterisations and figures as a kind of branding for a strain of film known to appeal to consumers, and also, in the studio era, for the sake of industrial efficiency. In these cases genre is enunciated in the filmic text itself, but genres do not spring exclusively from film production, nor solely from iconography and narrative structures. Through what Steve Neale calls the 'discursive relay', audiences, advertisers, journalists and critics (among others) also stake claims that shape the idea of a genre, but they can never do so definitively: new claims supplement the old, and what's been made one day might be changed or unmade the next. Furthermore, if these 'multiple groups who, by helping to define the genre, may be said to "speak" the genre', as Altman submits in a refinement of the syntactic/semantic model,[8] these plural discourses may send mixed messages, and gesture in divergent directions for listeners across historical moments. *Stagecoach* may most often be considered a western, but even this consensus is misleading when it obscures the diversity among constituents who invoke the genre in different ways and to different ends.[9] The discursive gestures that 'speak' genre and lend it an appearance of stability belie a fractured assemblage of plural and possibly competing pieces that, moreover, may shift over time.

Alongside film genre's epistemological and historical contingency, the idea that cinema expresses, reflects or divides neatly into national units also meets a critical challenge. Certainly, national interests have energetically policed or defended their own film industries, out of chauvinism, economics, propaganda, censorship concerns or to stake a beachhead against the Hollywood tide. A film's narrative may also promote and exploit assertions of the nation, and the alignment of a protagonist's plight with a national-historical mythology has proven a powerful and bankable ploy. The studio-era Hollywood western is here doubly emblematic: in style and mode of production it is the *cinéma américain par excellence*, while the narrative often reinforces a nation-building myth of the frontier and of 'manifest destiny'. The alignment of cinema with nationally marked narratives, styles and modes of production is not exclusive to the study of American film. Siegfried Kracauer identified nationalist motifs in German cinema that prefigure the rise of Nazism, for example, and Noël Burch discerned a distinct representational system in Japanese film.[10] Post-war art cinemas have been parcelled into distinct responses to Hollywood's global reach when invocations of the French New Wave, New German Cinema or Italian neo-realism, among other movements, divide films under national headings with their distinct practices, personnel and style. Even the recovery of popular European cinema may continue to position the 'domestic popular genres as a key to the national imaginary'.[11]

However, cinema does not spring *ex nihilo* in isolated national spheres, each industry cultivating an indigenous species of film whose unique savour is only later hybridised by cross-fertilisation. From its beginnings cinema has operated as a global enterprise.[12] National governments and industrial interests may subsequently have asserted control over film production and exhibition, in various modes and degrees of intensity across history, but the anxieties that drive these measures further confirm the ease with which film products, technologies, styles, profits and personnel migrate across national boundaries. National cinema persists as a powerful idea, but it is imposed on a fluid reality that extends beyond the filmic text, and its imagined coherence as an institution belies a loose and porous circumscription of diverse elements and localised practices.

The demarcation among national containers as a sufficient grid for plotting cinematic practices has been subject to robust interrogation. This re-oriented perspective on national cinemas demands a balance between recognising the enduring consequence of the national designation while also acknowledging it to be a ravel of heterogeneous assertions. For the study of French cinema, and of the French western specifically, it is instructive to revisit how Susan Hayward threads this needle in the monograph *French National Cinema*. An introductory passage frames this study with the contention that cinema enunciates the national in multiple registers, both within the filmic text and in broader contexts of production, industrial organisation, reception and promotion. Among the vectors of this enunciation, Hayward lists narratives, genres, codes and conventions, gesturality and morphology, stars, cinemas of the centre (Hollywood's global influence) and of the periphery ('indigenous' distinctiveness), and cultural institutions such as the *Cinémathèque française* and the Cannes Film Festival. Each voice in this chorus contributes its distinct aesthetic, social, economic, institutional or geo-political inflection to a polyvalent and dynamic idea of a 'French cinema' that results.

This ideation remains constitutively unstable. A given film might lack some of these assertions, or include others that gesture towards competing national referents. Moreover, point by point, each of the named sites of enunciation fails reliably to guarantee the singularity of a 'French cinema'. Certain narrative forms, filming styles and dramatic conventions may prevail in France, but they are unsure markers of a national cinema: the 'classical Hollywood style' became a lingua franca that inflects narrative cinema around the world, while signature traits of the French New Wave (for example) were rapidly imitated elsewhere. The provenance of directors and stars is not a safe determinant: French films have starred and been directed by non-French personnel, French directors and actors work in other industries, Hollywood included, and determining who qualifies adequately as 'French' is itself a fraught gesture. Language, gesture and 'morphology' are unreliable: dubbing allows for multilingual casts, and what is a 'look' or way of moving that is not a style, stereotype or mode of acting that another competent actor might adopt? Institutions like the *Cinémathèque française* or the Cannes film festival may be based in France and promote French cinema, but they both have an international focus. Ownership of the means of production, in an age of global capital and multinational co-productions, is an indecisive marker of nationality. Jurisdiction under French laws, regulation, censorship, union rules, taxation and qualification for subsidies may leave a mark on the final product, but to make these constraints the touchstone of national cinema risks restricting the meaning of 'French cinema' to legal or technical definitions. Finally, in the colonial and post-colonial dynamics under which the history of French cinema has unfolded, an indigenous French worldview begs interrogation. Cinema emerged in France against the backdrop of a colonial empire, which it outlived to see France become a member of the European Union. With the administration of vast territories from the *métropole*, a diaspora of ethnic French citizens, diverse peoples and populations who live under governments and educational systems that are or once were French, large-scale immigration from the former colonies (and elsewhere) to hexagonal France, and pan-European initiatives and co-production agreements, under which terms may a perspective be deemed French? Which combination and dosage of these diverse measures will qualify a film as sufficiently French?

Film scholars, too, lend voices to the chorus that enunciates a 'French Cinema'. Acts of determining what is decisive, relevant and representative – and what is exceptional and excluded – give shape to the cloud of assertions that, without this labour, remains formless. While recognising its diverse and moving parts, Hayward mobilises certain films, practices, institutions and personnel to confer provisional contours on a characterisation of 'French cinema'. Genre is a key vector of this enunciation. In a departure from studies that align French cinema with classic masterpieces or art house auteurs, *French National Cinema* includes a substantive discussion of the popular and more commercial films that drew French spectators in greatest numbers: among them crime films, historical dramas, thrillers, war films and serials.

However, even this polyvalent and genre-friendly characterisation of French cinema meets a hard and fast line when it comes to the western. 'What is least evident [in French Cinema], apart from epics, is the adventure film, to say nothing of the western', and indeed, a few references to pre-1914 cinema aside, nothing is said about the French western film. The omission might plausibly be ascribed to a determination that later French western films are of such minor importance that they do not 'make the cut' in a book of a few hundred pages, had not the consideration of the films – indeed, the very possibility of their existence – also met summary foreclosure. Unlike more 'universal' genres that transpose easily to French cinema, the western (along with the musical) is declared 'relinquished to the Americans' and 'totally effaced' from French cinema after World War I.[13] Hayward does not elaborate on these assertions, but their terms support the inference that the post-1914 French films with western themes remain *faux* or otherwise generically compromised to the extent that they are no longer recognisably 'westerns'. *French National Cinema* opens with an invocation of Benedict Anderson's characterisation of the nation as an 'imagined community': individuals imagine their participation in a vast but finite group, a singular and sovereign 'us' differentiated from all of 'them' out there in the world.[14] Hayward suggests that a national cinema, too, prompts the ideation of an 'ours' (or, for an outsider, a 'theirs'): a group of films, practices, people and institutions whose coherence and collective identity demand prior acts of imagination. One of the multiple acts that lend shape to this imagined French cinema, for Hayward as for others before her, is the exclusion of the western genre.

The epistemologies of cinema that lend meaning to 'French' and 'western' have tended to set them on divergent courses: train your sights on one and the other is diminished or disappears from view. The national cinema and the film genre are therefore not only similar in this respect, but are also complicit when each plays its part in constituting the other.[15] In both arenas, 'The French western', at least in the sound era, is marooned as an effectively meaningless notion: a conjunction of genre and national cinema not only unimagined but, under some of these terms, unimaginable.

The transnational frontier

Recognising films that harbour enunciations of both a French cinema and the western genre presents a choice. One might arrange this neglected corpus within the established and now more comprehensive folds of both the western genre and of French cinema, but there is another approach by which the aim is not to locate a home for these films within the received logics that have girded the genre and the national assertion. It is not a matter of redressing decades of critical neglect with a more thorough empirical study. On the contrary, it is to recognise that the critics are on to something when they evince the French western's unimaginability, and to lend this discursive blind field a heuristic function. What do these films expose about genre classifications and national cinemas as adequate prisms for differentiating cinematic practice? And which specific practices does the French western's unimaginability allow and reveal?

This critical orientation aligns with the conviction that parsing film into discrete national containers marginalises a broad spectrum of cinematic practices, and obscures other organising logics that emerge between, across and within national cinemas. Despite stark and persistent imbalances of power and scale, the tension between Hollywood and other national industries may, for example, also foster a mutually beneficial symbiosis that generates new possibilities for production and reception.[16] National enunciations also vary widely in nature and scope, and cinemas of smaller countries and of the developing world invite consideration separately from larger and more established industries that have historically dominated the study of film.[17] Local practices of film production and consumption fragment the idea of a univocal national assertion, regional cinemas may straddle national boundaries, and other transnational cinematic enunciations are only heard and understood when the frame of a national cinema is loosened.[18] Diasporic cinematic practices may have no clear national home,[19] and new geo-political formations engender distinct modalities in, for example, the idea of a 'European cinema' under the European Union's administration and subsidies. A transnational perspective nuances and revises assertions of Hollywood's hegemonic, homogenising empire often implied in the term 'globalisation'.[20] As this diversity of practices dislodges the study of cinema from a priori national frames, the nation remains a powerful regulator; few foresee a post-national cinema, and Hollywood often remains the elephant in the room. However, while the consequence of a national attribution persists, it is shown to be a mesh of plural modalities among others for which it cannot fully account.

The cinematic West is not exempt from this line of inquiry. A recent anthology of new scholarship on the transnational western opens with Neil

Campbell's axiomatic assertion: 'To examine the West in the twenty-first century is to think of it as always already transnational.'[21] In place of geographical or taxonomical grids, with their linear borders and separate containers, Campbell locates the West, and the western film genre, in a dialogic encounter of heterogeneous elements at proliferating points of contact. Austin Fisher, the editor of the volume, notes how in studies of the western, as in other areas of film studies, 'this line of enquiry is now flourishing', and the arguments in the collection expose 'how the western narrative format and its various iconographies have been deployed for the negotiation of multifarious national and subcultural identities since before Hollywood's golden age'.[22] This collection joins other writing on transnational and international western films in positioning the genre in a broader interrogation of national assertions in film industries around the world.[23] Untethering the genre from the 'Hollywood centre/derivative other' binary exposes diverse inflections that spread across national, regional and local contexts, and moves the western film from a site of national expression onto an ever-receding horizon of mutations and negotiations.

The transnational perspective would appear accommodating for examining the points of contact between a French national referent and the western genre. Indeed, the spectacle of the French western's volatility seems ripe for comment when it so plainly demands a discursive space beyond what has heretofore been provided. Nonetheless, the encounter of 'French' and 'western' continues to draw scant attention even as a transnational critical orientation reveals the diversity and variegation of the genre's expressions. In a pithy summation of deconstruction (one of many), Jacques Derrida once asserted the 'baseless necessity' of representation, a condition that might aptly characterise both national cinemas and film genres in the current theoretical climate: they remain powerful ideas for shaping thought on cinema, even as they are revealed to be constitutively contested.[24] The French western amply evinces discursive baselessness, often to the point of finding no foothold at all, but there appears to be little of the necessity that drives the imposition of meaning nonetheless. Unlike established couplings of national cinemas and film genres whose pilings beg interrogation, this denegated conjunction enjoys scant support or stability in the first place. How can one deconstruct what has never been constructed?

Herein lies the challenge and the interest – and the dissonance, the vitality and in some cases (let's just say it) the weirdness – of French western films. Collectively, their lack of belonging in accounts of both the western genre and French cinema opens a critical perspective on how film genres and national assertions act in concert as imagined groupings of film. The interest therefore lies not in pinning down the French western like an insect under glass, to document the identifying traits and evolutionary development of a previously unexamined species of film and to arrange it within existing taxonomies of genres and national cinemas. Nor does it reside in elucidating the logic of a new synthesis that replaces them, in elevating these films to the rank of great or even good works of cinema, or in situating these films in the lineage of writers from Alexis de Tocqueville to Jean Baudrillard who characterise the United States, its history, or its people from a perspective positioned as French. It lies instead in how the cinematic conjunction of 'French cinema' and 'western genre' evinces unsteadiness in both terms, and where the resulting instability is not simply a deficiency but also an opening that has been navigated cunningly and clumsily, on discontinuous and divergent trajectories, and to diverse ends. A study of these films participates in the ongoing recovery of popular cinemas that have been overlooked in film scholarship, but the purpose is not to make the French western film exist *per se* as a sub-genre, as an expression of a national cinema, or even as a freshly revealed hybrid with greater explanatory scope. This conjunction instead reveals cinema to be an echo chamber of plural and sometimes discordant enunciations, and exposes the acts of imagination to which more stable logics of French and western owe their coherence: acts that fail repeatedly, productively and sometimes spectacularly.

Notes

1. Rick Altman, 'A Semantic/Syntactic Approach to Film Genre', *Cinema Journal* 23, no. 3 (1984): 6–18. The studies cited in the previous chapter illustrate these two axes: Warshow compiled core traits that define the western protagonist, and Wright distilled the root narrative architecture of the western's 'syntax'. In both cases, evidence collected from chosen films anchors the genre's definition.
2. Andrew Tudor, 'Genre', in *The Film Genre Reader III*, ed. Barry Keith Grant (Austin: University of Texas Press), 5.
3. Ibid., 5.
4. *The Great Train Robbery* was 'not primarily perceived in the context of the Western'. Charles Musser, 'The Travel Genre in 1903–1904: Moving toward Fictional Narratives' (1987), in *Early Cinema: Space Frame Narrative*, ed. Thomas Elsaesser and Adam Barker (London, British Film Institute, 1990), 131. Screwball comedy and *film noir* similarly earn their names retrospectively.

5. 'Melodrama' is a contested term. Linda Williams considers melodrama a fundamental mode of American cinema and a paradigm that accommodates diverse thematic inflections: the Western is one mode of melodrama among others. See Linda Williams, 'Film Bodies: Gender, Genre, and Excess', *Film Quarterly* 44, no. 4 (Summer 1991): 2–13. In other usage 'melodrama' narrowly acts as a synonym of the 'weepie' or 'women's film'. Altman considers the sliding meanings of melodrama emblematic of the historical nature and fluidity of film genre definitions. On the term 'Western melodrama' specifically, see Altman, *Film/Genre*, 52.
6. Altman, *Film/Genre*, 101.
7. One could assert that genre is performative, insofar as in production and reception it is something one 'does' every time it is recognised and invoked. 'Genre is a process rather than a fact, and one in which different perspectives, needs and interests can and do deliver widely varying outcomes [. . .] genres are not born, they are made.' Barry Keith Langford, *Film Genre: Hollywood and Beyond* (Edinburgh: Edinburgh University Press, 2005), 5.
8. Altman, *Film/Genre*, 208.
9. The studio's publicity materials recommended against promoting *Stagecoach* as a western in a bid to expand the audience beyond a demographic of young males.
10. Kracauer and Burch, emblematic theorists in this vein of thought, identify ideological and stylistic national referents invoked in the filmic text. See Philip Rosen, 'History, Textuality, Nation: Kracauer, Burch, and some Problems in the Study of National Cinemas', in *Theorising National Cinema*, ed. Valentina Vitali and Paul Willemen (London: British Film Institute, 2006), 17–28.
11. Tim Bergfelder, 'Transnational Genre Hybridity: Between Vernacular Modernism and Postmodern Parody', in *Genre Hybridisation*, ed. Ivo Ritzer and Peter W. Schulze (Marburg: Schüren, 2013), 43.
12. The scale of the world, not of the individual country, 'reveals an essential gestalt of cinema's ambition during its era of novelty and innovation'. Tom Gunning, 'Early Cinema as Global Cinema: The Encyclopedic Ambition', in *Early Cinema and the 'National'*, ed. Richard Abel, Giorgio Bertellini and Rob King (New Barnet: John Libbey), 13.
13. Hayward, *French National Cinema*, 10.
14. Benedict Anderson, *Imagined Communities: Reflections on the Origin and Spread of Nationalism*, revised edition (London and New York: Verso, 2006).
15. The structural similarity and collusion of national cinemas and genres would bear out Altman's conjecture that 'against all expectations, genre theory might actually help us think about nations'. Altman, *Film/Genre*, 206.
16. On the meeting of a Hollywood genre and French cinema specifically, see Vanessa Schwartz, *It's so French: Hollywood, Paris, and the Making of Cosmopolitan Film Culture* (Chicago: University of Chicago Press, 2007). Schwartz's argument is taken up further in Chapter 7.
17. Mette Hjort and Duncan Petrie, *The Cinema of Small Nations* (Edinburgh, Edinburgh University Press, 2007).
18. This uneven transnational exchange is evinced in the essays collected in *Je t'aime...moi non plus: Franco-British Cinematic Relations*, ed. Ginette Vincendeau and Catherine Wheatley (Oxford and New York: Berghan, 2010). Mette Hjort enumerates diverse modes of this vein of inquiry in 'On the Plurality of Cinematic Transnationalism', in *World Cinemas, Transnational Perspectives*, ed. Nataša Ďurovičová and Kathleen Newman (New York and London: Routledge, 2010), 12–33.

19. Hamid Naficy, *An Accented Cinema: Exilic and Diasporic Filmmaking* (Princeton: Princeton University Press, 2003).
20. Miriam Bratu Hansen investigates local rearticulations and receptions of Hollywood-style film as a negotiation of a new 'horizon of experience' traced by cinema as a manifestation of modernity. See Miriam Bratu Hansen, 'The Mass Production of the Senses: Classical Cinema as Vernacular Modernism', *Modernism/Modernity* 6, no. 2 (1999), 59–77; and 'Fallen Women, Rising Stars, New Horizons: Shanghai Silent Film As Vernacular Modernism', *Film Quarterly* 54, no. 1 (Autumn 2000), 10–22.
21. Neil Campbell, *The Rhizomatic West: Representing the American West in a Transnational, Global Media Age* (Lincoln: University of Nebraska Press, 2008), 4. Also quoted in Austin Fisher, ed., 'Introduction', *Spaghetti Westerns at the Crossroads: Studies in Relocation, Transition, and Appropriation* (Edinburgh: Edinburgh University Press, 2016), 3.
22. Ibid., 3.
23. See Miller and Van Riper, *International Westerns*, and Klein, Ritzer and Schulze, *Global Perspectives*. Available at <https://ebookcentral.proquest.com/lib/rochester/reader.action?docID=5288273> (accessed 7 July 2023).
24. Jacques Derrida, 'The Theatre of Cruelty and the Closure of Representation', in *Writing and Difference*, trans. Alan Bass (Chicago: University of Chicago Press, 1978), 250. On the inexorability of genre designations in a literary mode, see Jacques Derrida, 'The Law of Genre', in *Acts of Literature*, ed. Derek Attridge (New York and London: Routledge, 1992), 221–52.

II
The Wild, Wild *Midi*

3

The curious geographies of Arizona Bill

In his 1962 memoirs, the French actor and director Joë (Jean) Hamman bestows the distinction of 'the first western' on *Le Cowboy*, a film he claims to have made in 1906. He then muses on his role in founding the genre: 'It is rather curious to note that it was a Frenchman who provided the impetus in a genre where the Americans were to become unbeatable.'[1] This assertion has been repeated over the years by fans, critics, scholars and even politicians as a surprising and overlooked fact of film history. On the internet it has gone viral, and in certain precincts it is received knowledge that the most ostensibly American of film genres traces its origin to an amateur film made in the Paris suburbs.[2]

The French claim to the first western may rest on firmer footing than mere Gallic chauvinism. Hamman boasted of a connection to the American West that few filmmakers, French or American, could rival in 1906. In his memoirs he recounts how as a young man in 1904, barely ten years after the frontier had been declared closed, he spent time on a ranch in Montana, visited the Pine Ridge reservation in South Dakota and called on Buffalo Bill Cody at his home in Nebraska. Hamman's recollections do not always square with the historical record, but whatever the journey's precise length or itinerary, at some point he acquired western riding and roping skills as well as a collection of western objects (a western saddle, cowboy clothes, Native American clothing and artifacts) that would later serve as props in his films.[3] However embellished the accounts of his early filmmaking, it is clear that by 1909 Hamman was directing and acting in western-themed films for the Lux company in Paris[4] and soon thereafter he would be the featured player in a series of films from Gaumont named 'Scènes de la vie de l'ouest Américain' ('Scenes of life in the American West', 1910–1912). He would garner his greatest recognition on both sides of the Atlantic playing both Native Americans and the recurring character 'Arizona Bill', a cowboy detective, for the Eclipse company between 1912 and 1914.[5] In 1914 Hamman signed with the Éclair company to make films at the studio's new facility in Tucson, but Arizona Bill never made it to Arizona: World War I began before his departure and he was quickly mobilised.[6]

If the French western has a golden age, it is undoubtedly the years immediately preceding World War I when the five most important French studios were all making western-themed films. In New Jersey, Texas, Arizona and California the Pathé, Méliès and Éclair companies had subsidiaries charged with producing films to meet the public's appetite for one- and two-reel films depicting the American West. The Gaumont and Eclipse studios made western films in France, the only moment in cinema's history when western-themed pictures were in serial production on French soil. Hamman was a frequent leading actor in these films, with the quarries of Arcueil, the Fontainebleau forest, and the Camargue region on the Mediterranean coast playing the role of the American frontier. Hamman's film career follows and in great degree shapes the fate of the silent western made in France: production began sometime around or shortly after 1906, continued for a few years, and then abruptly ceased with the onset of the war. The production of westerns made in France, and of films featuring Hamman, would never again match the volume and regularity of the period from 1909–1914.

Golden age, frontier travel and semi-stardom notwithstanding, Hamman's claim to the first western remains, to use his term, *curieux*, and measuring its credibility leads deep into the murky waters of genre formation. If the 'western' designation simply means themes, situations or personages associated with the frontier-era American West, the genre would date from the earliest days of cinema, well before Hamman ever claimed to have set foot in America or to have made a film. Edison produced western subjects for his Kinetoscope device (*Bucking Broncho, Annie Oakley, Ghost Dance*, all from 1894), the Lumières' *actualités* included western-themed views as early as 1896, and the Selig Company was filming scenic western 'panoramas' on location in Colorado by 1902. Edwin S. Porter's popular *The Great Train Robbery*, often dubbed the 'first western', had already recreated a fictive West in 1903. Numerous other American films, from *Cripple Creek Barroom* (1898) to *Life of an American Cowboy* (1906), depict cowboys, Native Americans and other western types in comedies, action sequences, chases and frontier battles.[7] Pathé's *Indiens et cowboys* (1904) already showed audiences a stagecoach attack that develops into a rescue story. By 1906, representations of the American West would not have been new cinema fare for spectators in either France or America.

The term 'western' was not widely used as a stand-alone genre designation until around 1910, and these earlier films may be classified under other generic rubrics.[8] Moreover, filmed images of the American West may not, on their own, suffice to constitute a 'western', a designation that by some definitions demands narrative or ideological structures more stable, developed and distinct than what these early films could support: for example, a meaningful opposition between east and west (divided by the frontier), a desert/garden binary that structures the narrative or a 'manifest destiny' registered in the conquest by Americans of European descent over other peoples and the lands they occupy.[9] Hamman's claim invites more serious consideration when 'western' designates more integrated structures of narrative and character psychology than the earlier films delivered. The dates of Hamman's silent French westerns (c. 1907–1914) are significant in cinema historiography and coincide with a period of rapid change in film production, distribution and exhibition. In the previous decade, cinema's first publics thrilled at what Tom Gunning calls the 'uncanny agitating power' of the new medium's 'aesthetic of astonishment': a 'cinema of attractions' that addressed the spectators directly, bidding them take in a visual display – a landscape, a stunt, a panoramic view, a gag – rather than follow the development of character psychology or a linear plot.[10] However, cinema quickly responded to its audience's thirst for narrative, and by 1906 the American Nickelodeon boom was fuelling a rapidly expanding production of films that drew the spectator into a spatial and temporal continuity established within and between shots. Cinema's 'transformational' or 'transitional' period,[11] in Gunning's terms a cinema of 'narrative integration', would last until around 1915 with the coalescence of the classical Hollywood narrative style that still, in great measure, dominates mainstream film and television today.

With the movie-going public showing an insatiable appetite for ever longer story films and exhibitors changing programmes several times a week, even daily, French film producers, like their American contemporaries, seized upon *Le Far-West* as a rich and ready source of scenarios to meet the burgeoning demand. Insofar as the integration of familiar western tropes into new storytelling strategies marks the incipient consolidation of the western genre itself, one might plausibly situate its origin somewhere around 1906, when Hamman claims to have made his first film. Hamman characterised its novelty: 'I was in fact trying not just to gallop around on horseback. It's very pretty to ride a horse, but it is not everything, one must try to bring something more, an idea or, in a word, some poetry, if you like.'[12] If we accept, for a moment, that *Le Cowboy* existed as Hamman describes it (conveying ideas and 'poetry' beyond a simple chase film), that its more developed aesthetic and ideological dimensions were indeed novel, and that these new elements are identifiable as constituents of the western under a credible definition of the genre, Hamman's claim to the first western is more defensible. The conditions this claim demands are also weighty enough to crush it. Any ideas or poetry that may have distinguished *Le Cowboy* will remain unknown; like most of its contemporaries, *Le Cowboy* is lost, and the western films from the Gaumont and Eclipse series that have survived are contemporaneous with a flood of American productions – the films of James Young Deer and Max 'Broncho Billy' Aronson, among hundreds of others – that by 1914 had established the conventions that allowed a film to be recognised as simply 'a western'.

Quibbling over which film, person or country claims the first western might seem an inconclusive exercise in jingoist hair-splitting. Indeed, the profusion of western-themed films produced and distributed in both the United States and France by French and American (and other) companies, from Edison and the Lumières through Broncho Billy and Arizona Bill, would more readily show that the genre's origins are transnational and that no single national industry, French, American or otherwise, may definitively claim them. Asserting the validity of Hamman's or anyone else's claim to being 'first' demands a further caveat, as most of the films of the era are lost and the need for speculation dooms the gesture to be indecisive.[13]

A separate interest in Hamman's claim lies not in measures of its plausibility, but in how the uncertainties that thwart its substantiation are a vital constituent of the cinematic depictions of the American West made in France before World War I. Hamman's films merit consideration apart from their American contemporaries for the distinct light they cast on 'transitional' cinema. The term itself may be misleading, for it carries a suggestion that 'transitional cinema did nothing save pave the way for classical Hollywood practice in the late 1910s'.[14] Film scholars have reconsidered the loose and uneven narrativity of films from this period as not merely 'a shift between paradigms, but also a paradigm in itself', with its own defining traits.[15] For the study of American westerns this re-adjusted perspective presents a challenge: the transitional paradigm may exist in its own right as a distinct cinematic practice, but at the same time it represents the developmental stage of a prolific genre that will comprise some of the most iconic films of the Hollywood studio era. For the French production of westerns, the years between 1906 and 1914 mark neither a gestation towards generic coalescence and a stylistically mature French western, nor an evolution or 'missing link' between early cinema and later consolidation. On the contrary, these dates frame a window of possibility that seems to slam shut with the consolidation of 'classical' narrative conventions. With no brilliant future illuminating them with retrospective explanatory light, their distinct features are less susceptible to being 'experienced as a rush to what came after'.[16]

The surviving films from the 'Arizona Bill' cycle reveal a permissive cinematic textuality that accommodates what, in hindsight, are startling incongruities.[17] Unsteadily integrating the visual display of landscapes and the narrative, they do not unequivocally show the American West, nor, often, do they tell its story. What they show and tell in its place is no more consistent: a loose alignment of rudimentary narratives, spectacular stunts, appealing landscapes and markers of other film genres, alongside an uneven semantics of 'westernness.' A growing demand for the tighter integration of these elements doubtless diminished the viability of *le Far-West* made in France and contributed to the end, after the war, of the serial production of westerns in the Camargue. However, in their day these films were well received in both the United States and in France, and though it may seem counterintuitive when measured by later standards, the glaring inconsistencies in these films may have less hobbled than enhanced their appeal. Could the imperfect integration of 'French' and 'western' be considered not a shortcoming but a positive trait of transitional cinema to which the films owe a measure of their success?

The western landscape in transition

By the time Hamman began playing Arizona Bill for the Eclipse studio in 1912, a western filmed anywhere other than the American West faced a formidable handicap. Pictures made by independent producers on western locations in the early 1910s were so popular, profitable and numerous that they could guarantee American exhibitors a reliable alternative to films licensed by the Motion Pictures Patent Company (MPPC, also known as 'The Trust') at home and flood markets abroad. Their success contributed to the defeat of Edison's Trust, and to the consolidation of the cinema industry in American hands.[18] The American-made western enjoyed a powerful double advantage in the spectacular visual interest and the alibi of authenticity a western location confers. Critics and spectators began to expect nothing less than the variety and beauty of the Sierra Nevada, the Great Plains, the California coast, or the Arizona desert; the pejorative term 'Jersey scenery' described the ersatz western settings of films made near Eastern cities.[19] Nonetheless, despite this inhospitable climate of reception, between 1912 and 1914 the George Kleine Company distributed a selection of two- and three-reel western-themed films, made in France, to exhibitors in the United States; four of the five films featured Hamman playing the cowboy detective Arizona Bill.[20] The often protectionist American critics received these films favourably, with praise for Hamman's performances despite obvious inconsistencies in the filming location and other details.[21] How, against the tide of purportedly more authentic American films made on location, could French-made westerns overcome their disadvantage to garner critical acclaim and their leading actor become a recognised figure rising towards international stardom?

Arizona Bill's appeal is less a conundrum if we approach these films as their contemporary spectators would have done, with little expectation that diegetic westernness will seamlessly align with or exhaustively contain the visual display of the filming location's landscapes. By 1908 D. W. Griffith may have been able to film a landscape that was 'not simply visually pleasurable, but is taken up by the symbolic system of the film's story and thoroughly narrativised'.[22] However, Griffith was an exceptional director, and many of his contemporaries struggled with making even the basic story of their films clear to the spectators.[23] The unevenness of narrative integration permitted what Charlie Keil has called the 'sustained appeal of attractions' to persist as an important feature of transitional cinema.[24] As late as 1913, a critic for *Le Courrier cinématographique* could still name panoramic landscape films cinema's most 'perfect' genre, a preference conferred at the expense of the creaky dramatic narratives endemic in the cinema of his time and in which these images are sometimes embedded:

> The most perfect genre currently is certainly the 'outdoor' ['panorama'] film, which naturally benefits from the perfections that have been slowly realised by 'pure' photography [...] These landscapes manage, in certain dramatic works, to mask the poverty of

the action; unfortunately it is not always this way, and the dramatic art, in the cinema, often verges on mediocrity, despite the exceptional resources it has at its disposal.[25]

The critic's remarks evince the tension between narrative and attraction. The visual appeal of a landscape does not submit to the narrative, but (if the spectator is lucky) compensates or even eclipses the weak dramatic action as the film's primary interest. Moreover, the critic does not locate the perfection of cinema in the successful bending of the landscape to narrative imperatives, but in an attraction-like appeal purified of such purpose. The smooth integration of the classical Hollywood film style might be just a couple of years away, but meanwhile narrative and visual display persist in following their own logics and may even compete.[26]

The transitional landscape's slack connection to the narrative prerogative hinders the inclusion of pre-1914 films under later definitions of the western genre that demand unconditional, immediate and complete integration of these elements. In *Sixguns and Society: A Structural Study of the Western*, one of the first theoretically informed monographs on the genre, Will Wright describes a landscape that 'does not simply present a familiar setting, it envelops the setting in social and moral meanings which are immediately understood'.[27] The gendered dynamic that structures Jane Tompkins's reading of the western requires a similarly saturated landscape 'so rhetorically persuasive that an entire code of values is in place, rock solid, from the outset, without anyone's ever saying a word'.[28] Richard Slotkin charts an imaginary frontier where white men regress to a more primitive state to regenerate, through acts of violence, an American society both stronger and more racially pure. The tight consolidation of image and narrative allows this mythic meaning to suffuse 'an imagined landscape which evokes authentic places and times, but which becomes, in the end, completely identified with the fictions created about it'.[29] The immediate and comprehensive integration of the visual landscape into the psychology of characters, mythic structure and the narrative overdetermines an exclusion of pre-1915 films, which do not guarantee such tight alignment. Neither Wright nor Tompkins considers silent film, and although Slotkin accedes to *The Great Train Robbery*'s claim to the 'first' western, the first film he analyses as an adequate vehicle for the American myth is, tellingly, Griffith's *The Birth of a Nation*, a film hailed as a watershed moment of narrative consolidation that heralded the end of cinema's transitional period and that is not a western.

Some transitional films may anticipate more developed structuring principles and ideological investments: Griffith's *Battle of Elderbush Gulch* (1913), for example, or even Broncho Billy's 'good bad man' persona. However, as the *Courrier cinématographique* critic observes, as late as 1913 a visual display could be lauded for an attraction-like appeal independent from the ideologically charged narrative structure – masculinist, nationalist or otherwise – that would exhaustively seize it. This looseness of integration may be perceived as a 'paradigm' in its own right, but for American films it may also represent a transitional immaturity redressed by subsequent stylistic developments and consolidation. By later measures of both documentary authenticity and narrative verisimilitude it is a lack, a deficiency, a glass half empty. The Arizona Bill films, on the other hand, owe not only a vitality but their very possibility to the licence not to reconcile filmed location, narrative and ideological investment in their enunciation of 'westernness.' Two surviving films from the series reveal how the imbrication of plural purposes, rather than their imperfect integration, is also a surplus, a glass full of potential, and may be considered a positive structuring principle of the transitional paradigm that contributes to their commercial viability and appeal.

The Mong-Fu Tong / Le Mystère de la banque d'Elk City (1913)

George Kleine's promotion for Eclipse's *The Mong-Fu Tong* (released in France as *Le Mystère de la banque d'Elk City* [The Elk City Bank Mystery]) promises that 'it will stir your blood like old wine – like a tale from Poe!'[30] The opening shot fulfils the promise of *Grand Guignol* macabre: a murder victim lies prone on an office floor, his head obscured under a desk, an open safe in the background. A sheriff is summoned, and he brings in the cowboy detective Arizona Bill to solve the case. As Bill keeps watch in the office, a band of Chinese criminals releases a snake into the room from under a floorboard and a series of action sequences ensues. A horseback pursuit and gunfight in which Bill's mount is shot from under him is followed by a car chase and fistfight as Bill overtakes and captures the Chinese gangsters. Bill is subsequently kidnapped and taken to a remote cabin *cum* opium den. Mong-Fu, the gang's leader, drugs his prisoner and coerces him to write a letter summoning his wife, whose beauty was revealed in a photograph. The henchmen lead the unsuspecting woman

Figure 3.1 Pre-release advertisement for the *Mong-Fu Tong*. Source: *Moving Picture World*, 13 August 1913.

to the remote house, where Mong-Fu viciously assaults her. She stabs him and liberates the bound Bill. After more brawls Bill and his wife flee on horseback as the house catches fire. Mong-Fu crawls in agony from the burnt debris. Back in the office, Bill clears up the mystery.

The story of *The Mong-Fu Tong* unfolds through an uneven narrative flow characteristic of transitional cinema. A single sequence, the chase that takes Bill from the office to his kidnapping, includes over 21 shots, nearly half of the total (46) in the print.[31] In the chase's dynamic climax, a rear-view travelling shot shows Bill's car gradually overtaking the car of the Chinese before Hamman, in one of his showpiece stunts (known as *clous*, or 'nails'), jumps from one moving car to the other and engages in a fistfight as the vehicle continues to hurtle towards the receding camera. The varied editing, camera movement and breathless action of the chase sequence is notably lacking in the remainder of the film, where the characters face an immobile camera in full or three-quarter shots, aligned on a horizontal plane with an expanse of empty space in the foreground. Variations are few: a low-angle medium reaction shot of the Chinese men under the floorboards and two high-angle shots, of Bill cradling his dead horse and of the man crawling from the charred wreckage, are all that break up the static uniformity.

A comparison of *The Mong-Fu Tong* with D. W. Griffith's *The Lonedale Operator* (1911) reveals a marked disparity in narrative complexity. Griffith used ninety-eight shots, more than twice the number in the print of *The Mong-Fu Tong*. Furthermore, Griffith's rhythms of alternation and repetition are carefully structured. Most cuts in *The Lonedale Operator* take the spectator from one location to another, weaving together two and sometimes three separate places in a single sequence, and the return to a location often deploys a new camera distance and angle.[32] In contrast, *The Mong-Fu Tong*, even though it was made later, hews to a linearity more akin to early chase films in which the film cuts to a different location only to accompany a character who makes the same displacement in the fiction. To bring Bill into the film, the sheriff leaves the office in one shot and arrives at the farm in the next, and the sequence ends with the two characters leaving the farm. In the following shot, Bill arrives back at the office, and so on. Such punctilious successivity precludes Griffith-style parallel editing and the range of emotions it can reveal and magnify. Instead, the broadest of brushstrokes establish motivation: Mong-Fu's leer, for example, bluntly registers the criminal desire that impels his actions.

However, even this plodding bid for intelligible spatio-temporal integration stumbles over the film's ambiguous deployment of 'westernness'. The office in the opening shot (French doors and windows, a telephone, men in suits) suggests the modern world of circa 1913 France, but the spatial and temporal frames of 'Frenchness' and contemporary modernity are quickly controverted by the arrival of the sheriff sporting a broad-brimmed hat and a showy metal star: the police authority is not a French *gendarme*, but a western type who travels with two pseudo-cowboy deputies. This initial incongruity inaugurates a string of discordant visual tropes that evoke both modern France and the frontier-era American West, often in the same frame. In his first appearance, in the courtyard of farm buildings with terracotta tile roofs, Bill is decked in showy western regalia: enormous woolly chaps, a bandana, a loose-fitting vest, a six-gun on a belt and a broad-brimmed hat. In contrast, his wife wears a tailored outfit with a 1910s silhouette, but she is the odd one out, sartorially, once the sheriff and his deputies arrive. Their presence alone is telling; they do not call Bill on the telephone as the clerk called them, and they travel to the farm by horse cart rather than automobile. Semantically, the displacement from the modern office to Bill's rustic farm reads as a journey from a 1913 French city to a temporally and geographically ambiguous zone that houses markers of both the nineteenth-century American West and of rural but modern France. The personage of Bill most strongly evokes the western setting when, in his western gear, he gives his wife a flourishing farewell on horseback from his western saddle before pursuing the villains in an automobile. Modern cars also take Bill, and later the woman, to Mong-Fu's den, where European modernity again evanesces as the signifiers – a remote and rustic cabin, a cowboy captive, an escape on horseback – allow filiation to a competing diegesis of the American West. The denouement brings the characters back to the modern French office.

The location shooting contributes to the indeterminate geography of *The Mong-Fu Tong*. Though certain buildings have a distinct French aspect (the *pierre de taille* exterior of the office's building, Bill's tile-roofed farm), the majority of exterior shots show tree-lined roads à la 'Jersey scenery' that fail to anchor the locations with precision. The discordance between the French title's situation of the action in the presumably American 'Elk City' and the American release's reference to 'Bill, an American in France' (revised, perhaps, to deflect American criticism of the obviously non-western locations)[33] reveals that the ambiguity of the setting was evident, even advantageous, at the time: the landscape is the backdrop for both a modern French world of telephones and motorcars and an American West of six-shooters and horses. In this indecisive

Figure 3.2 A cowboy in a car: Hamman prepares to jump in *The Mong-Fu Tong*. The Library of Congress.

geography Bill functions less as a traveller in time and space, plucked from frontier-era America and dropped into an unfamiliar modern Europe to which he must adapt, than as an inhabitant of two spheres that simultaneously assert themselves. Intermittent 'westernness' shares the screen with a similarly unstable European modernity whose distinct orientalist inflection is redolent of circa-1913 colonial anxieties; the setting is as evocative of Pierre Loti as it is of Zane Gray and Owen Wister. Inexorable white/European dominance and fears of miscegenation might subtend the plots and characterisations of both diegetic spheres, but neither modern France nor the American West decisively claims primacy or exhaustively saturates the landscape.

By later measures of diegetic stability, the curious co-presence of French and American elements would represent a wobbly tentative step on the way to a more smoothly integrated stride. However, if the film's marketing is an indication, this dual mode of address appealed to both French and American spectators. For both audiences, one may ask if the glaring discrepancies enhance, rather than detract from, the visual interest of the film. The neutrality of the landscapes in many shots tempers these dissonances in *The Mong-Fu Tong*. In a second film from the series, the southern French landscape more assertively competes with the purported setting in the American West, permitting a clearer distinction between 'French' and 'western' and raising with greater force the question of whether it constitutes a deficiency or a surplus attraction for the circa-1913 spectator.

The Last Minute (1913)

Released in the United States five weeks after *The Mong-Fu Tong*, *The Last Minute (La Dernière Minute)* tells a similar story. Bill is summoned to the bedside of a dying man, who slips him a document to the dismay of a villainous eavesdropping nephew. In a lawyer's office, the reading of the document, a will, names a niece the man's heir provided she present the document in person within thirty days. Bill and his wife travel to the niece's farm, but a posse of masked men follows, attacks, seizes the document and kidnaps the niece. On horseback, Bill and his wife pursue the men and a gunfight ensues. Bill's wife chases the kidnappers who hold the niece hostage, while Bill follows the rest of the group. Bill's wife shoots the kidnapper and rescues the niece. The other men board a train, which Bill overtakes on horseback. A fight ensues. Bill escapes to the train's roof, rigs the engine, and as the train crosses a bridge he jumps off the top of a train car into a river before the train explodes. Bill arrives at the lawyer's office in time to present the retrieved document.

Like *The Mong-Fu Tong*, *The Last Minute* establishes its contrived pretext with static interiors and long takes, setting the stage for the *clou* stunts that constitute the film's most spectacular attraction. Bill chases the moving train on horseback and leaps from his saddle onto the caboose's gallery.[34] The more astonishing and dangerous feat follows: as the sabotaged train crosses a bridge Bill jumps off a moving railway car into a river at least 20 feet below, just missing a piling as he lands close to the riverbank.[35] In addition to death-defying stunts, some notably poor production values are common to both films: in the opening shot a servant character looks at the camera operator for direction and upon receiving it gives a nod of assent; in another a shadow of someone behind the camera conspicuously falls into the frame. *The Last Minute* nonetheless presents greater cinematic complexity. The deeper space of the bedroom set generates dramatic tension through the entrances and reactions of characters on various planes. There is some shot variation and at times a careful *mise-en-scène*: the shot of the kidnappers riding across the foreground while others gallop in silhouette on a distant ridge, for example, anticipates the opening credits of Anthony Mann's *Winchester '73* (1950). Parallel editing also breaks up the linear succession of shots. The ride of Bill and his wife is intercut with the kidnappers' flight, and a few shots alternate between the separate chases. The bravura bridge stunt is followed by cuts between the soaked Bill and the speeding train before a long shot, possibly from his point of view, shows the distant explosion. The film also shows greater control over period detail: no telephones or automobiles compete with the semantics of westernness registered in the antlers in the old man's bedroom or the chaps hanging in Bill's kitchen, though some modern clothing and decor persist.

Nonetheless, despite greater sophistication and consistency in some components, the filmed landscape fractures the western diegesis more decisively than the film's predecessor. Though explicitly set in the American West, in contrast to the non-descript trees and roads of *The Mong-Fu Tong* the photography amply features panoramic views of the Camargue, the picturesque and geographically distinct region of the Rhône river delta known for desolate marshes, salt-water ponds and dunes populated by white horses and running bulls. The chase sequence includes long shots that become more extreme as the figures gallop away from the camera, their diminishing size in the frame giving way to sweeping views of grassy wetlands and copses. The landscape is featured in twenty-eight of the print's fifty-two shots, and another eight shots show exteriors of stucco and stone buildings characteristic of the region: the niece, for example, lives in a farmhouse with a steep thatched roof typical of a southern French *cabane*. The railroad bridge is constructed on stone pilings that little resemble the wooden trestles one would expect in the American West. A singularly aestheticised shot shows Bill riding through sand dunes in the mist. There is no evident effort to mask the distinct features of the Camargue scenery and the vernacular architecture of the region. On the contrary, they seem to be emphasised with pictorialist attention. The discordance between the Camargue filming location and the narrative's western setting did not escape the American commentator in *Moving Picture World*:

> The location of the story is the great West, but as so often happens in pictures made on the other side of the water and intended to reproduce the atmosphere of the land beyond the Rockies the task was too much for the producer. There are many apparent inconsistencies which weaken the story.[36]

The inconsistencies are undeniable, the ascribed intent less so. The panoramic photography suggests an intent more to feature the French landscapes than to bend them to a diegetic West.

The *Moving Picture World* critic's contention that the inconsistencies weaken *The Last Minute* also begs interrogation. Even the reviewer concedes that 'as entertainment the picture goes over', attributing the film's success to 'thrilling situations and sensational episodes'.[37] This ultimately positive verdict begs the question of whether the film succeeds despite the discord between filming locations and the western setting, or precisely because the visual display of thrills, sensations and appealing French landscapes does not fully submit to a thin and contrived narrative pretext. With hindsight one may easily imagine a more evenly integrated film that would minimise the discrepancies. A director could have again chosen to mute the landscape's distinctness by filming non-descript tree-lined roads throughout, or to bind Hamman's stunts more tightly to the story through intercut shots of the characters whose lives and livelihoods are at stake. But would neutral 'Jersey scenery' be more compelling than the visual interest of the panoramic display of plains, thatched roofs, marshes and dunes? By which measure would it enhance the film to channel the leap from the train through the threadbare conceit of a contested inheritance, rather than deploying a direct address whose 'aesthetics of astonishment' hails the incredulous spectator with a deliberate long take that precludes cinematic trickery, as if to say 'watch this, you are not going to believe your eyes, *this really happened*' when the small figure plummets from the railway car towards possible injury or death? Insofar as tighter narrative integration would not make a more compelling film, and even detract from it, the loose diegetic weave pierced by the attraction-like excess of stunts and landscapes constitutes less a lack than a surplus, less a crisis in narrativity than a positive trait of the 'transitional' paradigm: a generative cinematic textuality, permissive rather than primitive, rich rather than deficient, not a measure of failure but the conditions for the film's appeal to audiences at home and abroad.

A consequence of this surplus attraction, however, is that while these films may represent a golden age of the French western, they openly trade in the spectacle of the genre's incompleteness. The signifiers of the frontier-era American West are embedded in, and sometimes eclipsed

Figure 3.3 A bid to astonish: Bill's leap off the moving train in *The Last Minute*. The Library of Congress.

by, a setting that is registered not only as French but also as modern. Furthermore, the Camargue itself, as discussed in the following chapter, loads competing histories, narratives and traditions into these images. This fluidity unmoors a key parameter that, for theorists of genre as for many filmmakers, anchors a fundamental opposition: the frontier between East and West, garden and desert, or modern and rustic that ideologically charges the landscape in narratives of Western expansion, and through which a character's alignment with one side or the other decisively determines possibilities for speech and action.

The inconsistent connection to the American West also allows a filiation to other genre categories. In his publicity campaign Kleine marketed Hamman's series to American exhibitors as adventure films and, suggesting concern over the ambiguous diegesis, the advertising pitches again skirt mention of the western setting. The synopses and reviews in trade journals for the other films in the series that Kleine distributed further support the 'adventure' designation. *The Subterranean City* (*La Ville souterraine*) takes the character to an underground city 'that fairly rivals the wonders of *Aladdin's Lamp*', and in this fantastic setting Arizona Bill pursues jewel thieves while performing 'dare-devil exploits'.[38] The account of *Wrecked in Mid-air* places Bill back in a plausibly western setting of goldfields, horses and revolvers, but the stunts include a car chase and, for the centrepiece *clou*, by surviving accounts spectacular to watch, Hamman crashes an airplane and his character is rescued from the debris.[39] The films also bear close affinities to the crime or gangster genre. Bill is as much a detective as a cowboy, acting as the former in the modern French frame, the latter when the western setting reasserts itself, and as both simultaneously when neither diegetic frame prevails over the landscapes, buildings and situations seen in the films. Hamman's unrealised future career in Tucson was on a course towards crime films: in the never fulfilled agreement with the Éclair company he was slated to play the American dime-novel detective Nick Carter, not a cowboy named Bill.

The positive reception of the Arizona Bill cycle in both France and the United States bespeaks a tolerance for narrative looseness and ambiguity among both filmmakers and spectators. A rising star and some pretty scenery, a little narrative development here and some spectacular stunts there, a measure of both France and the old West, side by side, could in 1913 be entertaining, appealing and commercially viable for audiences in both countries. Later French western films will not enjoy similar 'transitional' freedom from the imperative to present a landscape 'completely identified with the fictions created about it'. When such integration – a cornerstone of the 'classical' narrative film style – becomes the goal, the viability of *le Far-West* made in a recognisable Camargue (or in the Landes, in Provence, or in the Fontainebleau forest) will be diminished.

The failure to meet the demand for more complete integration will nonetheless continue to present opportunity. Arizona Bill's curious geographies herald future meetings of the American West with French cinema – its stars, its landscapes and locations, its filming practices, and (in the sound era) its language – that generate a productive friction between the French and western elements. This tension will often steer the genre into an ironic or parodic mode, and when foregrounded may be harnessed to issue a sharp-edged critique of American-style film and American-style consumer culture. This critical blade cuts two ways, however, and the same discordance returns to muddy the coherence of the French assertion that fails, intentionally or not, either to overcome or smoothly to integrate the western element.

With the onset of the war in 1914, the production of westerns in France abruptly ceased and the genre would never see serial exploitation in France again. Although the pre-war films made on Camargue locations do not leave a legacy of continuous French production in the genre, they announce another strain of cinema that continued throughout the remainder of the silent era and into the early decades of sound film. The 'Camargue film' of the interwar years charges many of the same landscapes, personnel and situations seen in the Arizona Bill series with the traditions of a regional civilisation, preserved and set apart from the encroaching and homogenising centralisation of modern France. In the following chapter, a third surviving pre-war film featuring Hamman as 'Bill' will illustrate the constitutive paradox of this regionalist cycle: namely, that this traditional cinematic Camargue on film is, in significant measure, a modern creation, forged from tropes of the American West that owe their familiarity not only to a rustic frontier, but also to a modern world driven by new technologies of communication, travel and entertainment.

Notes

1. 'Il est assez curieux de constater que ce fut un français qui donna l'impulsion dans un genre où les Américains devaient devenir imbattables.' Joë Hamman, *Du Far-West à Montmartre: un demi-siècle d'aventures* (Paris: les Editeurs Français Réunis, 1962), 93. Hamman mentions a second film, *Le Desperado*, that he dubs 'one of cinema's

first westerns' ('un des premiers westerns du cinéma'). Ibid., 191. Francis Lacassin's research suggests *Le Cowboy* could not have been made before 1907 and places *Le Desperado* around 1910. Francis Lacassin, *Pour une contre-histoire du cinéma* (Institut Lumière/Actes Sud, 1994), 132.
2. Eric Leguèbe writes: 'En fait, la réalité du western a commencé à prendre corps au début du XXe siècle sur la terre de la France' ('In fact, the reality of the western began to take shape at the beginning of the twentieth century on French soil'). Eric Leguèbe, *L'Histoire universelle du Western* (Paris: Editions France-Empire, 1989), 252. Thierry Lefrançois cites the 'first westerns that, a surprising thing, were not made by Americans, but by our young painter (Hamman)' ('des premiers westerns qui, chose surprenante, ne furent pas tournés par des Américains, mais par notre jeune peintre). Thierry Lefrançois, *Les Indiens de Buffalo Bill et la Camargue* (Paris: Editions de La Martinière, 1994), 11. Michel Crépeau, the mayor of La Rochelle, observes that 'the first westerns were made in the Camargue in the silent era by a French filmmaker' ('les premiers westerns furent tournés en Camargue à l'époque du cinéma muet par un cinéaste Français'). In Lefrançois, *Les Indiens*, 7. Paul Bleton asserts that George Kleine's distribution of the Arizona Bill series 'made the nascent American cinema conscious of the cinematographic potential of the western universe' ('fit prendre conscience au cinema américain naissant du potential cinématographique de l'univers western.') Kleine did not begin importing these films until 1912, years after American western production was established. Paul Bleton, *Western, France: la place de l'Ouest dans l'imaginaire français* (Paris: Les Belles Lettres, 2002), 210. The claim is not exclusively French; Susan Hayward writes that 'although the genre originated in France, it was soon colonized by the Americans'. Susan Hayward, *French National Cinema*, second edition (New York and London: Routledge, 1993), 99. Numerous websites repeat the claim in various forms.
3. Hamman's accounts of his experience in America are discrepant. In a 1914 feature he states, falsely, that he was born in Canada and lived in the United States for 'several years'. *Le Courrier cinématographique* 4, no. 15 (11 April 1914): 44–5. In 1950 Hamman again claimed that he lived in the United States 'for years' ('des années'). 'Le Roi du lasso: le premier cow-boy du cinéma mondial', *Franc-tireur* (14 June 1950). Placed ironically under the rubric 'histoires vraies' (true stories), Hamman's account of how his horse and co-star (*Pieds Blancs*) was sent from America is fiction. Joë Hamman, 'Mon Cheval', *Film* (15 January 1920). Hamman attributes his first films to a studio that did not yet exist. The Buffalo Bill archives have no record of a visit from Hamman to Cody in 1904, leading Bernard Bastide to call Hamman's recollections 'seriously contested'. Bernard Bastide, *Aux sources du cinéma en Camargue: Joë Hamman et Folco de Baroncelli* (Avignon: Palais du Roure, 2018). Emily Burns further details how Hamman's accounts of his journey 'fall apart under scrutiny' in *Transnational Frontiers: The American West in France* (Norman: University of Oklahoma Press, 2018), 43–4. Burns also submits that Hamman and his friend, Folco de Baroncelli, likely acquired their Native American artifacts in France. Ibid., 44.
4. Lacassin, *Pour une contre-histoire*, 132.
5. A *Moving Picture World* reviewer praised Hamman's prowess in the 1912 *Red Man's Honor*: 'Joe Hamman will always be remembered as Red Hawk... He reminds one of that champion of all rough riders, Tom Mix, and must have punched cows and burned the plains with horse hoofs at some time in his career.' James S. McQuade, 'The Red Man's Honor', *Moving Picture World* 14, no. 11 (14 December 1912):

1064. An April 1914 issue of *Le Courrier cinématographique* features Hamman in a two-page spread. The critic notes his popularity in the United States. *Le Courrier cinématographique* 4, no. 15 (11 April 1914): 44–5.
6. For a biographical account of Hamman's activities before, during, and after the war, see Bastide, *Aux sources du cinéma en Camargue: Joë Hamman et Folco de Baroncelli*.
7. Nanna Verhoeff lists a number of surviving western films that would pre-date Hamman's *Le Cowboy* in *The West in Early Cinema: After the Beginning* (Amsterdam: Amsterdam University Press, 2006), 416–25.
8. Verhoeff observes that early western-themed story films were generally grouped under other genres: 'Romance of the West', 'Western Comedy', or 'Western Melodrama', among others; 'the western' did not emerge as a substantive until after 1910. Verhoeff, *The West in Early Cinema*, 114. As noted in Chapter 2, Charles Musser has argued that in 1903 *The Great Train Robbery* was 'not primarily perceived in the context of the western' and could be more accurately categorised as a crime film. Charles Musser, 'The Travel Genre in 1903–1904: Moving toward Fictional Narratives' (1987), in *Early Cinema: Space Frame Narrative*, ed. Thomas Elsaesser and Adam Barker (London, British Film Institute. 1990), 131.
9. Tom Gunning links the national narratives and the integration of film's storytelling capacity: 'The rise of nationalist discourse through and around cinema, while not absolutely absent from early cinema, seems rather to depend on narrative forms and the use of documentary to create ideological arguments that appear in the 1910s using complex editing-based structures of contrast and suspense.' Tom Gunning, 'Early Cinema as Global Cinema: The Encyclopedic Ambition', in *Early Cinema and the 'National'*, ed. Richard Abel, Giorgio Bertellini and Rob King (New Barnet: John Libbey, 2008), 15–16.
10. Tom Gunning, 'An Aesthetic of Astonishment: Early Film and the (In)Credulous Spectator', in *Film Theory and Criticism*, 6th edition, ed. Leon Baudry and Marshall Cohen (New York and Oxford: Oxford University Press, 2004), 864.
11. Charlie Keil prefers the term 'transitional' in *Early American Cinema in Transition: Story, Style, and Filmmaking 1907–1913* (Madison: The University of Wisconsin Press, 2001).
12. 'J'essayais justement de ne pas faire de la galopade. C'est très joli de monter à cheval, mais ce n'est pas tout, il faut tâcher d'apporter quelque chose, une idée, enfin de la poésie si vous voulez.' Quoted in Lacassin, *Pour une contre-histoire*, 260.
13. For Verhoeff, the inconsistent usage of the term 'western' betrays an inchoate generic consolidation that, with the incomplete archive, condemns the classification of pre-1914 films as 'westerns' to speculative anachronism. Verhoeff, *The West in Early Cinema*, 114.
14. Charlie Keil and Shelly Stamp, 'Introduction', in *American Cinema's Transitional Era*, ed. Charlie Keil and Shelly Stamp (Berkeley: University of California Press, 2004), 2.
15. Verhoeff, *The West in Early Cinema*, 117.
16. Ibid., 117.
17. The Gaumont 'Scènes de la vie de l'ouest Américain' have been shown at numerous festivals, been released on DVD, and drawn commentary. The present focus is on the surviving Arizona Bill films, which have garnered less attention and were believed by some to have been lost. The analysis is based on the reference prints of *The Mong-Fu Tong* and *The Last Minute* in the Library of Congress's collection in Washington, DC, and, in the next chapter the recently restored and digitised *Face au taureau* (*Facing the Bull*) at the *Centre National du Cinéma*.

18. Richard Abel asserts 'the unique significance of the western' for the dominance of American cinema in *Americanizing the Movie and 'Movie-Mad' Audiences, 1910–1914* (Berkeley: University of California Press, 2006), 62–79.
19. Eileen Bowser, *The Transformation of Cinema 1907–1915* (Berkeley: University of California Press, 1990), 155.
20. Under the name 'Kleine-Eclipse', Kleine released *Red Man's Honor* ('La Conscience de Cheval-Rouge', December 1912), in which Hamman plays the title role, followed by four Arizona Bill films: *The Mong-Fu Tong* ('Le Mystère de la banque d'Elk City', August 1913); *The Last Minute* ('La Dernière Minute', October 1913); *The Subterranean City, or, Trailing the Jewel Thieves* ('La Ville souterraine', November 1913); and *Wrecked in Mid-Air* (French title unknown, January 1914). Gaston Roudès directed some or all of these films.
21. James McQuade, a *Moving Picture World* reviewer, writes of *Red Man's Honor*: 'Monsieur Gaston Roudes [sic], the producer, is to be congratulated on having succeeded in giving us the atmosphere of Indian life and customs in years gone by, and he is also to be congratulated in having as his chief actor in the stirring scenes such an accomplished horseman and daredevil rider as Joe Hamman.' *Moving Picture World* 14, no. 11 (14 December 1912): 1064.
22. Tom Gunning, *D. W. Griffith & the Origins of American Narrative Film: The Early Years at Biograph* (Urbana: University of Illinois Press, 1994), 75.
23. Eileen Bowser observes a 'crisis in narrative' as the longer and more complex stories demanded by multiple reel films stumbled over the limited storytelling resources of many directors. Bowser, *The Transformation*, 42.
24. Charlie Keil, 'From Here to Modernity: Style, Historiography, and Transitional Cinema', in Keil and Stamp, *American Cinema's Transitional Era*, 54–5.
25. 'le genre actuellement le plus parfait est certes le "*plein-air*," qui a bénéficié, naturellement des perfections réalisées lentement par la photographie pure [...]. Ce sont des paysages qui parviennent, dans certaines oeuvres dramatiques, à masquer la pauvreté de l'action; malheureusement il n'en est pas toujours ainsi, et l'art dramatique, au cinéma, frise souvent la médiocrité, en dépit des ressources exceptionnelles dont il pourrait disposer'. 'Le Cinéma et l'art dramatique', *Le Courrier cinématographique* 3, no. 27 (5 July 1913): 4.
26. Verhoeff similarly observes a porous boundary between filmed location and diegetic setting, documentary and fiction, travelogue and story film, neither side exhaustively 'taking up' the other in its purpose. Verhoeff, *The West*, 110–11.
27. Will Wright, *Sixguns and Society: A Structural Study of the Western* (Berkeley: University of California Press, 1975), 4.
28. Jane Tompkins, *West of Everything* (Oxford: Oxford University Press, 1994), 74.
29. Richard Slotkin, *Gunfighter Nation: The Myth of the Frontier in Twentieth-Century America* (Norman: University of Oklahoma Press, 1998), 233.
30. 'A Smashing Kleine-Eclipse You Should Have!' *Moving Picture World* 17, no. 2 (2 August 1913): 507.
31. The number, length and order of the shots in a print from this era are susceptible to machine failures, burns, re-spliced fragments and editorial interventions over the years. The existing prints cannot be assumed to be complete or 'original'. Projection speed and running time are also subject to variation. For an account of these and other contingencies in studying prints of early films, see Paolo Cherchi-Usai, *Silent Cinema: A Guide to Study, Research, and Curatorship*, third edition (London: BFI, 2019).

32. Tom Gunning parses *The Londale Operator*'s 'grammar' in 'Systematizing the Electric Message: Narrative Form, Gender, and Modernity in *The Lonedale Operator*', in Keil and Stamp, *American Cinema's Transitional Era*, 15–50.
33. Another review also identifies Bill and his wife as Americans 'supposed to be stranded in Europe'. *The Exhibitors' Times* 1, no. 10 (26 July 1913): 18. The explanation fails to account for the tin-star sheriff as the agent of law enforcement.
34. Hamman had also performed this stunt for the Gaumont film *Le Railway de la mort* (*Their Lives for Gold*, Jean Durand, 1912).
35. Hamman performed what is reported to be an even more astounding feat in the (now lost) *Wrecked in Mid-air*: 'With his wife in the machine, the aeroplane blows up some seventy-five feet above the ground and falls to the earth, carrying the couple with them amid a shower of debris. There is neither subtitle nor film cutting to give an air of unreality to the scene. It is merely a hazardous and dangerous feat which would have constituted an Associated Press item, had it happened to a well-known aviator as it actually occurred before the camera.' 'Wrecked in Mid-Air (Manufacturers' Advance Notes)', *Moving Picture World* 3, no. 19 (17 January 1914): 298.
36. 'The Last Minute', *Moving Picture World* 18, no. 4 (25 October 1913): 380. In a study of the earlier Gaumont westerns, Mohr ascribes the ample featuring of the Camargue scenery to a bid to pass as the American West. Gregory Mohr, 'The French Camargue Western', in *Crossing Frontiers: Intercultural Perspectives on the Western*, ed. Peter W. Schulze, Thomas Klein and Ivo Ritzer (Marburg: Schüren Verlag, 2015), 92.
37. *Moving Picture World* 18, no. 4 (25 October 1913): 380.
38. James S. McQuade 'The Subterranean City'. *Le Courrier Cinématographique* 18, no. 7 (15 November 1913): 717.
39. The anachronism is not limited to the Eclipse 'Arizona Bill' series: in the Gaumont *Le Railway de la mort* the centrepiece chase sequence also includes a motor vehicle alongside horses and a train.

4

The modernity of tradition and the cinematic Camargue

When Joë Hamman returned to filmmaking after World War I, he formed his own production company, the *Films Joë Hamman*, and as a first production planned a western-themed adventure made in the Camargue region of southern France. He asked his friend, the marquis Folco de Baroncelli-Javon, to write the scenario.[1] Folco lived in the Camargue on his ranch-like estate (*le mas de l'Amarée*), and had often supplied land, lodging, personnel, horses and his herd of prized Mediterranean bulls to film crews in the pre-war years. Hamman proposed the idea:

> a good screenplay, grandiose, in the vein of *Cheval fantôme*, mixing in Indians, intrigues, the Camargue element, and well-dressed society people (something very much in demand, don't smile!). The latter is to vary the locations, decors, and costumes, but it is *not indispensable* if there is good action and some *clous* [showpiece stunts]. [...] Not too many roles. I'll hire people on site. Am interested only in the story's hero, who will be me, and a young heroine. The role of a villain will doubtless enhance the action.[2]

The sketch would aptly characterise Hamman's earlier films investigated in the previous chapter: cursory characters and plot provide support for the visual interest of scenery, decor and costumes. The 'Indians' stand out as a western motif whose justification alongside the 'Camargue element' is not immediately apparent, and the film would again feature Hamman performing his signature stunts. Hamman does not indicate how these diverse elements will come together as a coherent narrative. The pitch suggests more a mixed salad of appealing attractions lightly dressed with a thin plot – a western element here, some Camargue scenery there, spectacular feats and (why not?) a top hat or gown – than an integrated sauce thickened with narrative continuity: in short, a cinema characteristic of the films he made for the Gaumont and Eclipse studios before the war.

Hamman may have hoped to take up filmmaking much as he had left it, but cinema had not stood still in the intervening years. After 1914, Hollywood decisively dominated the global film market and the feature film had become an industry standard, its greater length sustained by causality, character psychology, and spatio-temporal orientation constructed through shot variations and smooth continuity in editing.[3] This new style did not eliminate the visual interest of stunts and landscapes, but bent them to the logic of narrative and character psychology. By the end of the war a spectator of a feature film could reasonably expect to know whether the action was unfolding in France or America, whether the setting was period or contemporary, why a cowboy named Bill was solving crimes in the Camargue, and if the Camargue landscapes were indeed representing the Camargue and not "Elk City" or other locations. The eventual scenario for *Le Gardian* indicates a willingness to adapt to the new style. The film is the story of a young *gardian* (a Camarguais rider and bull herder) caught between his humble fiancée and a more worldly but maliciously conniving woman. It's a conventional melodrama based on familiar sources, and is set unambiguously in the Camargue with ample scenery, action and regional character types.[4] Elements from Hamman's pre-war films persist, but they are integrated into the spatio-temporal parameters of the southern French setting, and the eponymous protagonist is clearly Camarguais, not an American named Bill.

The stabilisation of the Camargue setting might serve as a textbook illustration of the assimilation, or elimination, of attraction-like elements that a more integrated narrative film demands. The grassy expanses that once stood in for the Great Plains are now unambiguously the marshes of the Camargue, the thatched huts are not ersatz pioneer cabins but really are southern French *cabanes*, and the hero on horseback is now at home as a *gardian*. A casualty of this more coherent Camargue would seem to be the permissively ambiguous spectacle of westernness that the earlier cinema displayed, and that a more consistently integrated narrative necessarily excludes from the cinematic exploitation of the region. In a letter to Folco, Hamman promised to expiate the 'cinematic barbarities' wrought on the region in earlier films with a 'grand Camargue adventure with all the elements of its charm, violence, and legends'.[5] The Camargue on film could, it seems, simply be itself.

The above account of a more integrated Camargue setting aligns tidily with a linear evolutionary history of cinema's development, transition and narrative consolidation. However, it neglects the extent to which the cinematic exploitation of this region, engineered by Folco and filmed by Hamman, remains derived from an imagined American West. Specifically, Buffalo Bill's *Wild West* left a powerful impression on the noble rancher, and on the images of the region that he and Hamman, side by side but with different purposes, worked to bring to the screen.

The surviving footage of one of the last films to feature Hamman as 'Bill', *Facing the Bull* (*Face au taureau*, 1914), anticipates the muting of the western element in a cinema that celebrates the Camargue region and its past.[6] However, despite the evocation of a more traditional lifestyle, this Camargue on film is also inspired by an American spectacle that is the product of new technologies and new modes of mass production, distribution and consumption. A more consistently integrated 'Camargue itself' may appear to eliminate both the rustic westernness and the modern technologies (telephones, airplanes, motor vehicles) featured in the earlier films, but evocations of the frontier-era American West and of American-style modernity persist in filmed representations of the region even as it is positioned as a bastion of tradition. The 'de-westernisation' of the Camargue in the films of the 1920s and 1930s belies how the visual aspect of this region on film is a modern creation that, despite appearances, continues to exploit the uncertain geographies of Arizona Bill.

The missing link? *Facing the Bull / Face au taureau* (1914)

The restored footage of *Facing the Bull* runs approximately five minutes, less than a third of its original release length.[7] The lost footage appears to be primarily from the first part of the film, and the story's outline remains only partly intelligible: the vengeful Arbaud has a dispute with a widow, whose relationship to a character played by Hamman, identified in the intertitles as 'Bill', is unclear. Multiple shots of running bulls and *gardian* horsemen at work have no clear narrative purpose. The latter part of the footage remains sufficiently intact to trace a narrative. Arbaud poisons a watering hole, and when Bill investigates his horse drinks the water and dies. Bill sounds the alarm. Arbaud, stymied, lets loose a fierce bull that corners a woman, presumably the widow. Bill rides to her rescue and wrestles the bull to the ground. Arbaud frees the entire herd but is himself trampled, and men congratulate Bill as the widow is reunited with a young child. A promotional synopsis of *The Bull Trainer's Revenge* in a contemporaneous British publication fills the gaps in the story: a rich landowner, Raynaud, takes a mortal fall while riding and is transported to Arles where, on his deathbed, his soon-to-be widow promises to devote her life to caring for their child. Arbaud, the foreman of her cattle operation, wishes to marry her and to take control of the estate, but his courtship is repeatedly rebuffed and he seeks ever more devious ways of seizing the property. Hamman's character, the estate's executor, defends the widow's interests. Escalating tensions between the men lead to fistfights, sabotage and the poisoning of the horse, culminating with the raging bull's release, the climactic ride to the rescue and the murderous stampeding herd.[8]

Face au taureau hews to the formula of Hamman's prior Eclipse releases: chicanery after a contested inheritance leads to chases, daredevilry and rescue. The fragmented footage demands speculation, but the uneven editing and *mise-en-scène* also appear similar. Full and long shots dominate with few variations: a single reaction shot of Bill spying on Arbaud, and a medium shot of Bill with his dead horse. The shots appear to be edited in linear temporal succession, with the exception of a single shot of the cornered woman intercut with Bill's ride to save her. In the eponymous tauromachy, Hamman wrestles with the bull in a long take of 34 seconds; by contrast, the trampling of Arbaud is swiftly and unconvincingly executed with a trick substitution of a dummy. A telling discrepancy reveals persistent ambiguity in setting: much as the same location in *The Last Minute* signified Elk City for the French print but represented France for the American release, the intertitles name Hamman's character 'Bill', while in the English-language synopsis he is 'Mascaro', a name of Mediterranean provenance inconsistent with the American cowboy crime-solver from the other films.[9] The incomplete print demands speculation, but the visual display of the bulls also appears to impose more heavily than its narrative function would warrant. These shots establish the presence of the herd and of the raging bull, both important narrative agents, but their number, their repetitive nature, the absence of named characters, and the documentary quality of the images of herders at work permit the spectacle of the bulls, the *gardians* and the landscape to exceed a storytelling purpose. They are nearly identical to the images in a series of short *actualités* that Jean Durand filmed for the Gaumont company at approximately the same time, and suggest a similar intent to exploit the documentary visual interest of the region.[10]

However, *Face au taureau* differs from its surviving predecessors in the Arizona Bill series in that both narrative setting and filming location are unequivocally the Camargue and its environs. In the first shot of the surviving footage, a sun-drenched stone house with an ornate wooden door suggests a southern French exterior, likely from the part of the story set in Arles. With the exception of Hamman's Bill, the characters wear the traditional costumes of the region: the women's elaborate *fichus* and *coiffes* could plausibly have been borrowed from a production of *L'Arlésienne*, the riders sport the distinct print shirts and berets associated with Provence, and instead of a rifle or lariat they carry the tridents of the *gardians*. The brutish villain shares his name with Joseph d'Arbaud, an associate of Mistral who wrote lyrically of the Camargue landscape, and the landowner with Mathieu Raynaud, a bull-breeding confrère of Folco who had a *mas* in the region. The film documents the indigenous culture most forcefully in the images of galloping *gardians* and running herds of bulls (*manades*). An intertitle identifies the featured bull in the Provençal language as *Lou Cande*, 'the pure one', possibly the notorious animal of the same name that ran in early twentieth-century *courses de taureaux* in the region. In addition to the bull-herding images, Hamman's *clou* stunt demonstrates the Camarguais bull-wrestling traditionally performed at bull-branding festivals (*ferrades*). Bill prevails through his horsemanship and prowess handling bulls, talents he shares as much with the *gardians* as with an American cowboy. His simple coat and hat are less evidently evocative of a specific region than the showy chaps, bandanas and gun belts of *The Last Minute*. The film's westernness hangs on little more than Bill's name, and even it was, by the account, replaced by the name Mascaro in some releases. In either case, the character is clearly living not in the American West but in the Camargue.

With filming location, diegetic setting and culturally specific elements in alignment, *Face au taureau* may foreground the Camargue region's distinct cultural and geographical features unencumbered by the discordances that attended the previous films in the Arizona Bill series. The film all but completes the elimination of elements that sowed ambiguity in the earlier westerns, notably the semantics of lassos, tin-star sheriffs, woolly chaps and 'Indians'. In this respect it edges closer to the cusp between 'transitional' cinema and the consolidation of narrative continuity, clear spatio-temporal orientation and consistent characterisation that would shortly become an industry standard. *Face au taureau* was one of Hamman's last films before World War I, and its plot and visual components are closely consistent with the film he pitched to Folco when he returned to filmmaking in 1919: a Camargue setting, a simple plot, a hero and a villain, a reduced western element and a few characters who wear distinguished clothing. Subsequent production in the Camargue would seem to represent a further step in this evolution by eliminating any lingering reference to the semantics of the American West.

Western modernity in the traditional Camargue

However, situating *Face au taureau* as the 'missing link' between the pre-war westerns and the later dramas set in the region obscures the extent to which an ideation of the American West remains constitutive of the 'Camargue itself' on film. The traditional Camargue seen in *Face au taureau* is both less simple and more contested, and more modern and more American, than allowed in this evolutionary account, which neglects the extent to which the visual aspect of the region on film is a modern creation that sprang from the active imagination of Folco de Baroncelli.

Folco's involvement with the film industry dates at least to 1906, when Louis Feuillade negotiated the use of the marquis's bulls, sheep, horses and riders for the filming of Alice Guy's *Mireille*. In subsequent years he frequently hosted film crews at the *mas de l'Amarée*, acted as a consultant on the region and its customs, and facilitated the staging of bull herding, *ferrades* and other activities for the cameras. For filmmakers, Folco's hospitality, expertise, material, personnel, animals and access to shooting locations functioned like a small production unit for hire, ready to be deployed as called for by a scenario. His participation was sought by competing film companies and was not always available even for a friend like Hamman, who lamented the difficulty of filming in the region when his competitors had already secured Folco's services.[11]

However, Folco's consuming passion lay not in filmmaking but in the revindication of a Provençal identity in the spirit of Frédéric Mistral's *Félibrige* and other late nineteenth-century nationalist movements. As a young man he lived in Avignon (he inherited the *Palais du Roure*), married the daughter of a landowner in Châteauneuf-du-Pape and was a prominent figure in the *Félibrige*, writing Provençal poetry and serving as the editor of its mouthpiece journal, *L'Aïoli*. However, he left (and eventually lost) his palace and vineyards to live in the Camargue, at the time a remote enclave of dunes, marshy grasslands and ponds.[12] In this isolated and desolate region Folco believed to find the remnants of a civilisation preserved from, but threatened by, the homogenising and centralising pressures of a France governed from Paris. Where Mistral worked to codify the Provençal/Occitan language and to elevate it with literary works, eventually winning the Nobel prize for literature, Folco, though also a writer, strove to preserve, promote and, if necessary, confect a traditional Camarguais culture founded on the raising of cattle and horses.

Folco had a strategic eye for spectacle. Historian Robert Zaretsky documents the range of initiatives that bind Folco's political agenda to the creation of Camarguais tradition, with focus on the emblematic figure of the bull.[13] It was Folco, for example, who dressed the *gardians* in print cotton shirts whose eye-dazzling saturated colours led a younger generation to reject the drab work clothes of their forbears; they are today considered the traditional costume of the region. He also founded the *Nacioun gardiano* ('Gardian Nation'), a troupe of trident-brandishing riders that he featured in staged shows of 'traditional' horseback games (rules invented by Folco) to complement the *ferrades* and *courses* (Provençal-style bullfights). Even the Camargue landscape owes its singular appeal to Folco's lobbying for the conservation and restoration of what would become a regional park and nature preserve. Folco also devoted much of his life, and what remained of his depleted fortune, to restoring the genetic line of the Camarguais bull, an effort that drew symbolic urgency from the centralised French government's long history of antagonism towards Provençal/Occitan bullfighting traditions. The Camargue, analogous to the bull that is its emblem, represented to Folco a surviving remnant of the land, the 'race' of people, the language and the culture of a vast and powerful Occitan society that once stretched from Spain to Italy with, at its centre, the ancient kingdoms of Arles and Provence flanking the Rhône delta where the region lies. Never mind that the lost pure race of Mediterranean bulls may never have existed: Folco did not shy away from promoting a compelling myth when historical fact failed to deliver, and he created on the back of the bull a rallying figure for a traditional Provençal culture.[14]

The filmmakers and the marquis therefore found common interest in promoting a Camargue that is both visually compelling and distinct, an alignment that over-determines the images of the emblematic bulls. The bull incarnates the ideal breed that Folco sought to restore to its ancient integrity, and is the emblem of a Camargue that became a vivid spectacle through his interventions. Furthermore, in a setting firmly anchored in the Mediterranean *Midi*, there is no mistaking these small, lyre-horned bulls for an American steer on a ranch in Texas or Kansas.[15] In shots of *gardians* herding the animals across the plain, or of Hamman wrestling the animal, the bull simultaneously inscribes Folco's nationalist-regionalist fantasies and promotes a more continuously integrated Camargue diegesis.

Nevertheless, the picturesque and pre-industrial 'Camargue itself' seen in *Face au taureau*, however pristine or traditional in aspect, was not simply waiting to be revealed after the adulterating western trappings of earlier films had been stripped away. It, too, is in significant measure a modern confection that derives from representations of the American West. Before Hamman ever made a film or Folco founded the *Nacioun Gardiano*, the two men met on a field outside of Paris where Buffalo Bill's *Wild West* was encamped in the winter of 1905.[16] The *Wild West*, on its second European tour, was at this point a legendary phenomenon that attracted audiences on an unprecedented scale. The American West invoked in the spectacle was by 1905 already receding into history; for example, an attack on a stagecoach, a mode of transportation rapidly being superannuated by the train and the automobile, was a centrepiece feature of the show. However, the spectacular presentation of this wild and retro frontier depended on the exploitation of state-of-the-art technology: the speed and ease of travel enabled by steamships and motor vehicles, a travelling electrical plant that was the largest of its kind in the world, a publicity blitz that cannily deployed both lithography and photography, and a massive coordination of personnel and material that operated on a 'military-industrial scale'.[17] Furthermore, the technologies that enabled the show's transportation and distribution, as well as the publicity campaign in the print media, were promoted as part of the spectacle itself.[18] A large-format lithograph advertisement for the *Wild West* depicts horsemen lit by brilliant electric spotlights and reads: 'Buffalo Bill's Wild West and Congress of Rough Riders of the World In the Grandest of Illuminated Arenas, 2 Electric Plants, 250,000 Candle Power'.[19] The show not only incorporated modern industry as an attraction in its own right, but also as a theme in its positivist narrative. The electric lights became part of the attraction, and the conquest of the West (and, it was clearly communicated, the triumph of the white race with America as its standard bearer) was characterised in the programme as a *fait accompli* attributed to new technologies that include the railroad and the repeating rifle.[20]

Figure 4.1 Riders of the world – and two electric plants. The Library of Congress.

Hamman and Folco were both familiar with the *Wild West* outfit. As an employee of the show during its 1905 run in Paris, Hamman had ample occasion to study the entertainment potential of the western clothing and riding skills he would later display in his films.[21] For his part, Folco was impressed by the show's operation, and drew from it both practical and ideological inspiration for the theatrical displays of Provençal culture, bull-handling and horsemanship that he later staged in Arles and Nîmes. The admiration and imitation of the *Wild West* were also aspirational: Folco contacted the show's producers to propose having his *gardians* perform alongside the other riders of diverse nationalities under Buffalo Bill's spotlights (the offer was not accepted). Zaretsky concludes: 'just as the Wild West mobilized the techniques of modern entertainment, all the while insisting upon its authentic and didactic qualities, so too would Baroncelli seek, albeit at a far more modest level, the same effect in the Camargue'.[22]

On an allegorical plane, too, the American frontier experience brought to France by Cody's *Wild West* coloured Folco's conception of his own region's plight. The Native American performers in particular struck a chord, and after Hamman introduced Folco to his Lakota Sioux co-workers, Folco sought them out during the tour at various sites around France. One meeting allegedly took place in Le Cailar, on the edge of the Camargue, during the winter of 1905–1906. These encounters deeply affected Folco, who drew an analogy between the advancing American frontier and the encroachment of modernity on Provençal/Camarguais culture. In his imagination, the counterparts of his *gardians* were not only the cowboys to whom they are often compared, but also the Native Americans whose languages, traditional lifestyle and racial continuity were, in his eyes, similarly threatened.[23] Shortly after seeing the *Wild West* spectacle for the first time Folco composed a ballad in Provençal based on the Sioux Ghost Dance: the poem opens with the invocation of a 'red brother' and concludes 'my heart is red'.[24] Folco maintained a correspondence with Jacob Ištá Ská (Jacob White Eyes) for years thereafter.[25] With the elevated emotional pitch typical of his letters, he writes: 'I've the impression I was an Indian in a previous life. When I see you, I feel I am once again with my long-lost brothers. When I heard you, I shivered with the sense that I once spoke your language.'[26] The marquis adopted an Oglala name (*Zinktala Waste*, 'faithful bird'), posed for photographs in Sioux clothing and continued to compose poetry comparing the plight of the Native Americans to the defeat of the Occitan *Midi* by the northern French during the Albigensian crusade.[27] He even suggested that the Roma population of the Camargue region might have common ancestry with the Native Americans.

There is much more to say about both the *Wild West*'s reception in France and Folco de Baroncelli's fanciful, sometimes contradictory, and unapologetically nationalistic political and cultural agendas.[28] For the present account of films made in and about the region, suffice it to underscore two assertions. First, as inspiration, aspiration and allegory, an imagined American West provided 'both the catalyst and the vehicle' for the Camargue that Folco imagined, refashioned and, during his lifetime, effectively licensed to Hamman and other filmmakers.[29] Second, although Buffalo Bill's version of the West trafficked in legend and drew on the history of a rustic frontier, the show itself was a modern operation driven by cutting-edge technologies that enabled the international distribution of an entertainment product to be consumed by unprecedented numbers of spectators worldwide.

Cinema is one of these technologies. The *Wild West* was at the height of its popularity when commercial cinema was born, and some of the earliest films ever made show its performers in action.[30] Following Buffalo Bill's 1905–1906 European tour, the western film in America became a staple of the Nickelodeon-era cinema that eventually superannuated shows like the *Wild West*. Cody himself would try his hand at film production, though with little success. In France, the pre-1914 westerns, through the participation of both Folco and Hamman, sit in the lineage of the *Wild West* and represent a further transposition of its representational strategies to the screen.[31] So, too, does the 'grand Camargue adventure' of later Camargue films insofar as the region's traditional and more 'pure' aspect was reverse-engineered through environmental advocacy, taurine eugenics, imaginative revisions and a *mise-en-scène* inspired by the American mass entertainment spectacle. The interwar Camargue films made in the two decades after *Le Gardian* may suppress explicitly 'western' semantics, but the American West is not simply a veneer that may be peeled away to expose the Camargue's true and authentic aspect on film. The cinematic Camargue is cut from the same cloth as the movie cowboy, and if the Camargue piece forms the visible outside of this garment, it remains lined and supported by an imagined American West that will, in later years, continue to flash its distinct colours.

The 'de-westernised' Camargue film of the 1920s and 1930s

The French *Midi* (roughly the regions of Aquitaine, Languedoc and Provence) has provided a picturesque backdrop for filmmakers since the Lumières filmed the train pulling into the station at La Ciotat. The area is vast, however, and presents diverse characteristics on film: Marseille is a port city with a seamy underbelly, the Côte-d'Azur provides an elegant setting, and film adaptations of Marcel Pagnol's novels and plays constitute a substantial corpus in their own right.[32] In the 1920s and 1930s, the geographically and culturally distinct Camargue, in its traditional mode, was also exploited in a cycle of films. Drawing on literary works of the earlier century, filmmakers produced multiple adaptations of Mistral's *Mireille*, Alphonse Daudet's *L'Arlésienne* and Jean Aicard's *Le Roi de Camargue*; Folco's brother Jacques de Baroncelli directed versions of the latter two titles in 1930 and 1935. Other titles include Pierre Caron's adaptation of another Aicard novel, *Notre-Dame d'amour* (1923), and Baroncelli's *Gitanes* (1932).[33] These films feature many of the same Camargue 'semantics' that brought interest to the earlier western-themed films, but integrate the white horses, marshes, dunes, *gardians* herding bulls, and landscapes dotted with *mas* and *cabanes* into a narrative unambiguously set in the Camargue:

> If they are not westerns, all of these films draw inspiration from the adventure films made in the Camargue before 1914. But while the American cinema is henceforth dominant in the western, the Camargue is shown as itself and no longer as an ersatz Far West.[34]

The strategy seems clear: leave the frontier-era West to the Americans and let the Camargue, divested of foreign trappings, be itself.

The intentional 'de-westernisation' of the Camargue is evident in the adaptation of the source material for Jacques de Baroncelli's *Gitanes*. The inspiration for the film is a 1910 short story titled 'En Camargue: Coeur Ardent et Hirondelle Brune' ('In the Camargue: Burning Heart and Brown Swallow'), in which a Native American performer from Buffalo Bill's show meets a Roma woman in a tale of doomed interracial love.[35] However, by the time the cameras rolled Baroncelli had transformed the character of Coeur Ardent into a French sailor and had cast Charles Vanel in the lead role, muting references to the historical presence of the *Wild West* and its Native American personnel in the region. Later reprises of Hamman's bull-wrestling stunt further illustrate this transformation: Hamman repeats the feat he performed as 'Bill' in *Face au taureau* as an unequivocally Camarguais character in *Le Gardian*, and again in both the 1922 and 1933 adaptations of *Mireille*. A critic considers Hamman's 1933 performance a bright point in an otherwise bland film: 'Our national cowboy, whom I regret no longer seeing on the screen, portrays Ourrias as a solidly boorish bad guy.'[36] Indeed, spectators did, to an extent, see the same figure on the screen: Hamman again wrestles a bull to the ground against the backdrop of the same herds and *gardians* (Folco's *manade* is credited), and against the same characteristic marshes, ponds and grasslands that were featured in *Face au taureau* and other pre-1914 westerns. However, the cowboy character has become a fond memory, and the signifiers that once represented the Far West unambiguously represent the setting of Mistral's poem.

Traditional and rustic, with narratives frequently set in the nineteenth century, the 'Camargue itself' on film evokes the memory of a time and a place beyond the homogenising reach of a modernising world. However, this memory is selective, and its credibility and coherence also demand acts of forgetting. At the same time that *félibres* like Mistral and Folco were promoting the Provençal language and culture with urgency, their contemporary, historian Ernst Renan, was observing that for national ideations to attain cohesion and credibility, the mixed, inconsistent and contradictory parts of the past must be forgotten: 'forgetting, I would even go so far as to say historical error, is a crucial factor in the creation of a nation.'[37] The figure of forgetting would aptly characterise Folco's revindication of the bull as the emblem of Camarguais identity: to claim the restoration of a pure genetic line one must first forget all the generations of mixed-breed ancestors from which the animals nonetheless descend. The bulls, like other tropes of tradition in the Camargue films, belie the intentional labours of modern agents who, through contemporary interventions, shape them into the timeless emblems of an ancient civilisation.

Herein lies the paradox of the interwar Camargue films and their relation to the American West. A western spectacle realised through new technologies, new speed and ease of travel, and new modes of mass production and consumption is, in good measure, constitutive of the cinematic representations of the traditions, stories and people that Folco and others defended against the homogenising reach of modernity, industrialisation, standardisation and, later, Americanisation. Hamman claimed to eliminate 'barbarian' elements from his post-war Camargue films, and Folco, a political reactionary, freely embraced discourses of national and racial purity. However, this rhetoric of purification, and of divesting both modern and foreign trappings to recover a traditional Camargue, implies that the picturesque Camargue seen on film previously existed as an authentic historical referent. It effaces the contemporary labours, inspired by a state-of-the-art spectacle of the American West, that shape and inform it. It 'forgets', for example, that Folco's galloping *gardians*, before they ever rode for a movie camera in the remote Camargue, were pitched as a prospective act suitable for joining the cowboys, 'Indians' and other 'riders of the world' under Buffalo Bill's dazzling spotlights in Paris and other European cities.

It is therefore not only the cowboys, chaps, six-shooters and other elements of the frontier-era American setting that must be purged from this re-imagined Camargue on film, but also the airplanes, telephones, automobiles and other evocations of contemporary modern life that were also fixtures in earlier westerns made in the region. The elimination of Native Americans from the cinematic Camargue represents both vectors of this imperative. On the one hand, the 'vanishing Americans', romanticised or vilified in literature and film as the emblem of a pre-industrial mode of existence, are an indigenous North American element that no longer has a place in a more consistently integrated Camargue diegesis. However, the historical presence of Native Americans in the Camargue region is at the same time an index of modernity and its technologies. Jacob Ištá Ská and his compatriots travelled to Europe on a steamship, not by canoe. In the *Wild West* spectacle they worked under state-of-the-art electric lights, not by firelight, and by Folco's own account the Sioux men arrived at the meeting in Le Cailar not on horseback but in an automobile.[38] It is not only as denizens of the old American West but also as modern workers in a cosmopolitan and high-tech entertainment industry that the Sioux men must be 'forgotten' in representations of the traditional Camargue, a region they nonetheless visited and whose features on film were inspired by the show that they helped to bring to France.[39]

Memories fade over time, however, and through repeated acts of forgetting the new may gain legitimacy as the eternal, the natural or the universal. As John Ford's newspaperman observes in a transposition of Renan's assertion into the plain speech of the western, 'when the legend becomes fact, print the legend'. As early as 1925 Hamman was already calling his pre-war westerns 'distant memories' from a 'quasi-prehistoric' period of cinema that, by newer standards, would be sure to 'unleash laughter'.[40] The film artifact is also ephemeral, many of the early films are lost, and the industry's transition to sound relegated silent cinema to the past. Folco died in 1943 and Hamman ceased to play cowboys as his film career waned. With the passage of time, the experience of the early silent westerns fell outside the living memory of younger cinemagoers, and a new generation of spectators might detect no filiation to earlier westerns in the adaptations of *Mireille*, *L'Arlésienne* or *Le Roi de Camargue*. The 1953 film *White Mane* (*Crin-Blanc*, Albert Lamorisse), for example, features a wild Camargue of *gardians*, white horses, *cabanes* and marshes that are as removed from the industrialised world of electricity, automobiles and mass-produced consumer products as the legendary frontier in American westerns. However, an American cowboy in a western saddle with woolly chaps and a six-shooter would be a bizarre apparition in this film, no matter how much the galloping *gardians* in their broad-brimmed hats might have in common with him. *White Mane* was popular among children, who would have had no memory of a cowboy named Bill riding in automobiles or crashing airplanes in the same grasslands and dunes where the white horses run – unless, that is, they had seen other post-World War II evocations of the traditional Camargue on film, investigated in the following chapter, that position the region in the contemporary world and, with candid intention, exploit its filiation with the American West.

Notes

1. The marquis will hereafter be referred to simply as Folco, not to be confused with his brother, the film director Jacques de Baroncelli, or his nephew, the film critic Jean de Baroncelli.

2. Letter from Joë Hamman to Folco de Baroncelli dated 24 December 1919. Author's translation. Collections of the Palais du Roure. Quoted in Bernard Bastide, *Aux sources du cinéma en Camargue: Joë Hamman et Folco de Baroncelli* (Avignon: Palais du Roure, 2018), 59.
3. On the importance of westerns in establishing Hollywood's dominance, see, again, Richard Abel, *Americanizing*, 62–79.
4. The film is loosely a remake of Léonce Perret's *Le Gardian de Camargue* (1910). The story also evokes literary sources, namely Alphonse Daudet's *L'Arlésienne* and Jean Aicard's *Le Roi de Camargue*. Bastide's brief synopsis of the film, which he has reconstructed, contains no mention of the 'Indian' element. Bastide, *Aux sources du cinéma*, 59. See also <https://www.unifrance.org/film/37694/le-gardian> (accessed 5 July 2023).
5. Ibid., 58.
6. The surviving footage of *Face au taureau* is from a print with German intertitles (*Dem Stier gegenüber*), held at the *Centre national du cinéma et de l'image animé* (CNC). It has been restored and is available for streaming at the *Bibliothèque Nationale Française*.
7. A release announcement lists the length at 580 metres. *Le Courrier Cinématographique* 4, no. 6 (7 February 2014): 107.
8. Bastide cites this synopsis, from the film's British distributor (the Charles Urban Trading Co.), in *Aux sources du cinéma*, 168–9. Another trade journal indicates that the film was released in the UK by Urban-Eclipse on 11 March 1914. *The Bioscope* 23, no. 388 (19 March 1914): 1323.
9. Using the name from the English-language synopsis, Bastide refers to the character as 'Mascaro' in his analysis of *Face au taureau* and contends that the film is not part of the Arizona Bill series (*Aux sources du cinéma*, 44). However, in the surviving print Hamman's character is identified as 'Bill', which, along with a consistent persona and a similar narrative conceit, suggests continuity with the American character of Hamman's earlier films.
10. Durand directed *En Camargue*, *Ferrade en Camargue* and *Course de taureaux provençale*, all from 1913.
11. Bastide documents Folco's relation to filmmaking, including this recollection by Hamman: 'Quand je voulais aller en Camargue et qu'on le savait [. . .] Gaumont téléphonait à Baroncelli, j'arrivais . . . et je ne pouvais plus tourner! Ils avaient pris tous les chevaux, tous les taureaux, tous les gardians, tout ce que j'avais d'habitude.' ('When it became known that I wanted to go the Camargue [. . .] Gaumont would phone Baroncelli, I would arrive, and I would no longer be able to film! They had taken all the horses, all the bulls, all the gardians, everything I usually had.') Transcript from the Commission de recherches historiques de la Cinémathèque française, 24 June 1944, 11. Quoted in Bastide, *Aux sources du cinéma* 41, no. 87. Folco, for his part, would complain about competing ranch operations undercutting his fees. See Laure Marchis-Mouren and Estelle Rouquette, 'Wild South Camargue', in *Western Camarguais*, ed. Estelle Rouquette and Sam Stourdzé (Arles: Actes Sud, 2016), 17.
12. For a detailed account of Baroncelli's precarious finances and his ill-fated attempts to eke profit from the bull-breeding enterprise, see Henriette Dibon, *Folco de Baroncelli* (Nîmes: Bene, 1982).
13. Robert Zaretsky, *Cock and Bull Stories: Folco de Baroncelli and the Invention of the Camargue* (Lincoln: University of Nebraska Press: 2004).

14. Ibid., *passim*.
15. De la Bretèque observes that the diminutive breed of white Camarguais horses, like the bulls, also could not be mistaken for their American counterparts. François Amy de la Bretèque, 'Le Paysage de la Camargue dans les westerns français: un role discret', in Rouquette and Stourdzé, *Western Camarguais*, 111.
16. The *Nacioun Gardiano* was not officially established until 1909.
17. Robert W. Rydell and Rob Kroes, *Buffalo Bill in Bologna: The Americanization of the World* (Chicago: University of Chicago Press, 1994), 31.
18. '[A]s the show may have succeeded in embodying the "wildness" of the West, the show was as much a display of the products of nineteenth-century industrial civilization as it was of the savage life of the frontier.' Rydell and Kroes, *Buffalo Bill in Bologna*, 31. 'Contemporaries marveled at the speed with which the show could travel, build, and take down its arena, so it became a symbol of technological modernity as well.' Emily Burns, 'Taming a "Savage" Paris: The Masculine Visual Culture of Buffalo Bill's Wild West and France as a New American Frontier', in *The Popular Frontier: Buffalo Bill's Wild West and Transnational Masculine Culture*, ed. Frank Christensen (Norman: University of Oklahoma Press, 2017), 143. See also Venita Datta, 'Buffalo Bill Goes to France: French-American Encounters at the Wild West Show 1889–1890', *French Historical Studies* 41, no. 3 (August 2018): 525–55.
19. 'Buffalo Bill's Wild West and Congress of Rough Riders of the World in the Grandest of Illuminated Arenas, 2 Electric Plants, 250,000 Candle Power.' Library of Congress digital file. Available at <https://www.loc.gov/resource/ds.08325> (accessed 6 July 2019).
20. The programme notes 'underscored the expansion of the "white race" in the American West, facilitated by the railroad, and juxtaposed the Indians as opponents of that progress, claiming that they had now been tamed by the military power of the federal government and the rifle, which was presented as a symbol of modern civilization'. Datta, 'Buffalo Bill', 533.
21. 'De retour à mon pays, je compris tout le parti que l'on pouvait tirer de prises de vue de drames du Far-West [. . .] les aventures de Buffalo Bill – qui venait de faire une tournée triomphale en France – enflammaient les jeunes imaginations' ('Upon returning to my country I fully understood the advantage one could gain from filmed dramas of the Far West [. . .] the adventures of Buffalo Bill – who had just had a triumphant tour of France – kindled young imaginations'). Quoted in Albert Bonneau, 'Le Far-West en France', *Cinémagazine* 8 (May 1925): 222.
22. Zaretsky, *Cock and Bull*, 83.
23. Ibid., 67.
24. The poem, 'Soulòmi Rouge', is reprinted in Lefrançois, *Les Indiens de Buffalo Bill*, 76–81.
25. Burns contextualises this correspondence in *Transnational Frontiers*.
26. Cited in Zaretsky, *Cock and Bull*, 66.
27. 'A Iue-Blanc' was originally published in 1909. See Lefrançois, *Les Indiens de Buffalo Bill*, 81–2.
28. The literature on Buffalo Bill is vast. As for Folco, his conviction as both a Provençal nationalist and a French royalist suggests contradictory loyalties. A tension between the idea of France as the homogenising enemy and as the 'mother' country – between nationalism and regionalism – underlies the *Félibrige*, the latter impulse

becoming more characteristic of Folco's discourse over time. 'Le Félibrige ne donne pas naissance à un mouvement nationaliste, mais finit par s'arrêter au stade d'un régionalisme purement littéraire, bardé de déclarations de loyauté à la patrie française.' ('The *Félibrige* did not give birth to a nationalist movement but ended up stopping at the stage of a purely literary regionalism, larded with declarations of loyalty to the French *patrie*.') Philippe Martel, 'Le Félibrige: un incertain nationalisme linguistique', *Mots: Les langages du politique* 74 (2003): 43–57. See also Lefrançois, *Les Indiens*.

29. Zaretsky, *Cock and Bull*, 83. Laure Marchis-Mouren and Estelle Rouquette also observe 'a single mechanism constructs the myth of the cowboy and that of the *gardian*' ('un seul mécanisme construit le mythe du cowboy et celui du gardian'). 'Wild South Camargue', in Rouquette and Stourdzé, *Western Camarguais*, 17.

30. Edison had *Wild West* performers filmed for his Kinetoscope as early as 1894, and the Lumières catalogue of *actualités* included shots of Buffalo Bill's show by 1897.

31. A rich corpus of filmed representations of Cody and his exploits, on the frontier and as a showman, both pre-dates and follows his own brief career as a film producer. See Cynthia Miller, 'Performing the Iconic West: Wild West Shows', in *A Fistful of Icons: Essays on Frontier Fixtures of the American Western*, ed. Sue Matheson (Jefferson, NC: McFarland, 2017), 9–22. The frequent use of the character name 'Bill' in the French films is an evocation of his persona.

32. Colin Crisp, *Genre, Myth, and Convention in the French Cinema 1929–1939* (Bloomington: Indiana University Press, 2002), 59–60.

33. Not all early sound films made in the region are traditional period pieces: *Paris-Camargue* (Jack Forrester, 1935) for example, has a contemporary setting.

34. 'Si ce ne sont pas des westerns, tous ces films s'inspirent des films d'aventures tournés en Camargue avant 1914. Mais alors que le cinéma américain est désormais prépondérant en matière de westerns, la Camargue est montrée pour elle-même, et non plus comme un ersatz du Far West.' Rémi Venture, 'L'Aventure en Camargue', in Rouquette and Stourdzé, *Western Camarguais*, 63.

35. Hamman, who was also a visual artist, illustrated the volume that included the story, and it possibly provided the inspiration for his pitch for *Le Gardian*. He also played a Native American character named Coeur Ardent in a 1912 Gaumont western. Bernard Bastide, 'Jacques de Baroncelli, chantre de la Camargue'. Available at <http://www.cineressources.net/ressources/JacquesdeBaroncelli_ChantredelaCamargue.pdf> (accessed 5 July 2023).

36. 'Notre cow-boy national, que je regrette de ne plus voir à l'écran, a campé un Ourrias solidement rustre et mauvais bougre.' André de Reusse, *Hebdo-Film* no. 46 (16 December 1933): 13–14. Quoted in Bastide *Aux sources*, 76.

37. While much of Renan's work has diminished currency, the relocation of the nation to the realm of imagination continues to resonate widely.

38. The 1905 account, initially published in Provençal, is translated as 'La Défense d'une identité', trans. Rémi Venture, in LeFrançois, *Les Indiens de Buffalo Bill*, 35–7. Given the colourful filter of Folco's imagination, Zaretsky recommends caution in accepting such accounts as fact. Zaretsky, *Cock and Bull*, 161. The mention of the motor vehicle may draw credibility from the fact that Folco tended more to efface than to emphasise modernity in his references to the Native Americans.

39. Burns examines material and visual artifacts that reveal the complex modernity of these men: for example, Ištá Ská appears on the front image of a postcard in full traditional dress, but he also mails this same card as a tourist and professional whose business takes him to Europe. Burns *Transnational Frontiers*, 119–41. Regarding the visits to the Camargue region, sources place the Sioux men in Arles, Le Cailar and Marseille, but there is no record that they were ever able (or willing) to accept Folco's invitations to visit the *mas de l'Amarée*.
40. Quoted in Albert Bonneau, 'Le Far-West en France', 223.

5

The return of the western repressed

Like the train, the photograph, the telephone and the automobile, cinema has been characterised as a modern technology that enacts a new experience of time and space. In theorising cinema as a 'vernacular modernism', Miriam Hansen asserts that film, driven by a new technology and distributed for mass consumption on a global scale, activates 'new modes of organising vision and sensory perception, a new relationship with "things," different forms of mimetic experience and expression, or affectivity, temporality and reflexivity, a changing fabric of everyday life, sociability, and leisure.'[1] Hansen challenges the notion that the consolidation of greater narrative integration restored pre-cinematic ways of storytelling, or redressed the jarring discontinuities of an earlier cinema that traded openly in the amazement inspired by the newness of the medium. The standardisation of the 'classical' filmmaking style is instead the very 'incarnation of the modern, an aesthetic medium up-to-date with Fordist-Taylorist methods of industrial production and the promises of mass consumption, with drastic changes in social, gender, and generational relations, and with the restructuration of experience and subjectivity'.[2] To explain film style in the terms of a pre-cinematic past, by this reasoning, neglects the new modes of production, reception and perception engendered by this modern, technology-driven mass medium.

Hansen's challenge to existing accounts of film's development has not gone uncontested.[3] However, for the 'de-westernised' Camargue films of the 1920s and 1930s, examined in the previous chapter, the characterisation is fitting. Through the elimination of both rustic cowboys and modern telephones, or of Native Americans both on horseback and in automobiles, the cinematic *mise-en-scène* of the 'traditional' Camargue's landscapes, people and culture provides a 'cultural horizon in which the traumatic effects of modernity [are being] reflected, rejected or disavowed, transmuted or negotiated' – and, one may add, forgotten and remembered.[4]

This horizon, however, is not immutably traced in stone. It is an ever-receding zone of contest, and what once was rejected and disavowed may return in a new guise. In subsequent decades, after World War II, the traditional Camargue on film remains a site where the anxieties of the present are negotiated. However, in the positioning of the western genre, this restructuring of experience follows a tack nearly opposite to that of the interwar Camargue films. Far from muting or eliminating overt 'westernness', these films self-consciously inscribe, exploit and perpetuate the association of the cinematic Camargue with the western genre to the extent that they are sometimes classified as 'westerns', even when they are set in contemporary France with almost exclusively French characters. This western element, moreover, is positioned not only as a gesture towards a more primitive or traditional past, but is also aligned with the mass production, distribution and consumption of consumer goods in the newly modern and industrialised France of the *trente glorieuses*, the three decades of economic growth and rapid societal transformation following World War II. Two of these films, both commercial if not critical successes, stand out in this respect, one among the first of this sort and the other, arguably, among the last.

The re-westernised Camargue: *Vendetta en Camargue*

Vendetta en Camargue (*Vendetta in the Camargue*, Jean Devaivre, 1950) fulfils the title's promised exploitation of the region. The plot pits a group of Roma cattle thieves, led by the vampy and vindictive Conchita, against a Camarguais ranching operation, the *mas du Landre*, whose foreman, Krebs, is secretly Conchita's lover and accomplice. The absentee landlord of the *mas* has recently died and his daughter, Huguette, a circus performer from the northern city of Valenciennes, arrives to claim her inheritance. The employees' initial lack of respect for their new boss is swiftly corrected by her skills with a gun, her intelligence and her commanding demeanour. With the help of Frédé, a handsome neighbour, Huguette repeatedly thwarts the plans of the rustlers who wish to drive her away, leading to ever more vitriolic cries for vengeance from Conchita. The film culminates in a shootout between the rustler's fleeing caravan and Frédé's *gardian* riders, an all-out siege of the *mas*, and a vicious attempt to harm Huguette by lashing her to the back of a bull. Frédé rescues Huguette, captures Conchita, and order is restored. Huguette and Frédé kiss. The end.

If the synopsis seems a far-fetched amalgam of character types, situations and genre markers, the application for the film's financing shows that this treatment is intentional. In the characterisation of the film's commercial appeal, the emphasis lies squarely on variety: 'a series of heroic-burlesque episodes that will entertain the spectators and keep them breathless throughout', with 'perilous situations', and 'the whole will end with a marriage'.[5] The pitch also underscores the broad appeal of these diverse elements: 'the multiple and varied episodes teeming with humorous gags that constitute the framework of our film will make a spectacle likely to please all audiences'.[6] Director and producer Jean Devaivre, who also co-authored the script, was strategically casting a wide net. The meagre returns from a prior film had left his small production company, *La société des films Neptune* (a true 'mom-and-pop' operation: his wife was the company's production director), precariously in debt. His bid for financing turned on a simple, entertaining and predictably profitable film with appeal to the widest possible audience, including children.[7] He promised to use broad brushstrokes: 'a certain style of cinema, of open spaces and great horseback rides, of good guys and bad guys [*les gentils et les méchants*].'[8] The opening of the document sets the diegetic frame for this assemblage of attractions: 'The action of our films takes place in the "Land of the Bull" at the *mas du Landre*, in that Camargue whose immense plain under a fiery sky irresistibly evokes the endless spaces of the Far West.'[9] Devaivre thereby adds the picturesque Camargue and its connection to the West to the mix of genres and features – adventure film, melodrama, comedy, love story, gags, stunts – that will make the film worthy of financial backing. We are not far from Hamman's initial pitch for *Le Gardian*.

However, regarding the western element Devaivre had already tipped his hand. The working title of the film in his loan application was *Miss Cow-boy*, and he would later call his film a 'parody' of the western with the Roma and *gardians* standing in for the Native Americans and cowboys.[10] His approach may more accurately be characterised as analogy, however, as he transposes his *gentils* and *méchants* into a Camarguais frame. The Roma, for example, amply present the pejorative traits frequently bestowed on the 'Celluloid Indians' of studio-era American westerns.[11]

Devaivre's script includes a Roma 'tribal chief' (*chef de tribu*) who exiles the thieving members of his community, but whether wise or evil, these 'native' characters are unidimensional, transient, primitive (cooking on open fires at a rustic campsite, sleeping on the ground) and, in the case of Conchita, semi-nude and eroticised. They are bloodthirsty and vengeful but also naive, and are easily manipulated: the smiling Huguette and the courteous Frédé thwart the conniving criminals at every turn. The film also repurposes a familiar *mise-en-scène* from American westerns. The circle of caravans around an open fire out in the wilderness, a stray dog, people sitting on the ground, boxes of stolen rifles and the elderly chief could have been modelled on the tee-pee village of Griffith's *The Battle of Elderbush Gulch* (1913). So, too, could the siege of the *mas*: the *gentils* barricade themselves inside while the *méchants* circle the building, crawl on their bellies to sneak nearer, and set fires to smoke out their adversaries in a reprise of the attacks on ranch houses, cabins and wagon trains that are staple situations in American westerns. Conchita's seductive dance also bears a likeness to the opening sequence of the recently released *Duel in the Sun* (King Vidor, 1946), in which the camera lingers on the orgiastic gyrations of a Native American character.

The most elaborate citation of an American western occurs when the cattle thieves flee in a caravan pulled by six horses, pursued by a posse of *gardians* across a flat open plain. The reference to the chase sequence in John Ford's *Stagecoach* is unmistakable: a man fires over the coach's roof from the vehicle's 'shotgun seat', and men from both sides of the gunfight jump onto the coach's two lead horses and engage in a fistfight. In both films one of these men executes a stunt by dropping to the ground as the caravan runs past and the editing cuts between tracking shots of the wagon, the point of view of the driver over the backs of the galloping horses, and frontal shots of the pursuers. Where gags in other parts of the film approach slapstick farce, Devaivre's homage to Ford seems more a reverent bid to recapture its breathless action.

Nevertheless, it remains clear that the speeding vehicle is a cattle wagon in France, not a stagecoach in Arizona. The more jarring evocations of the American West, and of the western genre, are introduced into the film without transposition into a Camargue analogy. They, too, are unmistakable. When Huguette arrives in the region in her ramshackle circus truck, she is wearing fringed buckskins, boots, a holster with a pistol on her hip, and elaborately tooled gauntlet-like sleeves. The showy outfit would be worthy of Dale Evans, Roy Rogers's co-star and spouse, to whom

Figure 5.1 Homage to John Ford.

Huguette bears a close resemblance with her wavy blond hair spilling from under a wide-brimmed hat. The shooting script is explicit ('a lovely young woman dressed as a cowgirl'),[12] and the costume's western reference is not lost on the other characters: Frédé teasingly dubs Huguette 'Miss Cowboy', to which she responds by calling him by the name of the American western star, Tom Mix. When she first steps out of her truck at the *mas* the *gardians* stare at this alien arrival, mouths agape, the outlandishness of her attire verbally registered as Krebs jokes 'l'Amérique à la rescousse!' ('America to the rescue!').

Huguette's appearance as an American-style cowgirl further collapses the Camargue–West analogy when she performs skilled acts of marksmanship to assert her authority. She shoots the centre of targets that the men at the *mas* are unable to hit, and then, to dispel any lingering doubts, shoots a cigar out of the mouth of a ranch hand and fires at a playing card tossed into the air: the ace of hearts lands with a hole in its centre. Demonstrations of sharpshooting skills on film are a western trope that dates from Edison's kinetoscope loop of Annie Oakley and continues through Anthony Mann's *Winchester '73*, released the same year as *Vendetta en Camargue*, where the superior talents of the antagonists are established in a shooting contest. With her western gear and superb aim, Huguette's character is not the transposition of an Annie Oakley-like persona into a Camarguais analogy; she is, in fact, a western-style Annie Oakley-like performer dropped unexpectedly into the circa 1949 Camargue (Oakley also shot cigarettes out of men's mouths as part of her act).

Devaivre nevertheless wrangles these incongruous western figures into a Camarguais frame: lest there be question that this land is Texas or Arizona, the film opens, like many of its predecessors, with documentary-like shots of running bulls, *gardians* and landscapes that have, effectively, become shorthand for establishing a Camargue setting; a credited *manade* (of Emile Bilhau, a successor to Folco) again lends these images the stamp of authenticity. Huguette's circus background also provides a plausible alibi for her prowess, though the film does not explicitly offer this explanation for her showy western outfits and her sharpshooting skills.

However, in the *ferrade* sequence, halfway through the film, the evocation of the American West-as-spectacle imposes so heavily that it arguably outstrips the Camargue diegesis. A montage shows men riding bucking horses and roping cattle under brilliant sunshine while spectators watch from outside a rail fence that encloses the arena. Huguette arrives in full western regalia, including voluminous woolly chaps and a cowboy hat. Frédé, wearing a broad-brimmed hat and a bandana, takes a place alongside her on a rail fence, and a lasso wielder spins a loop around the couple and tightens it until they are bound in an embrace. The *mise-en-scène* could easily pass as a representation of a rodeo at a ranch in the American West, though these images remain situated in the spatio-temporal continuity of the narrative: the ranch is identified as Frédé's *mas*, and the *gardians* and Roma from other sequences in the film are among the spectators.

This ambiguous diegetic container strains to the point of collapse, however, when the stunts culminate in what the shooting script designates a 'number' (*un numéro*) by performers identified as 'Les Colorados', who execute 'extraordinary lasso tricks'. These anonymous men in boots and broad-brimmed hats jump through spinning lassos, spin a rope around a horse while standing in the saddle, and perform other tricks for the onlookers who witness the act along with the filmgoers. The performance is marked with a change in register: music replaces dialogue, the narrative grinds to a halt, and the focus shifts from the characters and the plot to a performed attraction whose interest lies in an 'aesthetics of astonishment' rather than continuity grounded in logical cause-and-effect or

Figure 5.2 'Miss Cow-boy' and 'Tom Mix'.

psychological motivation. The 'number' interrupts the rodeo/*ferrade* with an act one might expect in a Will Rogers review, or in Buffalo Bill's *Wild West*. Indeed, its appeal and direct address are akin to Edison's kinetoscope films of Buffalo Bill's performers: a bucking bronco rider, a lasso thrower, and a sharpshooting woman in showy western clothes, all of which are featured in *Vendetta en Camargue*.

Which logic justifies the presence of the western-themed elements in *Vendetta en Camargue*? The probability and necessity of 'classical' narrative causality cannot reliably account for them, nor can the Camargue setting. By these measures, their eruption into the film is jarring, and would seem to re-inscribe the kind of 'cinematic barbarities' that had been eliminated from the Camargue films of the prior decades. Their purpose lies elsewhere. Certainly, caution is advisable in seeking governing logic in a film intentionally conceived as a portmanteau of genres and schtick, but the evocations of the West in this film are far from random farce. With its shooting cowgirl, stagecoach chase, 'natives' in the wilds, bucking horses, lassos, riding stunts, gags and the attack on a ranch, *Vendetta en Camargue* deploys point-by-point features that a typical *Wild West* programme would have delivered, that impressed Folco and Hamman, that inspired

Figure 5.3 Huguette and Frédé (on the fence) take in the show.

earlier stagings of the region for the movie camera, and that Hamman's silent westerns imbricated but did not fully integrate into a Camargue setting.[13] Even the chosen views of the Camargue landscape are plausibly the same as those found in the silent western-themed films: Devaivre hired Hamman as the film's *régisseur général* specifically for his familiarity with the best shooting locations in the region.[14]

Furthermore, the re-westernised elements of this cinematic Camargue are, in their more overt manifestation, aligned more with modernity than with regression to a rustic mode of existence that characterises life on the American frontier in many western films. Huguette arrives in this far-flung region as a cosmopolitan stranger from the world outside. Her B-western clothing, her motor vehicle, and her assertive challenge to traditional masculine authority register both a modernisation and an Americanisation that in 1949, in the early years of post-war industrialisation, were fuelling a radical transformation of French society. The tensions between this modern cowgirl intruder and the traditional society drive the plot of the film. However, insofar as this traditional Camargue on film already derives from the American West as a modern spectacle, a memory that Devaivre self-consciously stokes, this sharpshooting, truck-driving, American-style cowgirl from the north is not a random or surprising alien from the outside world; she was always already at home among the filmed images of horses, riders, vistas, sunshine and cattle of the cinematic Camargue. For their part, French spectators in 1949 were not put off by the unexplained western elements in the Camargue setting: *Vendetta en Camargue* turned a profit sufficient to erase the debts of its predecessors and to put the *Société des films Neptune*, in Devaivre's words, 'back in the saddle'.[15]

An Oldsmobile in the old Camargue: *Where Are You From, Johnny?*

The intrusion of modern French society into a rustic and traditional Camargue again provides the narrative scaffolding for *Where Are You From, Johnny?* (*D'où viens-tu Johnny?*). The film was conceived as a vehicle for Johnny Hallyday, the foremost figure of American-style rock-n-roll in France, who had recently burst onto the music scene and by 1963 was a major star at the age of twenty. The narrative opens in Paris, where a rock band led by Johnny (also the character's name) rehearses in a club owned by a mobster; within minutes Hallyday delivers a hip-shaking performance that would justify his moniker 'the French Elvis'. Johnny runs an errand for his boss, but when he discovers that the briefcase he is transporting is full of illegal drugs he dumps the contents into the Seine river. Pursued by both the police and the gangster's hit men, Johnny decides to hide out in his native Camargue. In an abrupt switch of location, and from black and white to colour, a montage shows bulls running and *gardians* herding, followed by shots of a *ferrade* festival with bull-wrestling, cattle-branding, and meat-roasting on spits. The cheerful local inhabitants speak with broad *midi* accents, dress in colourful clothing and carry on affably under a brilliant blue sky. Johnny arrives at the party on foot from across the Camargue plains with only a guitar in his hand. He is received warmly by his friends and relatives, and within minutes sheds his drab Paris clothes for white jeans and a brightly coloured shirt and, proving that he has not become an effete Parisian, exhibits *gardian*-worthy toughness by wrestling a bull to the ground. Initially, the only fly in the ointment is some tension with his friend Django, a half-Roma who is jealous of the attention Johnny receives from Magali, Django's fiancée and the daughter

Figure 5.4 Nowhere to hide: Johnny is pursued through a *noir* Paris.

of the *mas*'s owner. This pastorale of love in the farmlands ends when Gigi, Johnny's Parisian girlfriend (played by Hallyday's future spouse Sylvie Vartan), blows his cover when she arrives unexpectedly in the region with the Parisian hit men secretly trailing her. They kidnap and torture Johnny, but with the help of Gigi he is rescued by his family and friends, and when the gangsters seek revenge they are trampled by a herd of bulls. In the closing shot, Johnny leaves the *mas*, again on foot, to return to Paris.

The stark contrast between the two shooting locations establishes a crucial opposition that structures the film. In the opening set in Paris, black leather jackets and louche surroundings lend Johnny's friends a veneer of delinquency. The action plays out against a modern city of cafés, pinball machines, cars and motorbikes, a modern train station, and the basement nightclub. With gangsters and police detectives, illicit drugs, guns, a dimly lit bar and a smoky train platform, the black-and-white filming of the Paris sequences lends the claustrophobic city the mood of a *film noir*. In contrast to the nervy and suspenseful music that accompanies the images of the Parisian train tracks during the credits, the abrupt cut to a brilliantly coloured Camargue is announced with a trumpet flourish that one might easily mistake for the opening bars of the theme to *Shane*, over which are heard cries of 'yippee' and 'yee-ha' as riders herd cattle across a river: if the Paris opening is a gritty gangster picture, the Camargue, unmistakably, evokes the western. The *ferrade* sequence is accompanied by diegetic Roma guitar music, but when a maverick bull escapes, Magali, in jeans and a broad-brimmed hat, races on horseback to rope it accompanied by a brisk, Copland-esque 'hoe-down' riff in a bright major key. It's one of many shots in which the music and *mise-en-scène* pastiche American westerns. For example, the sight of tall, blond, lanky Johnny arriving alone with his guitar evokes the title character of Nicholas Ray's *Johnny Guitar*, in which a similarly tall, blond, lanky Johnny (Sterling Hayden) shows up alone, armed only with his guitar.[16] Within minutes Hallyday delivers a song, the optimistic and folksy 'Pour moi la vie va commencer', on horseback: he has, effectively, become a singing cowboy. The bookend arrival and departure of Johnny from the *mas* – approaching the stationary camera from across the plain and then walking away from it at the end – reproduces the device from John Ford's *The Searchers*, as does the sub-plot of the 'mixed-blood' Django and his relation to Magali. Screenwriter Yvan Audouard was explicitly charged with writing a western for Hallyday. However, the only direct verbal reference to the American West or the western genre occurs when the gangsters mockingly call Johnny 'cowboy' as they torture their captive near the end of the film. The 'westernisation' of the Camargue in *Where Are You From, Johnny?* resides not in Audouard's dialogue, but implicitly in the choice of music and the *mise-en-scène*.

The elements that earlier Camargue films shared with the western are amply featured in *Where Are You From, Johnny?*: bright sun, big skies, horses and riders, bandanas and broad-brimmed hats, corrals and bulls. These images evoke a Camargue removed from the outside world in distance and, if not in time, then in the degree of modernisation: on the *mas* farm there are no telephones (messages are delivered in person), and the oil lamps hanging in the house suggest it has no electricity. Throughout the film, transitions between sequences are marked with shots of bulls running, *gardians* with tridents, and horses splashing through the grassy marshes; a *manade* of bulls and riders is again credited.

Figure 5.5 Johnny sings of a new life under brilliant blue skies.

However, this rustic and rural Camargue setting is limited to the sequences set at the *mas* and in the fields. Much of the latter half of the film takes place against the backdrop of the annual festival in Saintes-Maries-de-la-Mer, a town that serves as a liminal space between the outside world (namely, modern Paris) and the isolated, traditional lifestyle of the ranch-like *mas*.[17] These sequences feature a *course de taureaux* in a seaside arena (Johnny saves the day when Django is in danger), women in traditional costume, and Roma music and dancing. However, they also include gawking crowds of British, German and American tourists in garish shirts and shorts with cameras hanging around their necks. The intrusive reach of the outside world is underscored by the motorcoach that brings Gigi (along with more tourists) to the region, trailed by the menacing black, chrome-trimmed and finned Oldsmobile Super 88 convertible carrying the hit men in dark suits and sunglasses. Both the car and the Parisians stand out in the village, and the attention they draw becomes a plot element. The breached barrier between the modern world of Paris and the western-tinged Camargue, registered by the arrival of the bus and the showy American car, volatilises the oppositions that up to this point structured both the narrative and the style of the film: *noir* invades the western, distant Paris is only a day's drive away, and the Camargue is not a remote and impregnable bastion of tradition but an easily accessible attraction consumed by crowds of tourists from the outside world.

By thematising the tension between a modern industrialised consumer society of cars, guns and tourist cameras and a rural lifestyle from a previous century, *D'où viens-tu, Johnny?* taps the contradictions of its time. The film was made near the mid-point of the *trente glorieuses*, the three post-war decades during which, after years of depression and war, American-style consumer culture, driven by new technologies and technocratic industrialisation, was rapidly altering the experience of everyday life in France. In her study of this period, Kristin Ross identifies the tension between the seductive conveniences of modernisation, urbanisation and standardisation, and the anxieties that follow the radical 'reordering' of traditional lifestyles and communities that this new way of living entails. The automobile thematises this moment: still aspirational for many French citizens in the early 1960s, cars represented speed, power and convenience, and became a fetish item associated with the stars who frequently crashed them (among others, Hallyday). However, the automobile also enacted the 'reordering' of the formerly distinct geographical centres of community and multigenerational family units – the village, the neighbourhood – where the inhabitants live side by side and know each other by name. 'The destruction of such "traditional" societies through the creation of a space/time structured by the car', Ross argues, provoked a sense of loss and anxiety.[18]

Cinema also provides an arena where the tensions wrought by the new consumer culture are symbolically staged. Ross observes how the automobile emblematises the seduction of the new, but also the dangers it entails, in *Lola* (Jacques Demy, 1961), *Breathless* (Jean-Luc Godard, 1960), *La Belle Américaine* (Robert Dhéry, 1961) and other films that are close contemporaries of *Where Are You From, Johnny?* Like the automobile, cinema itself, Ross insists, also reconfigures the perception of time and space, and in its American (Hollywood) iteration it, too, is a mass-produced and technology-driven consumer item, standardised by genres and the Hollywood style: 'the two technologies [car and cinema] reinforced each other. Their shared qualities – movement, image, mechanization, standardization – made movies and cars the key commodity-vehicles of a complete transformation in European consumption patterns and cultural habits.'[19]

Where Are You From, Johnny? both illustrates and complicates Ross's argument. On the one hand, the representation of the region can be read as a reverse-shot reaction to the modernisation and reordering of society. The car, for example, recasts the experience of distance by making the formerly remote Camargue accessible to Parisians, tourists or whoever has a vehicle. The big black Oldsmobile is therefore doubly menacing: it represents a threat by bringing the killers to the region, but also a modern incursion into the rural, unindustrialised and culturally distinct bastion of tradition celebrated in the film adaptations of the 1920s and 1930s. The intrusion, however, is roundly defeated when the killers drive the car out to the *mas*: once they leave their vehicle, these hunters become the prey. The community, in which everyone knows and helps each other, proves stronger than the over-confident and violent outsiders. So, too, do the horse and bull, which in the end prevail with vengeful force in contrast to the abandoned car, tilting motionless on the shoulder of the road. At the close of the film Johnny leaves on foot. The sight of Hallyday slowly walking away from the camera across the plain effectively re-establishes the pre-industrial experience of time and distance that had been collapsed by the speed of motor vehicles: Paris is once again a long journey away, and the Camargue, or at least the *mas*, is again remote and purged of alien elements. Watching Johnny leave, Magali and Django, in each other's arms, prefigure future heirs to a place that has, so far, warded off the violent incursions of modernity, urbanisation, and the reach of a homogenising consumer culture that flattens regional difference and disrupts community and familial networks. The rural Camargue of *Where Are You From, Johnny?* is a fantasy of the defeat of the modern: like a Brigadoon, or collection of Provençal *santon* figurines in a box, the old Camargue will, it seems, still be there when Johnny needs it, with its reassuring community of colourful characters, traditions and unconditional solidarity, even as the world outside lurches anxiously into a new era.[20]

However, for this opposition between a modern France centred in Paris and the remote Camargue to hold, one must forget the extent to which this westernised Camargue itself is already inspired by modern American spectacles that French spectators consumed en masse. In the early 1900s, it was Buffalo Bill's *Wild West* that informed images of the region; after 1945 it was the American westerns, musicals and crime pictures that were flooding into France and that *Where Are You From, Johnny?* evokes.[21] As Ross notes, American films, like the automobile, were a standardised product exported by a technology-driven industry: both products were objects of fascination and unease, slick and seductive in their American iteration, bigger and in the eyes of some (the critics at the *Cahiers du cinéma* in the 1950s, for example) better than their French-made counterparts. In this respect the western elements associated with the region's traditions are not antithetical to the Oldsmobile convertible that intrudes into the region; they are analogous to it insofar as both bespeak the reach of mass-produced American consumer products

Figure 5.6 Johnny returns to Paris on foot.

into even this remote corner of rural France. If Paris has been invaded by American-style modernity, so, too, has the 'traditional' Camargue through its foregrounded kinship to the western film.

It is Hallyday himself, however, who most forcefully levels the opposition between modern Paris and the rustic Camargue. From his earliest recordings, Hallyday unabashedly imitated the sound of American popular music and the style of Hollywood film stars. He covered Elvis Presley's hits and imitated his moves, and adopted both the black leather jacket of Marlon Brando and the styling of James Dean, to whom he bore a marked resemblance. David Looseley characterises the constitutive Americanness of Hallyday's star persona: 'His entire act was obviously indebted to Elvis, James Dean, and the tropes of American popular culture generally.'[22] Hallyday was often scorned for his 'methodical mimicry of successive American styles', but was enthusiastically received by his French fans. Initially, Hallyday's image was threatening and he was perceived as an associate of a feared strain of juvenile delinquents in the late 1950s. However, as he became more mainstream he began to soften his image with a more wholesome presentation, a transformation enacted in the plot of *Where Are You From, Johnny?* Loosely traces this transformation: Hallyday's relation to Vartan would shortly culminate in a well-publicised marriage, the couple would have a son and he would submit to his obligatory military service during the Algerian war and, like Elvis, perform in uniform. His music also evolved:

> To defuse the dangers of rock'n'roll – its associations with dissident, working-class youths presaging both class and generational conflicts – rough diamonds like Johnny were swiftly polished up and transformed into the voice of the much more docile yéyé, whose ideology was that all young people, regardless of social position, were brought together as *copains* by their charmingly innocent love of pop music.[23]

The two locations of *Where Are You From, Johnny?* chart this transition: in Paris his friends wear black leather jackets and Johnny's costume, a plaid wool waist-length jacket, is similar to Brando's in *On the Waterfront* (Elia Kazan, 1954). He escapes this dark urban world of motorcycles and drug trafficking to croon under flowers on a country veranda at night: he has gone from a delinquent rocker mixed up with the mob to a down-home cowhand singing optimistically of life and love.

Still, despite the sharply drawn contrast between these registers, Hallyday's persona is drawing from the same well in both. Whether he is mimicking the Elvis of *Jailhouse Rock* (Richard Thorpe, 1957) or of the westerns *Love Me Tender* (Robert Webb, 1956) and *Flaming Star* (Don Siegel, 1960), the Brando of *The Wild One* (Laslo Benedek, 1953) or of *One-Eyed Jacks* (Marlon Brando, 1961), the James Dean of *Rebel Without a Cause* (Nicholas Ray, 1955) or of *Giant* (George Stevens, 1956), on a motorcycle or on horseback, embedded in *noir* Paris or in the western-tinged Camargue, Hallyday's image remains modelled on the stars and genres of Hollywood and the American culture industry. It is a great irony of Hallyday's career that his popularity never translated to the Anglo-American world where, if he was known at all, he often met indifference or ridicule. Despite the American inspiration, Hallyday's star appealed primarily to the French. He is both an emblematic product of a global culture industry, and the mark of persistent parochial precincts of taste and the unevenness of circulation in a transnational public sphere.

In this colourful western-tinged Camargue, like a land of Oz where Johnny briefly sojourns to discover who he really is, a telling detail nonetheless sounds an elegiac note. In the opening shots set in Paris, as Hallyday steers a toy car in an arcade game an iconic soft-drink bottle sits on the console while rock music plays loudly from a jukebox. The film's first intelligible line is from one of his friends, in a black jacket, who pounds on the bar and demands *un coca* while the older patrons of the café lament the behaviour of these 'kids'. Automobiles, rock music, unruly youth and the American soft-drink brand are tightly aligned. Later, in the Camargue, an American tourist in a Hawaiian print shirt and a straw hat, a camera around his neck, approaches a café's bar in Saintes-Maries-de-la-Mer and demands loudly, in English, a Coca-Cola ('All I want is a Coca-Cola. You understand, Coca-Cola?'). The bartender responds, in French, that he has no Coca-Cola and dispatches the bewildered man with the vernacular apéritif of the *Midi*, a pastis. The Coca-Cola/pastis conceit seems to reinforce the opposition of the modern outside world of rock music, black jackets, Oldsmobiles, Americans and Coca-Cola, with a traditional Camargue which still lies beyond the reach of an American-style consumer culture and global brands to which Paris, it seems, has thoroughly succumbed.

This opposition has already been defeated. Where in elegiac American westerns the appearance of an automobile heralds the end of the old West, in *Where Are You From, Johnny?* it is not the cars and buses that most emphatically mark the arrival of modernity but the people they convey, not the soft drink but the presence of the American himself who, even with a pastis in hand, registers the transformation of the Camargue into a tourist destination and a consumer commodity in a global marketplace. By 1963, the Camargue was no longer isolated and remote. The automobile had made the region easily accessible, and the French flocked to Mediterranean beaches on their extended paid vacations. The region is only a short drive from Marseille on one side, and on the other it abuts La Grande Motte, the planned resort community where the construction of futuristic seaside condominiums was beginning as *Where Are You From, Johnny?* was being filmed.[24] Tourism had become the principal industry of the region, and even in the film the mayor greets the arriving tourists and steers them towards the town's attractions. Today the scale of tourism is staggering: in 2010 the *Parc naturel régional* had fewer than 9,000 permanent inhabitants, of which less than 6% worked in farming, while in 2013 it welcomed over 5.5 million visitors, a million more than the Grand Canyon in the same year.[25]

Folco de Baroncelli's wish to cultivate and promote the appeal of the region was realised, one might surmise, beyond his wildest dreams. *Where Are You From, Johnny?* is not the last film made in the Camargue, but the incursion of automobiles, buses, hordes of tourists and globalised brands sounds an elegiac knell that pushes the persistence of this remote enclave, sheltered from the anxieties of the contemporary world, onto the threshold of fantasy. However, insofar as this traditional Camargue on film remains self-consciously fashioned through tropes of the American West, disseminated in France by spectacles from Buffalo Bill's *Wild West* through the post-war Hollywood western, it is constitutively alloyed with new technologies, a new speed and ease of travel, new modes of distribution and consumption and a transnational public. The running herds, lassos and singing cowboy join the American cars, Coca-Cola and rock-n-roll as projections of the same horizon of experience, not as holdouts against the traumatic effects of modernity but as the fruit of their negotiation.

Notes

1. Miriam Bratu Hansen, 'The Mass Production of the Senses: Classical Cinema as Vernacular Modernism', *Modernism/Modernity* 6, no. 2 (1999): 60.

2. Miriam Bratu Hansen, 'Fallen Women, Rising Stars, New Horizons: Shanghai Silent Film As Vernacular Modernism', *Film Quarterly* 54, no. 1 (Autumn, 2000): 11.
3. Hansen's stance may be grouped alongside other studies of cinema's modernity. See, among others, the articles included in Leo Charney and Vanessa Schwartz, eds, *Cinema and the Invention of Modern Life* (Berkeley: University of California Press, 1995). For a pointed rebuttal to this strain of thought, see Charlie Keil, 'To Here from Modernity: Style, Historiography, and Transitional Cinema', in Keil and Stamp, *American Cinema's Transitional Era*, 51–65.
4. Miriam Bratu Hansen, 'The Mass Production of the Senses', 68.
5. Synopsis for *Miss Cow-boy*, Fonds Crédit National, Archives of the *Cinémathèque française*, Référence: CN422-B293.
6. 'Les épisodes multiples et variés fourmillant de gags humoristiques qui constituent le trame de notre film doivent en faire un spectacle susceptible de plaire à tous les publics.' Ibid., no page number.
7. 'Les choses seront peut-être plus faciles si nous nous portons sur des sujets moins complexes, plus publics, plus accessibles à tous et surtout aux financiers potentiels.' Ibid., no page number.
8. '[U]n certain style de cinéma, les grands espaces et les grandes chevauchées, les gentils et les méchants'. Ibid., no page number.
9. 'L'action de notre film se déroule au "Pays du Taureau" au Mas du Landre, dans cette Camargue dont l'immense plaine au ciel de feu évoque irrésistiblement les espaces illimités du Far-West.' Ibid., no page number.
10. Jean Devaivre, *Action: mémoires 1930–1970* (Paris: Nicolas Philippe, 2002), 251.
11. On the stereotyped depiction of Native Americans in Hollywood westerns, see Jaquelyn Kilpatrick, *Celluloid Indians: Native Americans and Film* (Lincoln: University of Nebraska Press, 1999).
12. 'une ravissante jeune fille vêtue en "cow-girl"'. Jean Devaivre and René Mejean, *Miss Cow-boy*, shooting script, Archives of the *Cinémathèque Française*: 12.
13. The sample programme posted on the website of the William F. Cody Archive includes, among other acts, sharpshooters, horse races and equine acts, an attack on a stagecoach, a lasso act, 'Indians' showing their customs and riding skills, comic skits and an attack on a settler's cabin. Available at <http://codyarchive.org/memorabilia/wfc.mem00278.html> (accessed 1 March 2022).
14. Devaivre, *Action*, 242. Hamman's fee (100,000 francs) is significant given the low budget of the film, and suggests his importance. Auber (who five years later will play opposite Cary Grant and Grace Kelly in Hitchcock's *To Catch a Thief*) receives only 200,000 francs for her leading role, and Daniel Sarano, in his first film role, only 50,000.
15. 'Les recettes seront en conséquence ce qui aidera Neptune à se remettre en selle.' (Devaivre, *Action*, 257). In the year of its release *Vendetta en Camargue* outperformed many of its American western competitors. Its box office returns were comparable to those of the French release of the big-budget *Annie Get Your Gun* (George Sidney, 1950) the following year.
16. Similarly posed publicity material further underscores this reference.
17. François Amy de la Bretèque observes that the commercial centre of a *Midi* village serves as the contact zone between the local traditional culture and the outside world (and its tourists). François Amy de la Bretèque, 'Images of Provence: Ethnotypes and Stereotypes of the South in French Cinema', in *Popular European Cinema*, ed.

Richard Dyer and Ginette Vincendeau (London & New York: Routledge, 1992), 58–71.
18. So, too, Ross contends, did the fact that the car was mass produced with dehumanising assembly-line production by immigrant labourers who were kept invisible in this newly re-ordered society. Kristin Ross, *Fast Cars, Clean Bodies: Decolonization and the Reordering of French Culture* (Cambridge: MIT Press, 1995), 53.
19. Ibid., 38.
20. *Santons* are the traditional ceramic figurines of Provençal villagers, recognisable types each with their iconography, in a Christmas *crèche*. De la Bretèque notes the frequent evocation of these familiar types in films set in the Camargue. See de la Bretèque, 'Images of Provence'.
21. Powrie and Cadalanu note the 'American flavour' brought to the film by director Noël Howard, who had worked in Hollywood, and observe its 'curious amalgam of film noir, French western, and singer film'. Phil Powrie and Marie Cadalanu, *The French Film Musical* (London: Bloomsbury, 2020), 152.
22. David Looseley, 'Une passion française: The Mourning of Johnny Hallyday', *French Cultural Studies* 29, no. 4 (2018): 380.
23. David Looseley, 'Fabricating Johnny: French Popular Music and National Culture', *French Cultural Studies* 16, no. 2 (2005): 202. The 'cleansing' of Hallyday's image in the film is also noted in Jacques Durand, 'Lost Paradise', in Rouqette and Stourdzé, *Western*, 136–7.
24. This massive project, launched under president Charles de Gaulle to promote tourism, is hailed as 'one of the most important touristic and urban planning projects carried out in France and in Europe during the period called *les trente glorieuses*'. [C'est l'un des projets touristiques et urbanistiques les plus importants réalisés en France et en Europe dans la période dite des '30 glorieuses'.] Available at <https://www.lagrandemotte.fr/cadre-de-vie/decouvrir-la-ville/histoire-de-la-grande-motte> (accessed 3 March 2022).
25. The numbers indicate an approximately 10,000:1 visitor-to-farmer ratio. 'Les clientèles touristiques de la Camargue', 2013, <https://en.calameo.com/read/001239688ebf5e4cf111f> (accessed 19 August 2021).

III

Chez nous on the Range

6

Little colony on the prairie

An old-world France tinged with nostalgia for belle-époque elegance and a picturesque demi-monde of bistros and cabarets has inspired some of post-war Hollywood's most celebrated films: *An American in Paris* (Vincente Minnelli, 1951), *Moulin Rouge* (John Huston, 1952) and *Gigi* (Vincente Minnelli, 1958), among others. These musicals featured both French and American stars and were widely seen by audiences in both the United States and France at a moment when the French film industry was still finding its post-war footing.

The Technicolor, wide-screen, singing-and-dancing spectacles would appear to testify to the global dominance of genre-driven Hollywood production that could out-muscle other national film industries even in the representation of their own people, locations and culture, while appropriating their stars and audiences in the process. However, this corpus also provides grounds for revising characterisations of Hollywood's global hegemony and local French resistance, of centres and margins, and of industrial-scale production and a rival industry struggling to hold its own. In *It's So French!: Hollywood, Paris, and the Making of the Cosmopolitan Film Culture*, Vanessa Schwartz challenges the perception that post-war French cinema was the besieged victim of a one-way Americanisation imposed by its outsized Hollywood rival, and builds the argument on the big-budget musicals set in France.[1] The idealised Paris in *An American in Paris*, *Gigi* and other films bespeaks instead a calculated coordination between French and American film industries that becomes visible when their production and distribution are considered through a transnational lens. Through a mutually beneficial alloy of French and American shooting locations, economic interests, screens, stars and publics, these films 'construct an imagery that transcended the nation as an imagined community'.[2] They join the cult of Brigitte Bardot, the Cannes Film Festival, and 'cosmopolitan' productions such as Mike Todd's *Around the World in Eighty Days* (Michael Anderson, 1956) as evidence of a dynamic transatlantic film culture, and of a strategic symbiosis, of a new 'organising category' that demands a term of its own: a transnational 'Frenchness', distinct from both American and French cinema, whose logic more completely explains the creation and reception of these films.³

At the same time that the 'Frenchness' musicals were exploiting *fin-de-siècle* Paris, a group of French-language star vehicles drew inspiration from the frontier-era American West. These period films are also framed in the conventions of an established genre, and they, too, feature well-known performers: Fernand Raynaud (*Fernand cow-boy*, 1956), Luis Mariano (*Sérénade au Texas / Texas Serenade*, 1958) and Fernandel (*Dynamite Jack*, 1961). This small cycle opens an inverse perspective on film genre as a transnational zone of contact: 1950s Hollywood romanticises belle-époque Paris in lavish musicals, while nineteenth-century America provides fodder for comedy in post-war French westerns.

The apparent symmetry in this exchange quickly buckles under scrutiny. The 'Frenchness' cycle evinces cooperation between the French and American film industries in production, distribution and exhibition. The French westerns were filmed in France without the direct cooperation of Hollywood studios, and address a public that effectively excluded American filmgoers: although they were dubbed and distributed in Europe, none had theatrical release in the United States. Where the 'Frenchness' musicals include some of the most famous films in Hollywood's history and reaped a harvest of accolades (*Gigi* alone won eight Oscars), the French westerns were generally derided or ignored by critics. The stars of the 'Frenchness' films garnered fame on both sides of the Atlantic, and some became part of the Hollywood star system.⁴ In contrast, Mariano, his co-star Bourvil, and Raynaud were (and remain) unknown to most American spectators, and the films of Fernandel, ubiquitous in 1950s France, only occasionally reached American shores.

The positioning of star performers within an emblematic genre further distinguishes these films. Although he plays an ex-patriot in Paris, Gene Kelly is comfortably on home turf as he sings and dances for the camera on a sound-stage set; there is nothing dissonant or surprising about his appearance in a movie musical, be it set in France or elsewhere. Indeed, *An American in Paris* and some of its 'Frenchness' contemporaries are often considered the *summa* of the genre. The French westerns, on the contrary, cast their stars as interlopers in the genre twice over: their characters are hapless foreigners transplanted into the American West, and the humour of these situations is amplified by the discordant sight and sound of the French performer playing cowboy in a genre that Hollywood decisively dominated.

In short, the transnational transcendence of national cinemas looks vastly different from the reverse shot of the post-war French westerns, which do not similarly evince a cosmopolitan film culture (an 'Americanness') whose organising logic supersedes the French/American binary. One could say that the French western films failed to 'translate' for American audiences. The word's etymology is apt: the films were not 'carried across' the ocean from Europe, but the term is also fitting in its linguistic meaning, for these films remain resolutely French in a crucial respect so obvious that its consequences easily go unexamined: the actors in these films, with few exceptions, deliver their lines in French.

Transnational success and a French-language film are not *per se* incompatible. Dubbing and subtitling make films accessible to spectators worldwide, and the emblematic star of Schwartz's cosmopolitan film culture provides a signal example: Bardot rose to stardom with the success of *And God Created Woman* (*Et Dieu . . . créa la femme*, Roger Vadim, 1956), and in her subsequent leading roles she delivered her lines in French (with a notable exception, a western, discussed in the following chapter).[5] Nor is it surprising that a production with a French-speaking cast would substitute French for the language of the region in which a film is set. After all, in the 'Frenchness' films set in Paris actors often deliver their lines in English, even when they are native French speakers and the characters they portray are French. It would seem reasonable that the inverse could be the case when a French-language film is set in America: the spoken French would represent diegetic English, just as Leslie Caron's and Louis Jourdan's English dialogue in *Gigi* signifies French speech and not an inexplicable outbreak of English as the lingua franca of Paris.

However, the use of the French language in the western-themed vehicles for Raynaud, Mariano and Fernandel acts as more than a bid to be understood. Their characters are not American cowboys, bandits or sheriffs whose speech renders English in translation. Through a shared conceit, they play native French speakers who travel from France to the American frontier, bring their language with them and discover that in great measure the population of this distant land also speaks it. This ploy is doubly expedient: it enables a French-speaking public to understand the characters without subtitles, dubbing or the suggestion that this speech represents English filtered through French translation. Perhaps more importantly, the sound of the leading performers' spoken French is a salient constituent of their star persona, and a conveniently francophone frontier allows the actors to speak freely in their signature style without the presumption that their speech is a second-degree rendition of an English original.

A closer examination of this French speech exposes the imbalance between the 'Frenchness' musicals and the French westerns. In the former, the movie musical is solidly enunciated in celebrated films from the genre's golden age. In the latter the use of the French language amplifies discordance between 'French' and 'western', and this intentional draw on the dissonance of French stars speaking with their signature inflections in Texas or Arizona has been characterised as a defiant French drubbing of a signature Hollywood genre.[6] However, the farcical illogic of these francophone frontiers does not spare the French assertion that competes with the western genre, and the ploys that allow the performers to speak in French destabilise not only enunciations of 'western' but also of the French referent evoked in these films. In the present chapter, the focus lies on linguistic mutations that register ethnic and racial difference in the Fernand Raynaud vehicle *Fernand cow-boy*. In the following two chapters, a study of westerns that feature some of the most visible French stars of their day reveals how language supports the logics of 'western' and 'French', but also, as a key constituent of the stars' image, undermines and defeats them.

Language and the Mythic West

Language is a salient and vital component of filmic texts. It streams through the voices of speakers seen and unseen, and addresses the spectator visually in signs, handwriting and other written words that appear in the frame. Virtually all narrative film includes language, if only in the title or the credits. In many films, a flood of verbiage bathes the spectator aurally and visually in a nearly continuous stream.[7]

One need only imagine the world's billions of spectators, year after year, choosing, viewing and responding to films made in one language or another, and in some far more than others, to begin to grasp the magnitude of language's consequence for cinema. Language enmeshes the spectator in the uneven hierarchies and multidirectional flows of global capital and geo-political power: government subsidies, protectionist measures, nationalist politics, censorship, import quotas, conventions of translation through dubbing and subtitling, and other pressures figure in a 'mix of economic and political factors deploying language to regulate much more than a path to comprehensibility'.[8] Beyond carving out markets and audiences in a global industry, language also acts as a powerful arbiter of public spheres, a catalyst for ideations of an 'us' versus all of 'them' who do not share the language in question. Through what Benedict Anderson calls the 'fatality of linguistic diversity' these imagined linguistic communities map onto nations,[9] but language also shapes publics on other scales: some are seldom heard (a rarely filmed minority dialect), others co-exist or compete under a national umbrella (in Indian cinema, for example), while English's outsized presence in a global industry addresses a vast transnational community of filmgoers whose measure of inclusion in the 'us' depends on local climates of reception.[10] 'Language' comprises not only diverse 'natural' languages, but also the registers, modes of address and pronunciations that further assemble and exclude, attract and repel, and shape and erode the borders between an imagined 'us' or a 'them', even among those who share a common idiom.[11]

Despite its importance as a mediator of a spectator's experience, there is no guarantee that a film's language will draw sustained attention in film scholarship, criticism and theory. Certainly, there are precincts where language is thrust into the spotlight. Accounts of subject formation, grounded in psychoanalytical theory, assert the power of language to interpellate a spectator.[12] The consequences of the world's many natural languages, often positioned under the figure of 'Babel', also draw scrutiny to the conversion to sound, the practices of dubbing and subtitling, multilingual or 'polyglot' films, and avant-garde or art films that revise familiar conventions for language use.[13] However, even in these cases language may act as an index for other aspects of cinema that remain the primary focus of study: sound recording technologies, international distribution and co-production arrangements or the tension between American and European cinema, to name a few. The specific words uttered or seen often elude consideration. Properties of the voice in film have been explored independently of, and at times in opposition to, the language they convey.[14] Studies of speech often limit the purview to one mode of language delivery and exclude the written word, and the structure and narrative function of a film dialogue may be considered separately (in translation, for example) from the precise language used. Elsewhere, language serves as a more general theoretical metaphor ('how does cinema act like a language?') that outstrips the study of the written and spoken words found in a film.[15]

Immanent in speech, made audible by the voice in cinema and more broadly participating in the category of sound in a medium whose study strongly favours the visual, as a distinct cinematic object language does not draw critical attention commensurate with its stature in film.[16] The notion persists that language is uncinematic, in cinema but not of cinema, the stuff of literature and not of a visual medium where authors write with the camera and not with the pen: 'Language is not cinema [. . .] cinema is expression through images', reads the programme for a recent film conference.[17] The dismissal is rarely so categorical, and some filmmakers (Jean-Luc Godard, for example) conceive of language as a constituent of the image itself. Nevertheless, critics who champion the study of language in film are compelled to characterise it as a 'neglected domain' and 'dark corner'[18] whose 'perverse' and 'strange occultation'[19] is perpetuated by an endemic 'logophobia' in cinema studies.[20] Language easily settles into a grey zone where it may be both ubiquitous and inconspicuous, indispensable but beside the point, a background support whose features are only indirectly lit by an inquiring beam trained on other aspects of cinema.

In western films, language looms large from this dim corner. More than any other major Hollywood genre, the western regularly foregrounds linguistic exchange among characters of diverse ethnic and language groups, including Native Americans, hispanophones and immigrants from Europe and China. In studio-era Hollywood, the negotiation of linguistic diversity generally acts to preserve comprehensibility for an anglophone spectatorship. However, the ploys for achieving this practical goal are deeply implicated in the myth of American expansion that shapes narratives in literature, film and historical discourse. In his characterisation of American exceptionalism, historian Frederick Jackson Turner aligned the ascendance of the English language with the expanding nation. Inhabitants on the harsh edge of civilisation regress to a more primitive state, an experience that over time begets a distinct American identity strengthened by a good measure of Darwinist selection. On this frontier, inhabitants of diverse backgrounds comingle in a new American 'stock' that is no longer recognisably German, Scots-Irish or English (the ethnicities Turner names), with a notable exception: the composite bloodline does not imply a composite language. English unquestionably prevails, as Turner recognises with a telling caveat: 'beware of misinterpreting the fact that there is a common English speech in America into a belief that the stock is also English.'[21] Monolingualism manifests cohesion in this new American identity, and for future generations English will prevail in this formerly polyglot territory.

As history, Turner's thesis has been subject to over a century of challenges.[22] It finds more enduring traction in the narratives that shape ideas of the American West in popular literature and film.[23] A teleology of English ascendency regulates this imaginary land. Consider the stock tropes that channel the English language and the future American nation onto a confluent course in western films. The preoccupation with building churches and schools and the arrival of Eastern preachers and schoolteachers, whose prim speech contrasts with the slang and linguistic diversity of the frontier, foretell of new generations who will speak, read and write proper English. John Ford's *The Man Who Shot Liberty Valance* (1962) draws deeply on this conceit, representing Swedish, African American, rustic anglophone and Spanish-speaking townspeople learning to read and write English together in a one-room school; the use of the United States Constitution as the text for the language lesson tidily conflates future citizenship and mastery of English. Often excluded from this community, Native American characters face not assimilation but annihilation or displacement, and the native languages are destined to disappear with those who speak them.

If the end of a film prefigures a monolingual future, westerns routinely represent encounters between diverse language groups. These negotiations follow predictable patterns of asymmetry. English seems naturally to prevail when the protagonist bears a phonetically chiselled Scots-Anglo-Saxon name: Dunson, Kane, Bishop, MacAdam. For other characters, language indexes narrative agency along gendered and racial/ethnic distinctions. The refined speech patterns of women and non-Western men, as well as denizens of the Word (lawyers, preachers, teachers), signify impotence in a land where, as Jane Tompkins observes, 'language is false or at best ineffectual; only actions are real.'[24] Mexican characters often speak English, perhaps delivering a few lines in Spanish whose precise meaning is insignificant (a decorative *váyase* or *adiós*) or redundant to visual cues.[25] The speech of Native American characters poses a greater challenge. When an 'Anglo' character converses in a Native American language the meaning is often translated by another character or is immediately obvious from context. Some films render Native American speech in English, creating ambiguity when the line delivery represents both English speech and a native language; others use gibberish, inarticulate grunts or simply leave these characters mute. The rare film that reproduces a Native American language does not always avoid un-modern formality in the subtitled translation of speech, and the over-arching alignment of future nation, Turner's stock, and the English language may remain intact. In *Dances with Wolves* (Kevin Costner, 1990), hailed for its use of spoken Lakota, the elegiac closing again charts an Anglo-Saxon and English-speaking future whose new generations, though they might mourn instead of vilify the vanishing Indian, will have no further need for subtitles.[26]

The 'international westerns' that began to appear in greater numbers in the 1950s and 1960s faced the compounded challenge of representing a multilingual, multi-ethnic region while filming in a language that, in some cases, few or none of the represented characters speak. Provided all characters are presumed anglophone, it may be established that the spoken lines represent English in translation, but even this simple premise quickly leads to incongruity and dissonance. Placards and posters that have attained iconic status as signifiers of the West ('Saloon', 'Jail', 'Wanted') often remain in English, creating discordance between the spoken and written word. The language scheme is further complicated when the setting is multilingual. Native Americans, Mexicans and other characters whose native language is not English might, though not always, affect an inflection to signify ethnic and linguistic difference; the West German *Winnetou* films present diverse inflections in the German language (though inconsistently), for example, while in East German *Indianerfilme* the stylised speech of the 'Indians' often bears no differentiating accent.[27]

The representational demands language imposes in these films do not always harmonise with American frontier ideology. In spaghetti westerns, multinational co-productions filmed with actors speaking multiple languages and dubbed for distribution in various world markets, indifference to any single original language may derail the 'natural' trajectory towards English monolingualism and load other political resonances into a film.[28] The phraseology of an idiom also bears a distinct cultural stamp. In *Die Söhne der grossen Bärin / The Sons of Great Bear* (Josef Mach, 1966), the chief's exhortation to farm, forge and plough voices the official discourse of the East German 'workers' and farmers' state'.[29] The Far-West of Karl May's stories places the social and moral discourses of late nineteenth-century Europe in the mouths of characters.[30] Diverse meanings may be generated and loaded into a film through localised practices of dubbing and reception.[31] *Limonádový Joe aneb Konská opera / Lemonade Joe* (Oldrich Lipsky, 1964) infuses Brechtian alienation into a parodic parable of capitalist exploitation, a distanciation intensified by the uncustomary sound of a cowboy speaking Czech.

A French-language western also delivers a jolt of the unexpected. Is it possible to dispel the irony of a gunfighter sidling up to a saloon's bar and growling '*une bouteille!*'? The answer will depend in some measure on whether the utterance signifies French or English speech, a distinction that remains ill-defined in the western-themed star vehicles. This instability destabilises continuity in the diegesis, and along with it the frontier narrative of conquest and expansion that the institution of English reinforces. For a certain audience, the speech will nonetheless remain familiar and consistent insofar as it reproduces the anticipated speech patterns of the performer who utters it. The enunciation of the genre competes with, and in some cases is defeated by, the foregrounding of language as a constituent of the French star's image. In turn, however, this assertion of a French cinematic referent remains yoked to the illogical machinations of an ambiguous language scheme.

The francophone frontier: *Fernand cow-boy* (1956)

The opening of *Fernand cow-boy* richly thematises the negotiation of language difference. The diffident Fernand Mignot, played by Raynaud, has inherited a hotel in Texas and bids his village in rural France farewell. The dialogue underscores the unworldly Fernand's lack of the English skills necessary to manage this foreign business: as he boards a train his mother implores '*profite de ton voyage pour travailler ton anglais*' ('take advantage of your trip to practice your English'). The following sequence establishes just how sorely Fernand's English needs improvement. Seated in a stagecoach he intones a ludicrous sentence from a phrasebook: '*le rosier de ma cousine est fleurie*; ze rose tree av ma-ee coo-zeen ees. . .', a phrase he never manages to finish due to the encumbrances of the cramped vehicle, the bumpy ride and, within minutes, an attack by Native Americans. A line has been starkly drawn between the meek French-speaking petit-bourgeois and the realities of the frontier.

If the opening sequences herald the worthlessness of French on the frontier, those that follow surprise both spectators and Fernand by revealing the uselessness of English instead. As the stagecoach pulls into the town, signs ('General Store', 'Barber Shop') mark it as English-speaking, and Fernand manages to utter a halting 'Zank you' and to ask directions to the hotel. At this point the townspeople communicate only with gestures or inarticulate grunts. However, when Fernand enters the hotel's saloon the language scheme takes a surprising turn. To his belaboured 'Good morning, sir' the bartender sternly answers, in French, '*Minute!*' ('Just a minute!'). Fernand persists with a timid 'excuse me' and the barman snaps '*La ferme!*' ('Shut up!'), again in idiomatic French. After a few more lines the barman barks a menacing '*Qu'est-ce que vous voulez, vous?*' ('What do you want?'). Fernand, flustered, begins reciting his 'ze rose tree…' phrase, and is again interrupted: '*Qu'est-ce que c'est que tout ce charabia?*' ('What's all this gibberish?'). Fernand finally grasps the pointlessness of persisting in his wretched English and the two converse in French. Thereafter, and throughout the remainder of the film, everyone speaks French: cowboys and saloon girls, bandits and card sharps, trappers and Native Americans, even a parrot, and with the exception of the bartender (played by Jess Hahn, an American who made his acting career in France) their pronunciation bears no trace of an American English inflection; even some of the written language – '*Recherché!*' ('Wanted!') – begins to appear in French

Figure 6.1 Fernand's struggle with English.

after this transition. Risible, useless, reduced to *charabia*, thirteen minutes into the film English fails as a channel of oral communication and French becomes the universal language of line delivery.

Fernand cow-boy is both a comedy and a western, and the logics of the genres meet and compete in the representation of language. The exchange in the saloon satisfies the expectations of spectators familiar with Raynaud, whose characters often become embroiled in awkward situations riddled with misunderstandings and humorous turns. The linguistic banter with the barman conforms to the comic style of Raynaud's stage routines. It also participates in a broader parody of the western's generic conventions that includes an undercranked bar-room brawl, oversized western hats and chaps, and a pastiche of the chase sequence in John Ford's *Stagecoach*. These gags invoke the western genre's history while also referencing the chase, slapstick and screwball modes of film comedy. The abrupt shift from English to French serves a practical purpose for the performer as well: embodying both the actor Raynaud and the character Mignot, Fernand may thereafter communicate freely with the inhabitants of this distant land with his own voice, and the delivery of this language will be both comprehensible and anticipated for French-speaking spectators familiar with the performer.

Nevertheless, the narrative of *Fernand cow-boy* never provides an explanation for the surprising and universal French speech of the region's inhabitants. It remains unclear throughout the rest of the film whether the language of the town and region is indeed French, or if the speech (Fernand's included) represents English in translation; one is as implausible as the other. However expedient, self-conscious or comical, the ploy comes at the price of endemic ambiguity and illogic in language use. The stability and continuity of what may be called the film's 'linguistic diegesis' is constitutively compromised.

One may ask, at this juncture, to what extent it matters if Fernand's speech represents French or English in an intentionally silly send-up of western settings and situations. However, Fernand's are not the only utterances enmeshed in the ambiguous language scheme. The speech of Native American characters, marked as non-native speakers of the dominant language (be it English or French), complicates the ploy with a demand to register racial and ethnic diversity in speech. The spoken French of *Fernand cow-boy* is not uniform and, as in American westerns, diverse modes of speech convey social stratification in the multilingual, multinational and multi-ethnic West. The servant Orissa and the bandit

Castor Prudent ('Prudent Beaver'), the two Native American roles with dialogue, both utter a French marked as non-native through foregrounded inflections in pronunciation and grammar: for example, at a climactic moment in the film Orissa encounters pronoun trouble when she discloses the identity of the murderer by exclaiming '*Lui a tué Richardson!*' ('Him killed Richardson!'). These distortions do not compromise the comprehensibility of the lines, but function as signifiers of ethnicity.

Sociolinguists have observed how dramatic dialogue in theatre and film indexes regional, ethnic and class difference by spotlighting and overplaying deviations from linguistic norms recognised as standard.[32] The rich variety of non-dramatic ('real') speech patterns is often simplified, or 'flattened', to a small number of salient traits that make these inflections and the social distinctions they signify easily readable.[33] Nonetheless, like all language, speech in film, however contrived, remains embedded in relations of identity, power, geography and status that shape social roles and situations. The resonance the mutations load into the film is not innocent, and the distortions that signify ethnicity also register attitudes and values. In a study of Disney animated features, for example, Rosina Lippi-Green measures how the distinction between 'Mainstream United States English' (marked as 'correct' and 'unaccented') and its 'others' (foreign accents, dialects, 'vernacular' usage, etc.) closely correlates to a character's measure of beauty, goodness and agency in the narrative. She concludes that the pattern not only mirrors prevailing social attitudes but also perpetuates them: 'what children learn from the entertainment industry is to be comfortable with the *same* and wary about the *other*, and that language is a prime and ready diagnostic for this division between what is approachable and what is best left alone'.[34]

The 'flattening' (or 'selectivity') of linguistic identity in a narrow repertoire of exaggerated features colludes with other similarly unnuanced stereotypes about class, gender, ethnicity and regional/national identity. Representations of such mutations in Native American speech have a long history that pre-dates cinema, and American westerns, both on film and on television, are notorious in this arena. Linguist and anthropologist Barbra Meek identifies specific linguistic features of 'Hollywood Injun English' (lack of tense, deliberateness of speech and omitted subject pronouns, to name only a few) that simultaneously confer both ethnicity and subaltern status on a character.[35] In addition to marking the characters' ethnicity, the inarticulate grunts, 'baby talk' and distortions also perpetuate an image of the speakers as primitive, unmodern, incompetent, naive and alien. Even in sympathetic portrayals, the simplified and ungrammatical speech registers the 'celluloid Indian' as 'linguistically and perhaps mentally deficient'.[36] The speech of the Native American characters in *Fernand cow-boy* presents similar distortions, and also conveys similar attitudes. Orissa's pronoun use provides a representative example: coupled with her ingenuous and obsequious demeanour, the distortion marks her ethnicity and a child-like affect that distinguish her from the more cunning and articulate white female characters: the conniving Mae (Dora Doll) and the pert Any (Nadine Tallier).

However, the ambiguity of the language scheme in *Fernand cow-boy* does not spare the caricatured representation of Native American speech. Throughout the film it remains unclear whether Orissa's and Castor Prudent's distortions signify imperfect English in French translation, or imperfect diegetic French. The mutations consequently load resonances into the representation of racial and ethnic identity along plural vectors. As a translation of English speech, the distortions reproduce a number of traits identifiable in Hollywood's 'Injun' speech.[37] However, as French speech they gesture elsewhere, and closely resemble a patois that would have been a familiar linguistic marker of non-white ethnicity for 1950s audiences: namely, the simplified pidgin dialect purportedly used for communication with and between indigenous populations of the French colonies that was commonly known as *petit-nègre* (or in some contexts *petit français* or *français tirailleur*).[38] The likeness is consistent as Orissa and Castor Prudent utter what could serve as textbook illustrations, point by point, of the traits linguist and ethnographer Maurice Delafosse catalogued in his 1904 treatise on the dialect: infinitive instead of conjugation ('*Elle vouloir tuer Orissa*'/'she to want to kill Orissa'); suppression of articles ('*Castor Prudent fils de Renard Subtile*'/'Prudent Beaver son of Subtle Fox'); object pronoun in place of subject ('*Lui a tué Richardson*'/'Him killed Richardson'); and suppression of the preposition 'de' ('*Vous aimer pas tête cheval?*'/'You not like head [of] horse?').[39] In a moment of frustration Fernand follows another of Delafosse's injunctions when he speaks in Orissa's manner to make himself understood: 'we must speak to Blacks by putting ourselves within their reach, that is to say, by speaking *petit-nègre*.'[40] Delafosse explains that this dialect, unlike diverse creoles, was relatively standardised across language groups and that indigenous populations spoke it 'in nearly the same manner in Tonkin and in West Africa'.[41] In *Fernand cow-boy* the colonial pidgin appears to have found a toehold among the native populations of the American West.

Exaggerated representations of this dialect were already generating criticism in 1904, when Delafosse himself lamented the hackneyed and simplified imitations of the mutations he identified. In ensuing years popular media and advertising seized on the linguistic stereotype. The *Y'a bon Banania!* ('There good Banania!') exclaimed by the grinning *tirailleur* in advertisements for the French breakfast food is an emblematic and often reviled example.[42] However, due to its purported reach across linguistic groups, the dialect could be used to represent the speech of characters from diverse ethnicities, becoming effectively a blanket marker of non-white, non-European speech, in cinema and elsewhere. Four years prior to the release of *Fernand cow-boy*, in the opening chapter of *Black Skin, White Masks*, Franz Fanon forcefully indicted its use in film. He singled out the practice of using the dialect to dub the speech of African American characters in American films into French, and likened the persistent and indiscriminate cinematic interpellation of the black man as a speaker of the dialect to 'tying him to his image, snaring him, emprisoning him'.[43] African American speech in the English-language cinema of the time was itself a similarly impoverished 'stereotyped and highly simplified fiction' that 'draws heavily on intertextual references to previous representations of this speech style circulating in popular culture'.[44] The use of the same stereotyped speech pattern both to dub Hollywood's African Americans into French and to represent Native American speech channels these well-worn racially indexed representations onto a confluent course: a shared linguistic 'mask' as bromidic as the brownface make-up and feathered headbands worn by the actors who utter the lines in *Fernand cow-boy*.

The use of this caricatured dialect in *Fernand cow-boy* therefore carves out a distinct experience for a French-speaking public. The film had no theatrical release in the United States, but one might imagine the consequences of dubbing it for the American market. Not only would translation eviscerate the humour, surprise and purpose of the linguistic negotiation in the saloon, but the rendering of the Native American speech in English also demands choices that would alter or flatten the relief of this sociolinguistic 'mask'. The stylised English of Hollywood's 'Indian' may also be impoverished and stereotyped, but in mid-century American films it remains distinct from that of screen African Americans.[45] Either of these representations, if chosen for the English translation, would diminish the plural resonances conflated in Orissa's and Castor Prudent's French speech.

The polyvalent and ambiguous inscription of ethnicity in the language of *Fernand cow-boy* muddies familiar frontier myths and narratives. Understanding Fernand's speech as English in translation would linguistically assimilate him into the melting pot of an anglophone community, attuning the film to the monolingual imperium of Turnerian frontier ideology. However, there is no clearly English-speaking Fernand here, be he the actor Raynaud or the character Mignot. The possibility that Fernand and everyone else on this frontier are speaking French participates in the diversion of the narrative from a course towards the Anglo-Saxon dominance, regeneration through regression, and American administrative and economic control that are confluent with the institution of a common English language. Fernand does not embody the silent, strong, independent masculinity of the western type who survives through natural selection. He is a comically effete middle-class provincial who goes west specifically to claim the inheritance of capital and to assume, rather than to earn, the privileged status it confers. What could be less 'western' than the triumph of a class-bound heir from France who arrives in this arid wilderness muttering of familial roses, intoning his alignment squarely with the eastern 'civilised' side of the garden/desert binary that structures the West in the popular imagination?[46]

Unlike the American myth of expansion into a land whose prior occupants must be eliminated or assimilated and where fear of miscegenation often drives the narrative, *Fernand cow-boy* culminates in a *métissage* that enacts what Ella Shohat and Robert Stam identify as a more typically French colonial 'demographic imperative of territorial domination' that polices, educates, controls and occasionally intermarries with native populations. The result is a community governed by, but distinct from, the *métropole*.[47] When Fernand couples with Orissa at the denouement, the imagined community shakily prefigured will be populated in some measure by multi-ethnic children who bear the name Mignot, have no native English-speaking parent, no apparent Anglo-Saxon lineage and live in a francophone (at least in some measure) outpost in which their French father is a leading property owner. The plot's resolution in *Fernand cow-boy* represents, both in images and through the manipulation of the French language, a French ascension over a distant region and its local populations, cowboys and 'Indians' alike. With its French star, French comic tradition, and nearly universal use of the French language, *Fernand cow-boy* stages a French colonisation of a sliver of both the American West and the western genre.[48]

Figure 6.2 A francophone future?

But how stable is this francophone enclave, and how viable is its future, when the language scheme that anchors it is riddled with illogic, ambiguity and contradiction? If, as Miriam Hansen has asserted, cinema is a 'matrix for the articulation of fantasies, uncertainties, and anxieties'[49] projected through a dynamic encounter between globally circulating forms and local contexts, *Fernand cow-boy* enunciates the western 'within and across geopolitically uneven and unequal formations' to rework the genre as a fantasy of colonial power, and carves out this experience in a distinct manner for French-speaking spectators. However, language, stardom and a national allegory, be it of the American frontier or a French colonial empire, are here an unstable alloy, and *Fernand cow-boy* does not deliver a coherent narrative of French domination and triumph. The same language that vouchsafes Raynaud's familiar image as a performer also sows uncertainty in the narrative through constitutive ambiguity and illogic. Insofar as it remains unclear how, when, and even whether the inhabitants of this imagined land are in fact speaking French, the language scheme unsettles both the Turnerian narrative of Anglo-Saxon ascension and a rival ideation of French domination that would take its place.

Notes

1. Vanessa Schwartz, *It's So French!: Hollywood, Paris, and the Making of Cosmopolitan Film Culture* (Chicago and London: University of Chicago Press, 2007).
2. Ibid., 7.
3. A number of French or Franco-European productions share characteristics of Schwartz's 'Frenchness'. Besides Renoir's *French Cancan*, there is *Casino de Paris* (1957), *Une nuit au Moulin Rouge* (1957) and *Folies-Bergère* (1956). See Thomas Pillard, 'Une "curieuse rencontre": la "francization" du musical hollywoodien', in *Voyez comme on chante: films musicaux et cinéphilies populaires en France (1945–1958)*, ed. Sébastien Layerle and Raphaëlle Moine, *Théorème* 20 (Paris: Presses Sorbonne Nouvelle, 2014), 97–104.
4. Louis Jourdan and Leslie Caron signed contracts with David O. Selznick and MGM, and Maurice Chevalier was a Paramount regular.
5. Bardot performed in English in a small role in *Doctor at Sea* (Ralph Thomas, 1955), and also played herself in an English-speaking cameo appearance in *Dear Brigitte* (Henry Koster, 1965). For *Helen of Troy* (Robert Wise, 1956), her speech was dubbed by an English-speaking voice.
6. See Chapter 1.
7. Even a punctilious refusal of language would constitute a self-conscious zero-degree deployment. Consider, for example, the wordless opening sequence of Michelangelo Antonioni's *L'eclisse* (1962).
8. Nataša Ďurovičová, 'Vector, Flow, Zone: Towards a History of Cinematic Translation', in *World Cinemas, Transnational Perspectives*, ed. Nataša Ďurovičová and Kathleen Newman (London and New York: Routledge, 2010), 94.
9. Benedict Anderson, *Imagined Communities*, 42.
10. See, respectively, Mette Hjort and Duncan Petrie, eds, *The Cinema of Small Nations*, Edinburgh University Press, 2007; David Lunn, 'The Eloquent Language: Hindustani in 1940s Indian Cinema', *BioScope* 6, no. 1 (2015): 1–26; and Ella Shohat and Robert Stam, 'The Cinema After Babel', in *Taboo Memories, Diasporic Voices* (Durham, NC: Duke University Press, 2006), 106–13. Ginette Vincendeau challenges the trend to untether cinema and language from the nation in 'The Frenchness of French Cinema: The Language of National Identity, from the Regional to the Trans-national', in *Studies in French Cinema: UK Perspectives 1985–2010*, ed. Will Higbee and Sarah Leahy (Bristol and Chicago: Intellect, 2011), 337–52.
11. What Mikhail Bakhtin termed polyglossia and heteroglossia. On Bakhtin and cinema, see Robert Stam, *Subversive Pleasures: Bakhtin, Cultural Criticism, and Film* (Johns Hopkins University Press, 1989), and Shohat and Stam, 'The Cinema after Babel'. Terms designating language vary according to translation and discipline. In the present discussion, 'language' will refer to the use of verbal language, spoken or written, unless otherwise indicated. When necessary, the term 'natural language' will designate distinct idioms: Russian, Spanish, etc.
12. See the articles in Stephen Heath and Patricia Mellencamp, eds, *Cinema and Language*, AFI Monograph series vol. 1 (Frederick, MD: University Publications of America, 1983).
13. Michael Cronin examines the practices of dubbing and subtitling in *Translation Goes to the Movies* (London and New York: Routledge, 2008). Multilingual films are taken up in *Polyglot Cinema: Migration and Transcultural Narration in France, Italy,*

Portugal, and Spain, ed. Verena Berger and Miya Komori (Berlin: LIT Verlag: 2010). Mark Betz studies avant-garde or art films that revise conventions for language in *Beyond the Subtitle: Remapping European Art Cinema*, 3rd edition (Minneapolis, University of Minnesota Press, 2009).
14. Through the lens of Lacanian psychoanalysis, the voice may haunt the experience of cinema as a disquieting maternal spectre from a pre-linguistic state. See Mary Ann Doane, 'The Voice in Cinema: The Articulation of Body and Space', *Cinema/Sound, Yale French Studies* 60 (1980): 33–50; and Michel Chion, *The Voice in Cinema* (1984), trans. Claudia Gorbman (New York: Columbia University Press, 1999).
15. A well-known example would be Christian Metz, *Language and Cinema* (1971), trans. Donna Jean Umiker-Sebeok (The Hague: Mouton, 1974). Vincendeau singles out Hamid Naficy's theorisation of an 'accented cinema', where this metaphor for diasporic filmmaking supersedes the consideration of accented speech itself. See Ginette Vincendeau, 'Acteurs européens et cinéma classique hollywoodien – Casablanca, accents et authenticité', in *Le Classicisme hollywoodien*, ed. Jean-Loup Bourget and Jacqueline Nacache (Rennes: Presses universitaires de Rennes, 2009), 189–202. Translation itself arguably receives insufficient attention as a critical function of a global industry. See Abé Mark Nornes, *Cinema Babel: Translating Global Cinema* (Minneapolis: University of Minnesota Press, 2007).
16. 'The reality of language difference, the world-wide babble of mutually incomprehensible tongues and idioms, entails consequences for the cinema which have yet to be explored.' Ella Shohat and Robert Stam, 'The Cinema After Babel: Language, Difference, Power', *Screen* 26, no. 3–4 (August 1985): 35.
17. 'Blind Date with Nitrate', Programme for *The 3rd Nitrate Picture Show*, 2017: 14. There are notable exceptions. See, for example, Amy Lawrence, 'Women's Voices in Third World Cinema', in *Sound Theory Sound Practice*, ed. Rick Altman (New York: Routledge, 1992), 178–90. Available at <https://drive.google.com/file/d/0B0T-TVsrv1oMQcmRacTMyU1VfYzQ/view> (accessed 8 January 2019). On the specific status of the written word in film, see Michel Chion, *Words on Screen* (2013), trans. Claudia Gorbman (New York: Columbia, 2017).
18. Rick Altman, *Sound Theory*, 171.
19. Vincendeau, 'The Frenchness', 342.
20. The term is used both by Stam (*Subversive Pleasures*, 60) and by Kay Richardson, 'Multimodality and the Study of Popular Drama', *Language and Literature* 19, no. 4 (2010): 386. A notable exception is the work of Michel Chion, but even here the focus lies more assiduously on the dynamics of sound, the voice and speech, often independently of the specific language conveyed. Chion's most direct study of language is also his most fragmented: *Le complexe de Cyrano: la langue parlée dans les films français* (Paris: Cahiers du cinéma, 2008).
21. Frederick Jackson Turner, *The Frontier in American History* (New York: Henry Holt and Company, 1921), 23.
22. See, for example, Patricia Nelson Limerick's *Legacy of Conquest: The Unbroken Past of the American West* (New York: Norton, 1987).
23. Richard Slotkin's *Gunfighter Nation: The Myth of the Frontier in Twentieth-Century America* (Norman: University of Oklahoma Press, 1992) offers a thorough parsing of the frontier myth in film and fiction.
24. Jane Tompkins, *West of Everything: The Inner Life of Westerns* (New York and Oxford: Oxford University Press, 1992), 51.

25. Sarah Kozloff, *Overhearing Film Dialogue* (Berkeley: University of California Press, 2000), 150.
26. On ploys used for negotiating native languages in Hollywood, see Jacquelyn Kilpatrick, *Celluloid Indians: Native Americans and Film* (Lincoln and London: University of Nebraska Press, 1999), 130.
27. Gerd Gemünden, 'Between Karl May and Karl Marx: The DEFA Indianerfilme (1965–1983)', *Film History* 10, no. 3 (1988): 400.
28. Austin Fisher examines the domestic politics of Italian westerns in *Radical Frontiers in the Spaghetti Western: Politics, Violence and Popular Italian Cinema* (London and New York: I. B. Tauris and Company, 2011). See also Christopher Frayling, *Spaghetti Westerns: Cowboys and Europeans from Karl May to Sergio Leone* (London and New York: I. B. Tauris and Company, 2006), 217–44.
29. Gemünden, 'Between', 400.
30. Tassilo Schneider, 'Finding a New Heimat in the Wild West: Karl May and the German Western of the 1960s', in *Back in the Saddle Again: New Essays on the Western*, ed. Edward Buscombe and Roberta E. Pearson (London: BFI, 1998), 141–59.
31. See Chelsea Wessels, '"Do I look Mexican?": Translating the Western Beyond National Borders', *Transformations* 24 (2014), online version. Available at <https://www.transformationsjournal.org/wp-content/uploads/2016/12/Wessels_Transformations24.pdf> (accessed 10 July 2022).
32. For example (among other studies), in *banlieue* accents in French films, African American Vernacular English on film, and speech of Native American characters in westerns. See Gaëlle Planchenault, 'Accented French in Films: Performing and Evaluating In-Group Stylisations', *Multilingua: Journal of Cross-Cultural and Interlanguage Communication* 31, no. 2 (May 2012), 253–75; Mary Bucholtz and Quiana Lopez, 'Performing Blackness, Forming Whiteness: Linguistic Minstrelsy in Hollywood Film', *Journal of Sociolinguistics* 15, no. 5 (2011): 680–706; and Barbra Meek, 'And the Injun Goes "How!": Representations of American Indian English in White Public Space', *Language in Society* 35, no. 10 (February 2006): 93–128.
33. The operative tropes include 'selectivity, mis-realisation (intentional or not), overshoot, undershoot'. Allan Bell and Andy Gibson, 'Staging Language: An Introduction to the Sociolinguistics of Performance', *Journal of Sociolinguistics* 15, no. 5 (2011): 568. See also Barbara Johnstone, 'Dialect Enregisterment in Performance', *Journal of Sociolinguistics* 15, no. 5 (2011): 658.
34. Rosina Lippi-Green, *English with an Accent: Language, Ideology, and Discrimination in the United States* (London and New York: Routledge, 1997), 103.
35. Meek differentiates 'Hollywood Injun English' (HIE) from 'real life' American Indian English (AIE). Barbra Meek, 'And the Injun Goes "How!"'.
36. Kilpatrick, *Celluloid*, 38.
37. A similar pattern is observable in the *bande dessinée*. In the *Lucky Luke* series, launched in 1949 and gaining in popularity as *Fernand cow-boy* was made, the 'Flathead' tribe ('les Têtes-Plates') also speaks with stylised distortions that have been characterised as 'un étrange langage anthropologique et asyntaxique' ('a strange anthropological and asyntactic language'). Manuel Meune, 'Quand Lucky Luke et les (Amér)Indiens parlent franco-provençal bressan: traduction et transposition, entre inaudibilité linguistique et visibilité culturelle', *TranscUltruAl* 10 (2018): 56.
38. These terms have no easy translation. *Nègre* is a dated term and in current usage is an injurious expletive, though the strength of its pejorative connotations may be

dependent on context. *Tirailleur* is a military term ('infantry') and here refers to the shared French dialect of colonial fighters originally from different linguistic groups.
39. Maurice Delafosse, *Vocabulaires comparitifs de plus de 60 langues ou dialectes parlés à la Côte d'Ivoire et dans les régions limitrophes* (Paris: Ernest Leroux, 1904). Gabriel Manessy observes that the dialect left virtually no written record of its early usage other than Delafosse's treatise. Gabriel Manessy, *Le Français en Afrique Noire: mythes, stratégies, pratiques* (Paris: L'Harmattan, 1994), 111.
40. 'Il nous faut parler aux Noirs en nous mettant à leur portée, c'est-à-dire de parler petit-nègre.' Delafosse, *Vocabulaires*, 264.
41. 'à peu près de la même façon au Tonkin et en Afrique occidentale.' Delafosse, *Vocabulaires*, 263.
42. The Senegalese poet and statesman Léopold Sédar Senghor defiantly wrote 'I'll tear the *Banania* laughter off all the walls of France ('Je déchirerai les rires banania sur tous les murs de France'). 'Poème luminaire' (1940), *Oeuvre poétique* (Paris: Seuil, 1964), 55–6.
43. Frantz Fanon, *Black Skin, White Masks*, trans. Richard Philcox (New York: Grove Press, 2008), 18.
44. Mary Bucholtz, 'Race and the Re-embodied Voice in Hollywood Film', *Language & Communication* 31 (2011), 259.
45. Meek identifies 'certain phrases and lexical items found only in HIE [Hollywood Injun English]' that distinguish this speech from other distortions. Meek, 'And the Injun', 96.
46. On this imaginary divide, see Henry Nash Smith, *Virgin Land: The American West as Symbol and Myth* (Cambridge, MA and London: Harvard University Press, 1950).
47. Ella Shohat and Robert Stam, *Race in Translation: Culture Wars around the Postcolonial Atlantic* (New York and London: New York University Press, 2012), 59.
48. This reading is advanced by Sorin. See Chapter 1.
49. Hansen, 'Fallen Women', 14.

7

The language of stars on the francophone frontier

The story is legend: when Greta Garbo made her first talking picture it was not certain her Swedish accent would appeal to American audiences. By 1930 a number of prominent European actors had already retired or returned to their home countries, and some Americans, including Garbo's frequent co-star John Gilbert, had seen their careers hobbled by a voice that did not correspond to the persona that had been established and adulated in the silent era. Garbo's husky voice played well. So, too, did her distinct manipulation of the English language. The Swedish accent became an important facet of her star persona: an inflected, world-weary 'I want to be alone' was soon shorthand for the star's identity.

A star's identity, however, extends beyond what may be seen or heard on the screen. Richard Dyer has named the persona that coalesces through films and other media (fan publications, publicity, newspaper columns and reviews, live appearances) the 'star image'.[1] Distinct from both characters in the films and a 'real' person, stardom draws from a range of images, discourses and modes of consumption; indeed, what a star consumes (in product endorsements, for example) may be an important constituent of the persona. Stardom is also historical, and its nature and types vary, ranging from the glamourous divinities of the silent era and the carefully dosed wholesomeness of studio-era Hollywood to later stars like Jane Fonda, whose image Dyer situates at a complex intersection of Hollywood history (through her father Henry and brother Peter), diverse star types (starlet, pin-up) and a polarising media presence as a political activist. However, the term 'image', Dyer concedes, is misleading, for despite its visual reference it also comprises 'a complex configuration of visual, verbal and aural signs'.[2] The term nonetheless remains appropriate for his study, as Dyer focuses primarily on what is seen – images and written texts – and only skims the aural contribution of a film star's distinct voice and manner of speech delivery.

However, as the transition to sound revealed, a star's voice quality, dialect and accent can strengthen or defeat the 'fit' of a star image and a role, something of which Hollywood producers were keenly aware. The case of another Swedish star is instructive. Ingrid Bergman's self-presentation might seem unmannered alongside the extravagant Garbo, but this image, too, was the result of strategic and detailed handling: Bergman's full eyebrows may have registered as 'natural' compared to Garbo's pencilled arcs, for example, but they remained unplucked only after intra-studio deliberations about the image she should project.[3] Producer David O. Selznick was also concerned with the language skills of his new star. He assigned Bergman a language coach with a clear directive: 'this is the woman you are going to live with, eat with, and sleep with; you're going to stay with her day and night, because you are going to get your accent and dialogue from her'.[4] Bergman later described the months of effort to get her English 'right'.[5] If Academy Awards and box-office receipts are the measure, this careful dosage of foreignness, grammatical English and studied 'Middle-Atlantic' pronunciation is unquestionably felicitous. This simultaneously natural and *soigné* inflection, beyond the qualities of the voice itself, suits Bergman's character in, for example, *Casablanca*, a film whose reception suggests a good 'fit' between her image and the role. This signature manipulation of English derives less from the identity of a character in the film, however, than from a strategically managed and shaped star property that Selznick licensed to the Warner Brothers, eager to feature this lucrative box-office draw uttering lines in a trademark delivery that listeners would recognise not only from other films but also from radio shows including *Lux Radio Theater*, *The Jack Benny Program* and *CBS Looks at Hollywood*.[6]

As with genres, a critical focus trained on Hollywood studios leaves the machinery of stardom in other contexts less sharply defined. In a study of 'classic' French cinema from 1930 to 1960, a period roughly contemporary to the sound era in the Hollywood studios, Colin Crisp notes that without a stable of stars under long-term contracts, French producers had little comparable interest in developing and promoting star properties. Publicity campaigns were instead mounted to feature roles in a specific film, not to promote the stars themselves, for 'any increase in the exchange value of a star would benefit other companies' who employ the performer in subsequent productions.[7] Nonetheless, movie magazines and events such as the Cannes festival (inaugurated in 1938) and later the César awards (France's answer to the Oscars) provided platforms for the cultivation of a public image beyond the films themselves. So, too, did the managed relay of a star's persona in journalism, photography, advertisement and other modes of dissemination to which many French stars 'cross over': the radio, the stage, the music hall, and later television. Although the meaning and function of stardom differs in the French context there are, nonetheless, mechanisms for generating and disseminating a 'star image': it may not be as focused or aligned with a studio's interests as its Hollywood contemporaries, but in France 'stars are absolutely central to the film industry'.[8]

The post-war western-themed star vehicles examined in this chapter each feature a leading actor whose voice and speech patterns, key constituents of the star's image, are consistent across films, media coverage and other modes of performance. Fernandel first honed his public persona in the café-concert and music hall, and Mariano's work in cinema is one facet of a longer career as a singer: his films are often adapted from stage operettas, and on the screen he croons the same songs he performed for live audiences. Fernandel and Mariano had successful recording careers, and both could be heard on the radio. In addition to the timbre and quality of the performer's singing and speaking voice, a distinct articulation of the French language also conveys their star persona: Mariano's roles exploit his Spanish heritage and accent in films set in Spain, Mexico and the Caribbean, and Fernandel's star image was forged in films that foreground his Marseillais inflections.

And lest it go without saying, despite the Texas and Arizona settings in the western films, the language marked by these inflections is French.[9] The signature manipulation of the language remains intact, maintaining the integrity of the star image. However, an examination of these contrived language schemes reveals that the possibilities they enable in the service of stardom also come at a cost, and unsettle not only the western diegesis but also the assertion of a French national referent that openly competes with it.

Sérénade au Texas: an 'Americanness' musical?

The premise of *Sérénade au Texas* resembles that of *Fernand cow-boy*, examined in the previous chapter: Jacques (Luis Mariano), a timid provincial shop assistant, learns from his lawyer, Jérôme ([André] Bourvil), that he has inherited a Texas oil field from a distant relative. Ill-informed about the realities of frontier life, both men naively believe their legal documents will hold sway in this distant and lawless land. The disabused and penniless men meet an itinerant theatre troupe led by Silvia (Sonia Ziemann), with whom Jacques becomes enamoured. The middle-class Frenchman, through feats both accidental and heroic, goes on to prevail over the organised criminals who would usurp his claim, though instead of using his new fortune to settle the land Jacques creates a song-and-dance spectacle, the 'Big Bend Follies'.

The similarities between the films extend to the representation of language. Like *Fernand cow-boy*, *Sérénade au Texas* features an established performer of stage and screen whose character converses in the same idiomatic French in the opening sequence set in France as he uses to address the inhabitants of American West throughout the remainder of the film. The absence of any Native American speech eases certain demands on the language scheme, and there is no active negotiation of French and English as in the saloon exchange in *Fernand cow-boy*. The ploy nonetheless institutes a similar ambiguity, and persistent discrepancies disturb the premise that the French line delivery represents either universal French on the Texas frontier or diegetic English in translation. Written language is inconsistent and inconclusive: signs appear mostly in English ('Last Chance Saloon', 'Sheriff', 'Store') but when their meaning is essential for the plot they may be in French ('Feux d'artifice', 'Théâtre'). A language difference between the Frenchmen and the locals is suggested when Jacques and Jérôme communicate by gesture to purchase a horse, but this moment is exceptional and everywhere else they speak as if they shared a common native language with the Texans. A spectator might reasonably assume that conversations between the two Frenchmen represent French speech, while their verbal interaction with the Americans would be in English, yet these exchanges follow each other continuously with no marked transition. Throughout the film it remains unclear if the spoken language represents English that the two Frenchmen have somehow swiftly mastered to perfection, or if Texas has unaccountably become a francophone region.

Sérénade au Texas shares a strong comic impulse with its predecessor, drawing humour from the placement of two well-known French performers playing hapless but ultimately triumphant Frenchmen in a western setting. However, *Sérénade au Texas* is also a musical film and sits in a more variegated generic context. As in post-war Hollywood musicals with western settings – *The Harvey Girls* (George Sidney, 1946), *Seven Brides for Seven Brothers* (Stanley Donen, 1954), *Oklahoma!* (Fred Zinnemann, 1955) – the plot of *Sérénade au Texas* exploits a cultural dissonance between European/Eastern mores and the ethos of the American West to channel the western's conventions into the familiar narrative syntax of the film musical,[10] though with a notable gender reversal: on the one hand the effeminate Jacques and skittish Jérôme, on the other the strong and capable American women who wear trousers and possess superior gun and horse skills.[11] The film includes musical stage productions, deploying another familiar formula (the 'backstage' musical) that sets the preparation for the spectacle, the developing romance, and struggle with the antagonists on a common course that culminates in a celebratory production number. *Sérénade au Texas* elsewhere taps into the B-western singing cowboy tradition of Gene Autry and Tex Ritter when Mariano sheds his formal European clothes to croon by a campfire in a fringed cowboy outfit.[12]

Sérénade au Texas also presents structural affinities with the post-war 'Frenchness' musicals discussed in the previous chapter, most notably *An American in Paris*, through a homologous inversion of the French-American encounter. Mariano's character, like Gene Kelly's, seeks success, or at least his next meal, by practising his art in a foreign land. Both have a less optimistic sidekick (Bourvil, Oscar Levant) with whom they

Figure 7.1 Mariano as a singing cowboy.

share a nationality and a language, and both stage an amorous encounter between French and American characters. Where Kelly shakes up French decorum with boisterous jazz and athletic dancing, Mariano's first show, produced in a barn, brings the middle-brow entertainment of nineteenth-century France to rowdy Texas audiences: the programme includes operetta pieces, a ballet sequence, an overwrought melodrama in the Pixérécourt style and, in a gesture evocative of the 'Frenchness' films, a can-can dance number with a backdrop depicting the Moulin Rouge and Montmartre. The lavish production numbers that close both films set the characters in inversely anachronistic settings. In his dream ballet, Kelly rubs shoulders with *fin-de-siècle* personages against precise citations of paintings by Dufy, Utrillo, Van Gogh and Toulouse-Lautrec. *Sérénade au Texas* opens with Jérôme living in this same *fin-de-siècle* France, with art nouveau decor and specific references to Yvette Guilbert and Aristide Bruant, singers for whom Toulouse-Lautrec created the large-format lithographs that inspired the art direction of, among other films, *Gigi, An American in Paris, Moulin Rouge* and *French Cancan*. In his final number, however, Mariano is transported to a modern stage where, in a white cowboy outfit that could have suited Roy Rogers, he belts out his eponymous serenade against a schematic evocation of Times Square lit with electric light bulbs and neon signs that read 'Chevrolet', 'Woolworth', 'Snack Bar', 'Coca-Cola' and the name of Kelly's Hollywood contemporary and

Figure 7.2 A Parisian in America.

sometime co-star, Frank Sinatra. Where Kelly displaced waltzes with jazz in earlier sequences of *An American in Paris*, in the dream ballet he reconciles American modernity with old-world refinement. Mariano's operatic crooner finds himself among leaping cowboys and leggy cowgirls ('Les Blue-Bell Girls' from the Lido, a rival spectacle to the Moulin Rouge in the 1950s) in a fantasy number that conflates the French music hall, modern Broadway and a stylised Far West; the choreography and music all but quote Agnes DeMille's and Aaron Copland's 1942 *Rodeo*, the pioneering hybrid of classical ballet with vernacular American dances, themes and music that would inspire the choreography for *Oklahoma!*.

Again, the apparent symmetry is deceptive. *An American in Paris* was a commercial and critical success in both France and the United States, a signal work in a major Hollywood genre, and later becomes the emblem of a transnational 'Frenchness'. No inverse 'Americanness' in *Sérénade au Texas* accedes to a transatlantic, transnational film culture. Despite the title song's assertion that it has been circulating around the world *depuis toujours* ('since forever'), *Sérénade au Texas* had no theatrical release in the United States, and Mariano and Bourvil remained virtually unknown to American filmgoers. Moreover, even if the film had reached American cinemas, without prior familiarity with Mariano's star persona the final number, where the ambiguous representation of language colludes with unaccountable spatio-temporal inconsistencies, might easily strike a spectator as nothing short of bizarre. There is no 'dream ballet', backstage narrative, or other alibi to explain this abrupt displacement of the cast from circa-1890 Texas to a contemporary stage. Set against the discordance between written English on the signs and the French song lyrics, this unabashedly modern reprise of a number earlier performed on a horse-drawn wagon for a crowd of rustic Texans gestures towards both diegetic English and diegetic French, and evokes multiple periods and places: frontier-era Texas and modern France, belle-époque music halls and 1950s New York. These plural impulses integrate neither with each other nor into the rest of the film's narrative, creating not a culminating synthesis or a denouement but a detached coda of elements that are inexplicable and, in significant measure, dissonant with the rest of the film. The 'where', 'when' and 'why' of the diegesis are unmoored, and for a spectator unfamiliar with the 'who' in question the sight and sound of Mariano's sudden transport from Texas to a modern stage show, singing operatically in inflected French and surrounded by dancing cowboys and cowgirls in an electrified and colour-saturated evocation of Times Square, offers a logic-defying phantasm of both 'French' and 'western'.

Nonetheless, in another respect the jarring representational strategies of *Sérénade au Texas* sit comfortably in the French context of production and reception. Like the western, the genre of the film musical carries a strong association with studio-era Hollywood. However, unlike French westerns, French musical films were numerous in the 1940s and 1950s and count among the greatest box-office successes of these decades.[13] The most successful of them all were Mariano's singing costumed spectacles set in a sunny Spain, Jamaica or other picturesque locations tinged with a 'soft' exoticism.[14] *Andalousie / Andalusia* (Robert Vernay, 1951) and *Violettes impériales / Imperial Violets* (Richard Pottier, 1952) were the second-highest French box-office draws of their respective years, and in 1956 *Le Chanteur de Mexico / The Singer of Mexico* (Richard Pottier) was fifth. Mariano was one of the most bankable stars of the decade, and his most popular films drew more spectators than, for example, any Bardot picture in its year of release. He was also a highly mediatised figure. Mariano carefully cultivated a consistent star image, 'the fruit of an entirely conscious construction on the part of the singer and his entourage'.[15] Film magazine covers featured his toothy smile, for seven years he wrote a weekly column in *Cinémonde*, and he formed a 'club Luis Mariano' for the adoring fans who swarmed around him when he appeared in public.[16]

Furthermore, the context for Mariano's success, and for his star image, is broader than his work in film. Observing the 'extraordinary closeness of cinema and stage in France', Ginette Vincendeau cautions against the tendency to isolate the film careers of stars who were trained on the French stage and for whom the experience in cinema represents only one element of a long and diverse performing career.[17] Mariano honed his persona, performance style and distinctly accented French (initially a handicap, then a signature) on the stage, where he worked before, throughout, and after the span of his work in film.[18] Many of Mariano's films were filmed versions of his staged shows, including the exceptionally popular *Le Chanteur de Mexico*, which opened at Paris's Théâtre du Châtelet in 1951 and later toured France and its territories in a run of over 900 performances. In addition to his cinema and theatre performances, French spectators would also have known Mariano's voice and speech from recordings (some of them successful enough to go Gold), the radio, appearances on the new medium of television, performances at Paris's Olympia and Lido venues and, for those who lived in the provinces, from tours to their hometowns. In 1958, the year *Sérénade au Texas* was released, Mariano was performing with the Cirque Pinder, which featured him entering the arena on horseback and in costume while singing the theme song from *Le Chanteur de Mexico* in his signature style.[19] A devoted fan might therefore be able to hear Mariano at a live spectacle one evening, on the radio or television the next, and in the cinema on the following.[20] The sound and the sight of Mariano in a semi-exotic costume on a glittering stage, surrounded by dancers while he croons an operetta tune in his inflected French, would have been familiar to a broad cross-section of the French public who had seen similar performances not only in the cycle of musical film vehicles but also in other spectacles that demanded less regard for diegetic stability and narrative continuity.

The representation of language that appears jarring or bewildering in one context of reception may be smoothly continuous with a familiar star image in another. While the quality of *Sérénade au Texas* may be a matter of taste, measuring it against the touchstone of either transnational 'Frenchness' or classical Hollywood – its westerns, its musicals or even its western musicals – obscures the complexity of the exchange and the specificity of the French context, effectively enforcing an 'otherness reduced to sameness' that Roland Barthes decried as an insidious sleight of cultural myths.[21] Delineating a horizon of experience that can mean 'different things to different people and publics, both at home and abroad',[22] Mariano's performance in *Sérénade au Texas*, in its aural and linguistic dimension, demands a differentiated account of the uneven flow of globally circulating generic forms at multiple sites of production and reception.

Nevertheless, the framing of Mariano's star persona in this western vehicle sets the French assertion squarely in a realm of fantasy. The finale's amalgam of star and genre, of English and French, of modern New York and the belle époque, of contemporary Paris and Texas saloons, spectacularly stages a breach of logic that may easily strike a spectator as hallucinatory, or patently absurd. Even for French filmgoers in 1958 it is unclear whether this triumph of the star persona over the western genre meant much to many: *Sérénade au Texas* was a box-office disappointment compared to Mariano's prior successes, and effectively marked the end of his film career.

Dynamite Jack: Talking back

The premise of *Dynamite Jack* is familiar: a French émigré played by a prominent French star travels to the American West. Fleeing France after refusing to take part in a duel, the inept and cowardly Antoine Espérandieu (Fernandel) arrives by stagecoach in Arizona, here represented by the rocky slopes of the Montagne Sainte-Victoire near Aix-en-Provence. After a series of incidents arising from his strong physical resemblance to the murderous bandit Jack (also played by Fernandel, but dubbed with a different voice), the effete Frenchman triumphs more or less in spite of himself over his adversary: at the film's end the townsfolk hail Antoine as the heroic slayer of the villain, though it was the sheriff who discreetly fired the fatal shot. As in *Fernand cow-boy*, Antoine does not unite with a love interest of Anglo-Saxon descent: the rich widow of one of Jack's victims rejects Antoine after learning that he exploited the twin-like resemblance to seduce Jack's lover, the Mexican saloon owner Dolores (Eleonora Vargas). In the film's final sequence Dolores forces Antoine at gunpoint to redeem her honour by marrying her. *Dynamite Jack* again tracks the ascent of a bumbling French hero and property owner, and like *Fernand cow-boy* prefigures a future generation that will neither alloy with the Anglo-Saxon melting pot nor be raised by native English-speaking parents.

Dynamite Jack also displays, again, bald inconsistencies in language use, and the delivery of French lines in a presumably anglophone diegesis generates pervasive ambiguity. It is again uncertain which language is represented (do Antoine's delirious mutterings and asides represent French or English speech?), and the film presents discordance between spoken French and written language ('Barber Shop', 'Ale on Draught', and so on). The Native American characters' studious silence does not exempt them from the uncertainty: do they hear and react to diegetic French or English? In the film's sole sustained utterance of English the townsfolk sing 'For He's a Jolly Good Fellow' before immediately reverting to French to deliver their spoken lines. The friction in the linguistic diegesis intensifies when written English draws verbal reactions: Antoine and the presumably anglophone sheriff converse in French over a grave marker with an English epitaph, and both Antoine and Jack react to 'Wanted' posters bearing their common likeness above an English text. The film also casts American and British actors in a number of supporting roles, placing the marked accents of certain characters (the rich widow, the storekeeper, a sergeant played, again, by Jess Hahn) alongside the native French of others (the sheriff, a henchman, more widows, not to mention both Jack and Antoine); at variance with the characters' presumed nationalities, this distinction has no evident pattern or narrative purpose.

The doppelgänger conceit proves especially pernicious for logic and continuity in the representation of language.[23] Fernandel's Antoine and Jack unaccountably communicate with the ease of men who share a native

Figure 7.3 French speech, English writing.

language when, through the use of split-screen filming and body doubles, they meet, play cards and fight. Once Antoine changes into western gear, he passes for Jack visually and initially imitates Jack's speech, though he has very few lines at this point. However, the developing plot hitches its logic to an obvious distinction between their speech when both characters strategically fall silent to prolong the dissimulation: a mute Antoine controls Jack's henchmen and seduces Dolores by communicating with gestures, while the townspeople fête a studiously speechless Jack, believing him to be Antoine. The trait of speech that would betray their identities remains unclear. If the speech that would reveal Antoine's identity is French, how have the Arizonans been understanding it? If the speech represents non-native English, why do he and Jack communicate effortlessly with native pronunciation when some other characters speak with broad English inflection? Despite the emphasised variation between the two characters' speech (Jack's tone is gruff, while Fernandel's familiar voice conveys Antoine's lines), the premise suffers a further blow when the narrative course bypasses the identifying capacity of language so conspicuously established: threatened with hanging, a silent Antoine inexplicably fails to avail himself of the speech that would immediately exonerate him, while the townspeople disregard speech and rely instead on a corporeal index, a tattoo, to identify Jack.

The far-fetched language scheme of *Dynamite Jack* reinforces, along with other elements, the reputation of French westerns as cheapened parodies of a classic Hollywood genre. Reviewing the film's 2013 DVD

Figure 7.4 Antoine and Jack converse.

release, the critic for the *Nouvel Observateur* did not mince words: 'it's bottom-of-the-barrel cinema, filmed by a lad in need of a brain'.[24] Nevertheless, despite its shortcomings, in 1961 over 2,450,000 French spectators paid to see *Dynamite Jack*. The film's commercial appeal is doubtless due to its leading actor. Fernandel starred in some of the most successful films of the 1950s: only *Gone with the Wind* (Victor Fleming, 1939, French release 1950) and *Cinderella* (Walt Disney, 1950) drew more spectators in France than *Le Petit Monde de Don Camillo / The Little World of Don Camillo* (Julien Duvivier, 1952) in the decade. Fernandel's films, including multiple *Don Camillo* sequels, were prolific and popular. One of the constitutive traits of Fernandel's star image is the distinct sound of his voice. Richard Kuisel credits Fernandel's tremendous popularity among the French public to the re-assuring conjunction of a singular face and his familiar manipulation of the French language:

> To the extent French movie goers had a choice they preferred familiar 'French' films – a cinema program reminiscent of the 1930s and 1940s, with conventional plots and settings, narrated in their language, that featured French stars. In a word, they wanted to see Fernandel.[25]

Unlike Raynaud and Mariano, Fernandel attained a degree of transatlantic recognition. However, despite the international release of select films and a few Hollywood ventures, 'Fernandel's triumphal career remained, as a whole, national'.[26] He ultimately refused the lure of a Hollywood contract, but his characters could find themselves on American soil in films that intentionally evoke studio-era genres: notably, in addition to *Dynamite Jack*, the gangster film *L'Ennemi public no 1/The Most Wanted Man* (Henri Verneuil, 1953), set in modern New York. Regarding the latter, Thomas Pillard suggests that Fernandel's distinct voice, speaking in a genre film set in America, addresses plural publics differently: the gangster genre and the internationally known star maintain global appeal, while Fernandel's distinctive speech shapes an untranslatable and arguably richer experience that, Kuisel argues, French spectators craved. Pillard singles out the opening sequence of *The Most Wanted Man* where Fernandel, dressed as a cowboy against a painted backdrop of western scenery in a department store, plays a salesman hawking modern camping equipment. The incongruity *en abyme* between the French star and foregrounded generic markers announces how the film's nod towards both the western and the gangster film, emblems of a global film industry dominated by Hollywood, may nonetheless continue to address a French-speaking public in a separate modality with a familiar voice delivering lines in French, 'guaranteeing the continuity of French identity in the context of important sociocultural and cinematographic changes'.[27]

And changes there were. By 1959, the 'new wave' of cinema was breaking on both European and American shores, generating a new image of 'Frenchness' on film fuelled by the repudiation of the cinema in which Mariano and Fernandel had thrived. In mainstream media, fresh faces and new performance styles, some imported from America, were also rapidly dating the stage traditions that had shaped the personas of the performers; one need only compare the middle-aged Mariano crooning an operetta tune to the youthful 'yé-yé' rock-n-roll of the early 1960s to grasp the strong correlation, established by Pierre Bourdieu in his sociological study of taste, between a preference for Mariano and the most traditional, conservative values of an older and provincial demographic.[28] Nonetheless, the enduring appeal of familiar faces and voices speaking a familiar language may explain how, sham shop-fronts and cardboard cacti stuck into southern French landscapes notwithstanding, *Sérénade au Texas* and *Dynamite Jack* satisfied a certain section of the French public and maintained a modicum of box-office appeal.

Along with *Fernand cow-boy*, this small cycle of western star vehicles justifies challenges to the prevailing assertion that the French incursion into the western is a symptom of invasive Americanisation, and that Hollywood's hegemonic reach inexorably compels producers elsewhere to rehearse its powerful genres with deficient imitations or clumsy burlesque. The deployment of the French language follows other logics – of stardom, of other genres (comedy and musical), of performance styles rooted in French cabarets and music halls – that compete with that of the western genre.[29] With well-known stars playing French characters who bring their language to the mythic American West, these films do not merely 'speak' the Hollywood idiom imperfectly, nor do they smoothly meld with it in a transnational and transatlantic alloy, be it 'Frenchness' or an inverse 'Americanness'; they 'talk back', in French, leveraging the genre to carve out a distinct experience for a circumscribed public that, for the most part, excludes the American spectator.[30]

However, when these French westerns talk back, they don't always make sense. The stars may be comfortably at home speaking in a manner familiar from other modes of performance and recordings, but the language they utter binds this declension of French cinema to a far-fetched, unstable and at times bewildering ideation of a francophone frontier. The staging of this fantasy also exposes its incoherence. Which organising logic, be it of 'French' or of 'Frenchness', is asserted by the French language when the schemes that allow its expression so flagrantly exhibit their constitutive illogic?

There may, nonetheless, be a respect in which these unstable allegories of linguistic ascension over a distant land constitute a discerning enunciation of a French national referent. It is far from triumphant. The production of these films began in the immediate aftermath of the French army's defeat at Dien Bien Phu and continued through the escalation of the Algerian conflict. For the spectators of these releases, the stability and future of these French-dominated, French-speaking enclaves in the American West were, perhaps, as impossible to imagine as those of the French colonial empire in full crisis.

Notes

1. Richard Dyer, *Stars* (London: BFI, 2008; original publication 1979).
2. Dyer, *Stars*, 34.
3. David Selznick, *Memo from David O. Selznick*, ed. Rudy Behlmer (New York: Modern Library, 2000), 146–7.
4. Selznick, *Memo*, 70.

5. Ingrid Bergman and Alan Burgess, *My Story* (New York: Delacorte, 1980), 73–4. The passage of time has put her mannered diction's craft into relief. 'Staccato t's and accordion-stretched a's lend a musical flavor to Bergman's lilt . . . The grandeur and glamor in her voice, though, is a sham . . . a now-abandoned affectation.' Trey Taylor, 'The Rise and Fall of Katherine Hepburn's Fake Accent', *Atlantic Monthly* online, 8 August 2013. Available at <https://www.theatlantic.com/entertainment/archive/2013/08/the-rise-and-fall-of-katharine-hepburns-fake-accent/278505> (accessed 8 January 2019).
6. 'The voice is an integral part of the star system, and Ingrid Bergman's accent was an important part of her persona.' Amy Lawrence, *Echo and Narcissus: Women's Voices in Classical Hollywood Cinema* (Berkeley: University of California Press, 1991), 125.
7. Colin Crisp, *The Classic French Cinema 1930–1960* (Bloomington: Indiana University Press, 1997), 225.
8. Ginette Vincendeau, *Stars and Stardom in French Cinema* (London and New York: Continuum, 2000), 39.
9. While Mariano occasionally made both French- and Spanish-language versions of his films, *Sérénade au Texas* was filmed only in French.
10. Rick Altman identifies the 'dual focus' syntax in *The American Film Musical* (Bloomington: Indiana University Press, 1987), 16–27.
11. On the sexuality of Mariano's star image, Powrie and Cadalanu observe 'a curious tension between the effeminate and the chaste'. *The French Film Musical* (London: Bloomsbury, 2020), 142.
12. Autry's *Old Corral* (1936) was, coincidentally, released in the United Kingdom as *Texas Serenade*. Sorin also observes similarities between *Sérénade au Texas*, backstage musicals and the singing cowboy tradition.
13. Chion writes that the French musical films, despite their number, are, like the westerns, 'films rarely mentioned in histories of cinema' (my translation). Michel Chion, *La Comédie musicale* (Paris: Cahiers du cinéma, 2002), 61. Recent scholarship sheds new light on this genre. See *Voyez comme on chante! Films musicaux et cinéphilies populaires en France (1945–1958)*, ed. Sébastien Layerle and Raphaëlle Moine, *Théorème* 20 (Paris: Presses Sorbonne Nouvelle, 2014); Phil Powrie, 'The French Musical: Swing and Big Bands in the Cinema of the 1940s and 1950s', *Screen* 54, no. 2 (2013): 152–73; and Powrie and Cadalanu, *The French Film Musical*.
14. On Mariano's 'exoticism within everyone's reach' (my translation), see Phil Powrie, 'Luis Mariano et l'exotisme ordinaire', in Layerle and Moine, *Voyez*, 19–29.
15. Geneviève Sellier, '"Le Chéri des midinettes": Luis Mariano dans le courrier des lecteurs de Cinémonde (1949–1956)', in Layerle and Moine, *Voyez*, 37.
16. Ibid., 37.
17. Ginette Vincendeau, *Stars and Stardom in French Cinema* (London: Continuum, 2000), 7.
18. On Mariano's life and career, see Jacques Rouhaud and Patchi, *Luis Mariano: Une vie* (Bordeaux: Editions Sud Ouest, 2006), and Henry-Jean Servat, *Luis Mariano: Les mélodies du bonheur* (Paris: Hors-Collection, 2013).
19. Servat, *Luis Mariano*, 128.
20. Vincendeau observes how such 'crossover' between the theatre and cinema distinguishes the French film industry from the American, in *Stars and Stardom*, 7.
21. Roland Barthes, 'The myth today', in *Mythologies*, trans. Annette Lavers (New York: Hill and Wang, 1972), 151.
22. Hansen, 'Fallen Women', 12.

23. Fernandel frequently played more than one character in a film, a ploy that multiplied opportunities for the exploitation of the star's image. See Ginette Vincendeau, 'Fernandel: de l'innocent du village à "Monsieur tout le monde"', in *Genres et acteurs du cinema français*, ed. Gwénaëlle Le Gras et Delphine Chedaleux (Rennes: Presses universitaires de Rennes, 2012), 218.
24. François Forestier, 'Dynamite Jack: le western-bouillabaisse de Fernandel', *Le nouvel observateur*, 27, April 2013. Available at <http://tempsreel.nouvelobs.com/cinema/20130427.CIN4029/dynamite-jack-le-western-bouillabaisse-de-fernandel.html> (accessed 21 June 2016; my translation). A survey of other critiques following the release suggests that the reviewer voices a prevailing opinion.
25. Richard Kuisel, 'The Fernandel Factor: The Rivalry Between French and American Cinema in the 1950s', *Yale French Studies* 98 (2000): 127.
26. 'La carrière triomphale de Fernandel resta dans l'ensemble nationale'. Ginette Vincendeau, 'Fernandel', 207.
27. Pillard, 'Une voix de star française', 73.
28. Bourdieu contrasts Mariano with Johnny Hallyday (the 'French Elvis') in *Distinction: A Social Critique of the Judgment of Taste*, trans. Richard Nice (Cambridge, MA: Harvard University Press, 1984), 367.
29. This was Sorin's conclusion. See Chapter 1.
30. The most radical thrust of the Algerian comedian Fellag's redubbing of *Dynamite Jack* as *Dynamite Moh* (1996), an allegory of 1990s Algerian politics, may therefore be the sound of Fernandel speaking in Algerian. On this reinterpretation of the film, see Peter Bloom, 'Beyond the Western Frontier: Reappropriation of the "Good Badman" in France, the French Colonies and Contemporary Algeria', in *Westerns: Films Through History*, ed. Janet Walker (New York: Routledge, 2001), 197–216.

8

Cowboy and alien: the Bardot western

In the nineteenth-century Arizona desert, a western hero fights alongside his sidekick, an expert rider who wields weapons with deadly skill. The westerner's rugged and stoic presentation contrasts with his companion's broken English, painted face and wild unkempt hair. This extravagant character is not one of the film's many Apaches, but an alien presence that more powerfully threatens if not the western hero, then the generic frame of westernness that would contain him: she is Brigitte Bardot, playing opposite Sean Connery, in *Shalako* (Edward Dmytryk 1968).

Bardot made westerns – or at least films that have been called westerns. In addition to *Shalako* she starred with Jeanne Moreau in *Viva Maria!* (Louis Malle, 1965) and with Claudia Cardinale in *Les Pétroleuses / The Legend of Frenchie King* (Christian-Jaque, 1971). High-wattage celebrity and eminent directors notwithstanding, these films garner scant attention in most accounts of Bardot's film career, where commentary more assiduously dwells on the frank and youthful sexuality exhibited in *Et Dieu... créa la femme / And God Created Woman* (Roger Vadim, 1956), and her consecration as a *nouvelle vague* icon in Jean-Luc Godard's *Le Mépris / Contempt* (1963). Vadim's and Godard's films are hailed as signal events in Bardot's stardom and, each in its way, in the history of French cinema. When not overlooked entirely, the three western films are marginalised as curiosities of a spent film career slouching towards an undistinguished end.[1]

The relation between genres and stardom is complex. Richard Dyer has identified two axes in this dynamic. On the one hand genres and star images are complicit: genre serves as a mediator of 'fit' between a film role and a star's established image, and may be a signal constituent of it

(John Wayne and the western, for example, or Carole Lombard and the screwball comedy). However, they are also homologous: genres, like star images, are continuous with a relay of iconography, visual style, symbolic structures and discourse that exceed what appears on the screen.[2] This structural similarity snares the star vehicle in the same circular conundrum that has often vexed genre criticism: namely that the group of films that define measures of 'good fit' between a star and a genre will a priori exclude those that present ill-fitting characteristics.[3] When is a western not a western? When is Bardot not Bardot? These riddles share an answer in the Bardot westerns, which stray from the familiar relays that shape ideas of both the star and the genre. A reconsideration of these films yields a more differentiated understanding of Bardot's star image, and more broadly, when a singularly visible emblem of French cinema is cast in a genre closely associated with America and Hollywood, of the cinematic enunciation of the western.

A blazing star in the western sky

The convergence of Bardot and the western strikes a number of dissonant notes. In 1965 film critic Pauline Kael drew a distinction between Hollywood formulas and the cinema Bardot represented:

> By the late fifties movies had reached an all-time low: Educated people who still attended American movies did so furtively. The country that had pioneered the only great modern new art had mechanized and commercialized the art – and the interest – out of it; American movies had become a bad joke. And art or foreign movies had come to mean Brigitte Bardot in and out of towel and sheet and Italian Amazons in and out of slips and beds.[4]

Kael invokes Bardot as an emblematic figure in the well-rehearsed polarity between European cinema and the standardised industrial product coming out of Hollywood. The 'most photographed woman in the world' lent an alluring face to 'art and foreign' cinema. *And God Created Woman* rallied the future *nouvelle vague* auteurs and marked a breakthrough for the success of European film in the United States, and a few years later *Contempt* elevated her to the status of New Wave 'muse'.[5] In both films, Bardot's character notoriously cavorts in and out of towels and sheets.

However, Kael's complaint cuts on a different bias when it suggests that art cinema, too, becomes degraded when its distinction resides in sexual content impermissible under the American Production Code. 'Foreign' films, like their American contemporaries, seem also to suffer from an art deficiency in their bid for prurient appeal. It is unclear which films Kael is invoking, and Bardot appeared nude in both 'art' films and more mainstream productions. Indeed, an inclusive survey of Bardot's filmography reveals a preponderance of pictures that, nudity aside, are conventional, commercial and mainstream, and could easily be called genre films: successive cycles of 'sex kitten' comedies, 'dumb blonde' farces redolent of the films of Judy Holliday and Marilyn Monroe, and crime melodramas.[6] Bardot also played in peplum films, historical costume dramas and, later in her career, in westerns. Moreover, the directors and screenwriters of these films include Henri-Georges Clouzot, Christian-Jaque, Claude Autant-Lara, Jean Aurenche, Pierre Bost and Michel Audiard, figures whom François Truffaut and others decried as standard bearers of the cinema against which auteurist originality is defined: the French 'tradition of quality' and its stultifying conventions. Among French spectators, Bardot's strongest box-office draw in its year of release was not signed Vadim, Godard or Malle, but Clouzot for the *noir* courtroom drama *La Vérité / The Truth* (1960), followed closely by the light comedy *Babette s'en va-t-en guerre / Babette Goes to War* (1959) directed by Christian-Jaque with dialogue by Audiard.

Bardot's appeal in the United States also complicates characterisations of a pitched battle between Hollywood commercialism and European art cinema. The success of *And God Created Woman*, for example, is due in significant measure to an intentional alignment of French producers, the French Film Office, and the *Centre National Cinématographique* with American financiers, exhibitors and audience preferences. Bardot's allure on both sides of the Atlantic reveals how 'mutual dependence rather than antagonism' between film industries generated a cosmopolitan cinema that supersedes the Hollywood/European binary.[7] Nevertheless, as noted in the previous chapters, a symbiosis between national film industries does not as aptly characterise other strains of post-war films that knew success in France but remained virtually unknown to American spectators. The hyper-exposed Bardot was far from invisible, but the distinction remains consequential for her singular career in an important respect: her films include some of the most well-known 'art and foreign' films, but the others also represent the visible tip of a greater mass of popular European cinema whose recovery is an ongoing project in the study of film. Accounts of Bardot's stardom tend to overlook her westerns, and accounts of the western, even in its international and transnational declensions, tend to overlook Bardot and her compatriots: hence a dissonance when the exceptionally visible Bardot plays in a western film.

The conjunction of Bardot and the western strikes another unexpected note when the outsized star image is not only French but also female. The representation of gender is an important parameter of film genre, and the western is no exception.[8] Female characters in westerns are more diverse and complex than stereotypical saloon girl/schoolmarm and blonde/brunette caricatures allow.[9] Nonetheless, insofar as the mythic cinematic West serves as a proving ground where masculinity is formed and tested, when the focus is trained on male characters and their fixation on each other 'the power and presence of women is proportionally reduced'.[10] A strong leading female protagonist may, on her own, constitute a revisionist gesture, and when this role is played by a high-profile celebrity the star image may outstrip even the greater narrative agency and interest the character commands. Marlene Dietrich arguably 'overwhelms the narrative' of *Destry Rides Again* (George Marshall, 1939) and *Rancho Notorious* (Fritz Lang, 1952), despite efforts to mute her lavish persona.[11] Joan Crawford brings signature toughness to *Johnny Guitar* (Nicholas Ray, 1954), but the western situations and settings also warp under the heft of her star presence: 'The casting links the three terms western, Woman, and Star to another that has marked the picture ever since its release: Weird.'[12] The same might be said of Barbara Stanwyck's whip-wielding ranch owner in Samuel Fuller's *Forty Guns* (1957). If seasoned stars who made their careers largely within Hollywood studios are already excessive in the genre, Bardot's incandescent star image, the face of a 'Frenchness' forged outside Hollywood and in great measure off the screen by the unremitting publicity she attracted, has even stronger potential for overrunning the western's frame. Bardot's appearance in a western consequently poses a distinct challenge to filmmakers, who must devise a strategy for containing, harnessing or surrendering to the imposing star persona she loads into a film.

The task of managing the Bardot star image is further complicated when the performer who appears in these pictures has become, to a degree, discrepant with it. The starlet who initially inspired *Bardomania* provocatively joined a youthful and tomboyish *gamine* to a frank, unapologetic expression of sexual desire. Simone de Beauvoir observed the convergence of lithe androgyny and rapacious sexuality through which Bardot is 'as much the hunter as the prey'.[13] The *jeune fille* with a predatory libido flouted both societal values and the manufactured glamour of an older generation of actors who were often her co-stars. Bardot plays her blend of youth, sexuality and 'naturalness' (in speech, clothing and gesture) against older men, both sexual partners and father figures, and also alongside more mature women who are outraged by her insolence.[14] However, by 1959 her image had already begun to transform to a more adult figure: by the time Bardot made her first western the bikini-clad nymphet who frolicked for photographers on the beach at Cannes had become a thirty-something twice-divorced mother, and at the release of *Les Pétroleuses* she was nearing forty. Times, too, were changing, and the teenage Bardot's scandalous impertinence had become comparatively tame in the context of a more permissive cinema and the new social and political climate of the late 1960s.

In sum, there is something inferentially un-Bardot, un-western and by some accounts un-French about the Bardot westerns: hence a plausible explanation for their relative invisibility in discussions of both the western genre and the Bardot star image. For the Bardot western to find footing in these discursive arenas a looser and more variegated characterisation of the constitutive fields – of 'Bardot', 'western' and more broadly of French cinema – is warranted. This differentiation begins with the stark difference in the treatments of the star's image among the three films themselves.

And Malle created . . . a 'man's role'

The opening sequences of Louis Malle's *Viva Maria!* follow a young revolutionary named Maria (Bardot) from Ireland to Central America, circa 1910, where she joins a travelling circus and befriends a dancehall singer also named Maria (Jeanne Moreau). The two inadvertently invent the striptease after a serendipitous wardrobe malfunction during their routine, precipitating Bardot-Maria's sexual awakening. After the martyrdom of a young revolutionary leader (George Hamilton), the two Marias lead a peasant revolt against the military dictator and his Catholic clergy henchmen, prevailing through Bardot-Maria's anarchic dare-devilry and Moreau-Maria's inspirational incitement.

Malle had already plumbed Bardot's stardom in the quasi-biographical *A Very Private Affair* (*Vie privée*, 1962), and he again draws deeply on her established image in *Viva Maria!*. In the opening sequences Bardot reprises her *gamine* persona, dressed as an adolescent boy. Throughout, in contrast to Moreau's more refined gestures, Bardot runs atop moving train cars, swings from vines, throws bombs, discharges firearms (including a machine gun) and performs on stage dressed as a man; she observed 'I'm practically playing a man's role'.[15] However, within a few minutes of screen time this naive tomboy, who bemoans 'I don't know what love is',[16] is stumbling home from an orgy with three exhausted men, exhibiting an unmistakably adult body in a torn dress as she flaunts a hypertrophied sexual appetite; she will thereafter keep a growing list of lovers at her bedside. Pierre Cardin's tailored costumes further contrast with the oversized boy's clothes. Whether engaged in rough-and-tumble escapades or sexual exploits, Bardot resolutely remains the hunter, pursuing men both to kill them in the name of the revolution and to satisfy her desire. Where in *A Very Private Affair* Malle blended the star image with a screen presence in a tragic mode, here he buoyantly celebrates the constitutive components of Bardot's star persona: in addition to the uncouth adolescent with adult appetites observed by de Beauvoir, we also find elements of the 'blonde' persona noted by Vincendeau in Bardot's unschooled heroine,[17] who sports her signature hair and make-up and, as in some of her earlier films, both sings and dances.

In contrast to the familiarity of the Bardot star image, the national and genre affiliations of *Viva Maria!* are less sharply defined. The film is a Franco-Italian co-production financed in part by its American distributor,

Figure 8.1 Bardot in *Viva Maria!*: 'a man's role'.

and its international cast speak in diverse languages. The participation of two French stars, a French director, and French producers, along with a preponderant use of the French language and an initial release in France, nonetheless permit a qualified attribution of the film as 'French'. The film's genre profile is more fluid. Malle characterised *Viva Maria!* as 'a pastiche of an adventure film, a sort of big-budget tropical *Zazie dans le métro*'.[18] He acknowledges that the south-of-the-border western *Vera Cruz* (Robert Aldrich, 1954) sparked the idea of pairing Bardot and Moreau in place of Burt Lancaster and Gary Cooper, but he also claims to have drawn inspiration from adventure films, illustrated children's books, and comics showing 'intrepid characters lost in tropical forests'.[19] On the screen, the connection to the western remains similarly loose. While the film features familiar signifiers of the cinematic West (saloons, guns, horses), other semantic markers (phonographs, automobiles, palaces, jungles) establish a circa-1910 colonial setting distanced from the frontier-era American West in both time and place. *Viva Maria!* also exhibits scant preoccupation with the American nation-building narrative, garden-desert metaphors or the distinct gendered fantasies identified as constitutive structures of the western genre. Puzzled critics associated the film with personages as diverse as Jane Russell and Sergei Eisenstein, Mack Sennett and Richard Strauss, or Tintin and Shakespeare. They also struggled to characterise its genre affiliation. Henri Chapier's review is typical: 'Opera buffa, western parody, musical comedy, communist pamphlet, picture book, a serial in colour – animated by comic-strip heroines – pleasure cinema *à la* Max Ophuls, here are many labels for a film that refuses them all.'[20] Others dubbed it a burlesque, a road film, an action picture, a farce and an epic. Consequently, despite some common ground with certain American Viet Nam-era westerns (guerilla war tactics, Marxist sympathies), the film's connection to the genre is too ludic and slack to enact the systematic revisionist thrust of *Soldier Blue* (Ralph Nelson, 1970) or *Ulzana's Raid* (Robert Aldrich, 1972), or to support the elegiac weight that modern technologies (automobile, machine gun) and a Central American setting will carry a few years later in Sam Peckinpah's *The Wild Bunch* (1969).

In 1965, this quirky and (by Malle's own concession) uneven film enjoyed broad appeal across diverse constituencies. When box-office receipts are adjusted as a percentage of total yearly film attendance in France, *Viva Maria!* outperformed even *And God Created Woman* in its year of release and counts among Bardot's most popular films; it would

Figure 8.2 Moreau and Bardot: the hunters, not the prey.

also be Malle's second greatest commercial success after *Au revoir les enfants* (1987).[21] Daniel Cohn-Bendit, the leader of the 1968 student protest movements in Paris, named it his 'cinematic ideal',[22] and in Germany the founders of the *Kommune I* first formed the *Viva Maria Gruppe*, embracing a piece of popular culture that illustrated how a fun, sexy and anarchic anti-authoritarianism and an intellectual Marxism, personified by Bardot and Moreau, need not be mutually exclusive.[23] In the United States, the film sparked a censorship lawsuit that reached the Supreme Court, again making Bardot the face of a permissive foreign cinema.[24] The film's success, influence and rich discursive wake do not evince the decline of its featured star. Critics commented on a familiar and radiant Bardot, 'stunning with youth and ease, as seductive playing a young boy as being the blaring star',[25] who, more than Moreau, is at home in this strain of ebullient comedy: '*Viva Maria!* gives Brigitte Bardot one of the best roles of her career and Jeanne Moreau one of her worst.'[26] The appeal, however, may not be ascribed to the integration of the Bardot star image with the western genre. If the meeting of these two spheres in *Viva Maria!* is sympathetic, the Bardot star image shines brightly alongside a cinematic westernness that remains, in good measure, beside the point.

A bad fit

Three years later, Bardot's second western effectively inverts this imbalance between the star and the genre. *Shalako* opened on screens with a swell of symphonic music composed on American folk tonalities, a panoramic mountain landscape, a blue sky and a scrolling text: 'To the plains and the mountains of the American West came not only the pioneer, but the European big game hunter as well.' After listing historical figures who made this voyage, duly noting those guided by Buffalo Bill, the text continues: 'There were hundreds of others. Some came only to hunt and to travel, others stayed to ranch – one or two became outlaws.

Figure 8.3 *Shane*, the 'guiding light'.

Figure 8.4 The retro-Hollywood bid.

They and their descendants helped the peoples of North America to build the adventurous West.' The text is signed not by an historian, but by 'Louis L'Amour, Hollywood, California'. The image of the scrolling text then cuts to a shot of Sean Connery, clad in light-coloured buckskins, who mounts his horse and rides through a mountainous terrain. The metre picks up, a succession of ten names announces a star-studded film to come, and when the title appears a virile chorus sings about the man, his exploits and his pursuit of a woman. The song ends as the rider crosses a ridge behind the name of veteran Hollywood director Edward Dmytryk, glowing in saturated Technicolor red.

If the music, graphics and atmosphere of the opening strike a viewer as familiar, it is no coincidence. The credits evoke Hollywood westerns of the previous decades and specifically present similarities with George Stevens's 1953 *Shane*, a picture that producer Euan Lloyd called his 'guiding light' in conceiving *Shalako*.[27] Lloyd intentionally and unapologetically embraced the stories, style and personnel of the studio-era western. He claims it was through Alan Ladd (who played the title role in *Shane*) that he secured the rights to the story from L'Amour, whose western fiction had already inspired other film and television productions. For the title role Lloyd courted Henry Fonda, but when financial backers baulked at the actor's age he seized the opportunity to sign Sean Connery in his first post-Bond role.[28] Dmytryk, whose previous films include the westerns *Broken Lance* (1954) and *Warlock* (1959), was asked to direct, and rounding out the Hollywood western eminence the Apache chief's son was played by Woody Strode, who earlier in the decade had appeared in John Ford's *Sergeant Rutledge* (1960) and *The Man Who Shot Liberty Valance* (1962).

While instances of graphic violence, sexual suggestion and stylistic flourishes distinguish *Shalako* from studio-era production, the film's characters, situations, settings and style hew to a retro-Hollywood impulse. The hero is the tried-and-true 'Leatherstocking' intermediary between civilisation and the wilderness, a chase sequence pays shot-for-shot homage to Ford's 1939 *Stagecoach* (though here no cavalry arrives to save the day), and when the Apache chief proclaims 'there has been enough bloodshed', effectively ending the narrative, any revisionist note to his abrupt clemency provides scant counterweight to nearly two hours of vicious Apaches torturing, raping, murdering and, in a sympathy-quashing gesture that dates to D. W. Griffith, killing dogs. Further aligning with Hollywood's conventions, opening lyrics notwithstanding, the hero's struggle against male adversaries fuels the narrative more than his pursuit of Bardot's love. Only in the final minutes, with social hierarchies levelled, the ills of civilisation washed away, in a mountain hideaway evocative of the Edenic conclusion to Zane Grey's *Riders of the Purple Sage*, may Bardot and Connery finally (but off camera) get to work creating the survival-of-the-fittest alloy of European 'stock' that regenerates the nation in the Turnerian frontier narrative.

Lloyd's bid was a critical and commercial failure. In the preceding years Italian co-productions had renewed interest in the western by distorting and often vacating the conventions of Hollywood production. The spaghetti cycle – ironic, violent, stylish, stripped of optimistic frontier ideology – was at is zenith in 1968, and the American industry was pivoting out of the studio-era towards a 'New Hollywood' whose westerns better resonated with a new political and social climate. Alongside Sergio Leone's films and *The Great Silence* (*Il grande silenzio*, Sergio Corbucci, 1968), *Shalako* struck critics as 'unoriginal', 'routine', 'heavy', 'standard' and 'conventional', characterisations soon confirmed with the release of a spate of elegiac and revisionist westerns that include *The Wild Bunch* (Sam Peckinpah, 1969) and *Little Big Man* (Arthur Penn, 1970): 'The man called Shalako turns out to be just the kind of old-fashioned, virtuous westerner Eastwood (and the Vietnam War) had just consigned to the dustbin of cultural history.'[29] Ironically, the retro-Hollywood impulse of *Shalako* also strains against the fact that it is an exceptionally cosmopolitan film with a multinational cast and crew, an independent British producer, the same arid Spanish shooting locations as many of its spaghetti contemporaries, and an unprecedented financing arrangement that covered production costs from the advance sale of distribution rights in over thirty different countries. Bemused critics observed two highly exposed sex symbols of modern European cinema labouring under the Spanish sun in this earnest but ersatz Hollywood-style film. Connery's low-key performance garnered mixed recognition; Bardot's drew bewildered ridicule.

In *Viva Maria!* Malle exploited a powerful star persona he understood with nuance. The opening credits of *Shalako* announce a contrary strategy on the part of Dmytryk and Lloyd: to contain Bardot's screen presence in a retro-western frame with little concession to her established image. The scrolling text of the opening pre-emptively locks the star into a matriarchal role in the narrative of American national regeneration. The song's lyrics subordinate her character's narrative and sexual agency to that of the hero – the woman is not the hunter but the follower, the object, the prize. The song, the film's title, and the montage of Connery's ride further establish that the narrative of *Shalako* will be the story of his character's quest. The opening bears the imprimatur 'Hollywood, California', a place Bardot had never worked and in contrast to which her fame as a censurable sex-bomb, an art house feature and a New Wave muse drew energy. The credit sequence announces that *Shalako* will be a conventional western that happens to co-star Brigitte Bardot, not a vehicle for her familiar star image.

Nobody puts B. B. in a corner. From her first appearance, Bardot disrupts the retro-western diegesis that strains to contain her. Following the credits, the film opens with a group of men baiting a mountain lion before Bardot's character, the Countess Irina, shoots it for sport. In 1968 Bardot was already a well-known animal lover and often posed with dogs, cats, birds and other animals on the sets of her films; for later spectators the sight of the internationally known animal rights activist gleefully killing a mountain lion is nothing short of stupifying. The styling is also dissonant with her image. Bardot's heavily made-up eyes peer out from under a carapace of a costume – heavy black coat and skirt, high-necked blouse tied with a bow, hair pulled up tight under a top hat – that could not be further from the 'natural' look of the trendsetter who a few months earlier was photographed dining at Maxim's tousled and barefoot. If eventually the hair comes down and the coat comes off, the blouse remains modestly buttoned until the final minutes of the film (a short dressing sequence excepted). The prim costuming is consistent with the countess's traditional views on love and sex. When Connery's Shalako steals a kiss, Bardot's character talks of marriage and rejects his advances: 'It's impossible . . . no.' The casting of Honor Blackman as the sexually forward Lady Julia further pits Bardot against the traits of her own celebrity image. Blackman, who had recently played Pussy Galore in the James Bond film *Goldfinger* (Guy Hamilton, 1964), here acts as the calculating predator, flirting aggressively, abandoning her husband and bedding down with the hired guide. Bardot's countess sighs 'I wish I could be more like Julia, she takes what she wants', a chaste lament uttered by a star notorious for taking exactly what she wants both on screen and off: at the time she was carrying on an extramarital affair with singer Serge Gainsbourg, and the same sighing voice would soon be recording the breathy orgasm for his 'Je t'aime, moi non plus'.

It is little surprise, therefore, that Bardot's appearance in *Shalako* struck critics as a discrepant graft onto a tired western frame. Kael wonders why 'the girl who set the style for modern girls to look like amoral teen-age whores is cast as an aristocrat with a "code" and left stranded on the screen'.[30] A French critic writes that 'she seems as misplaced in this mess as a piece of porcelain in an elephant shop'.[31] In *Le Monde*, Jean de Baroncelli flatly declares a bad fit: 'She had the completely wrong script'.[32]

Bardot is nonetheless a performer hired to play a fictive character, to act, and one might (hypothetically) find spectators unfamiliar with the star image that clashes with the role. However, Bardot jolts *Shalako* not only through dissonance with her established image off screen or from other films; she also rattles it from within the diegesis itself. Specifically, the scenario about which she is 'wrong' is written in a language she spoke poorly, and she delivers her lines in a halting, strongly accented and at times barely comprehensible English. Three years earlier, when she played herself in *Dear Brigitte*, the inflected English speech amplified her thrall over the Americans who had travelled to France on a pilgrimage to her star image: natural, sexual, modern and French. She did not disappoint, receiving the Americans, again barefoot and tousled, in a simple dress as she coddled her beloved animals and flirted with her guests (played by James Stewart and Billy Mummy) in heavily accented English. In *Shalako* this same voice again asserts a foreign presence in a Hollywood-style film, but even if the accent could be considered a character attribute of the countess (whose nationality is not specified), Bardot's laboured speech is jarring and interferes with the comprehensibility of her lines. Anglophone critics note the 'impossible lines for Miss Bardot to speak in her still limited English'[33] and quip that 'Miss Bardot clearly has a lovely time speaking inflected American English'.[34]

Bardot's infelicitous encounter with the English language was not lost on French critics, either. Henri Chapier wonders: 'Are we to believe that her first words in English unleash laughter on purpose?'[35] The robotic blurts of tortured English phonemes lend credence to Bardot's claim that she learned the lines 'like a parrot', never read the full script, and understood nothing about her role. During coachings, she writes, 'I would listen while thinking about other things; I'd say "yes, yes," while smoking a cigarette.'[36] Whatever the cause, the spectacle of Bardot struggling to deliver intelligible lines compromises the logic of character, of narrative and of language use in this outdated western frame. The fit is doubly bad, as the

Figure 8.5 Having a 'lovely time' speaking English.

deliberate and forced English speech further clashes with the spontaneity and naturalness that are constitutive of her star image, on screen and off.

'Oh, what a man . . .'

The Legend of Frenchie King, Bardot's third western and one of the last films she would make, follows the story of Frenchie King (Bardot), a notorious bandit who, with her gang of female-to-male cross-dressed train robbers, gives up a life of crime and men's clothing to settle down on a Texas ranch as 'Dr Miller', the name on a deed acquired during a heist. The women encounter a hostile welcome from their neighbours, four half-Corsican brothers and their domineering sister Maria (Claudia Cardinale), who know there is oil on the property and wish to drive away the newcomers. The animosity culminates in a fistfight showdown between Bardot's and Cardinale's characters before the return of the real Dr Miller leads to their reconciliation, a quadruple marriage of Maria's brothers to Frenchie's sidekicks, and the reconstitution of an expanded King gang, now led by both Bardot and Cardinale.

Like *Viva Maria!*, *The Legend of Frenchie King* features a pair of high-profile European stars engaged in action sequences, cross dressing, musical numbers, firearm displays and slapstick gags. However, in its evocation of the western genre *The Legend of Frenchie King* is not a simple *Viva Maria!* knock-off. Unlike the earlier film, *The Legend of Frenchie King* is set squarely in the frontier-era American West and draws richly on settings and situations familiar from other western films. During the opening

Figure 8.6 Bardot as Frenchie King.

heist, the shot of a figure running atop the train faithfully quotes the film often called the 'first western', Edwin S. Porter's 1903 *The Great Train Robbery*, as do the subsequent murder of the engineer, the robbery, and figures dressed in black making their getaway. Threaded throughout are nods to a more recent predecessor, *Cat Ballou* (Elliott Silverstein, 1965), the send-up of the cinematic West whose title character, played by Jane Fonda, also leads a youthful gang on train robberies and other exploits. Beyond shared situations, parodic tone, and imbricated star images (Fonda had married Vadim and played the Bardot-inspired title character of his 1968 *Barbarella*), the connection between the films is sealed when, mid-heist, the camera cuts to a banjo player (uncredited) perched on the train's tender singing the 'Ballad of Frenchie King', much as Nat King Cole appeared alongside Fonda to sing the 'Ballad of Cat Ballou'. Finally, the Franco-Italian co-production, Spanish shooting location and participation of Cardinale, who had starred in Sergio Leone's *Once Upon a Time in the West* (1968), lend the film affinities with its spaghetti contemporaries. As an enunciation of the western genre *The Legend of Frenchie King* is firing on multiple cylinders.

However, at the same time, *The Legend of Frenchie King* also sits in the tradition of popular French cinema. Director Christian-Jaque had been working in film since the silent era, and played a crucial role in steering the French film industry through the Nazi occupation. Over the course of his career he directed an impressive roster of French stars: Fernandel, Martine Carole, Jean Marais, Gérard Philipe, Alain Delon and, among others, Bardot. Through numerous box-office successes – Fernandel's early breakthroughs, historical costume dramas, literary adaptations – Christian-Jaque earned a reputation as a bankable technician who could adapt to diverse genres. This competency, however, later became perceived as a shortcoming. Unlike the revered Howard Hawks, who adeptly left his mark on films across genres, for French critics Christian-Jaque's 'polymorphous filmography' lacked a distinct authorial stamp: his conventional style incited Michel Dorsday to lament that 'cinema is dead' in an article that has since been called the 'declaration of war' on the 'tradition of quality'.[37] A younger generation would scorn Christian-Jaque's films as stale and artless, and in the wake of the New Wave the veteran director fell out of favour among critics, scholars and the public.[38] Neither an auteur with transnational appeal like Malle, nor an A-list Hollywood director like Dmytryk, Christian-Jaque might serve as an emblematic figure of the cinema that falls through the cracks when criticism aligns art films with Europe and commercial or genre films with Hollywood production. Despite his status as a 'pillar of French cinema', by the time Christian-Jaque directed *The Legend of Frenchie King* 'no one was interested in the filmmaker, histories of cinema neglected him entirely, [and] the specialised press and cinephiles were purely and simply unaware of him'.[39]

The film's reception did little to rekindle interest in its director's legacy. A sympathetic critic could muster backhanded praise by calling the director 'a skilled tradesman who knows the effectiveness of his craft and seeks only to win over, without guilty indulgence, a broad public'.[40] Others freely unleashed contempt for the apparent lack of authorial intelligence. Henri Chapier panned 'a film made in the manner of a bad TV soap opera: dreadful photography, no attention to framing, provincial *mise-en-scène*, music galore that underscores the inane script, absence of ideas on every level'.[41] He continued mercilessly: 'to dare present such an affront to the very notion of spectacle one should be fined!'[42]

Nonetheless, Christian-Jaque was playing to a strength by remaining adeptly attuned to his stars' established images. Where *Shalako* doubled down on genre conventions and consigned Bardot to a supporting role that stripped away constitutive traits of her star persona, *The Legend of Frenchie King* takes the opposite tack, celebrating Bardot and Cardinale in a revisionist lampoon where studio-era Hollywood westerns are the butt of the joke. The script, styling and direction systematically grant the stars the agency and screen time conventionally reserved for male characters in westerns: 'Oh! What a Man was Frenchie', the banjo player sings, and throughout the women are tough leaders, exhibit superior skills with firearms and horses, and change in and out of men's clothing. An inverse divestment of wherewithal from the town's male citizenry puts the women's authority into relief. Besides the childish Sarrazin brothers the only sizeable male roles are the villainous Dr Miller and the diminutive sheriff, played by Michael J. Pollard, who struggles to mount his horse, misplaces his guns and whom the two women repeatedly reduce to a blushing simper. The lack of a male lead or credible heterosexual love interest allows Bardot's Frenchie and Cardinale's Maria to fixate on each other, and as with male characters in earlier westerns (and unlike *Viva Maria!*), their rivalry drives the narrative. The revisionist logic of this gender reversal is punctuated by gags, gimmicks and episodic stunts – bicycle races, flashes of breasts and buttocks, Pollard's schtick, narrative-halting songs by Cardinale and Micheline Presle in a cameo – whose attraction-like address strains an already weak chain of dramatic probability and necessity. However, the main attraction remains unquestionably the spectacle of Bardot and Cardinale romping across the screen. Commentators both appreciative and disappointed note how the film openly serves as a vehicle for the two stars, and that the plights of Frenchie King and Maria Sarrazin merely provide scaffolding for this *duel d'actrices*.[43]

The rivalry between the leading characters culminates in a climactic fistfight during which the two actresses slam and kick each other around a farmyard in a dance-like brawl, a literal bodice-ripper in which the exaggerated sound of tearing fabric accompanies a visual crescendo of undergarments and brimming décolletage. The characters then reconcile abruptly upon the return of the real Dr Miller. As the closing credits run, Bardot and Cardinale, dressed as men, gallop on horseback across the desert at the head of the expanded King gang of four newly-wed couples, relinquishing dreams of oil and domesticity for life as gender-bending outlaws. But there has been no closure: no victory, no culminating kiss for either star, no indication into which sunset this French-speaking *maquis* is riding. One could project multiple meanings into this lack. Could it be, as in other French westerns of the post-war decades, a diversion of frontier narratives away from an Anglo-Saxon or anglophone future? An anarchic revolution to nowhere as an allegory of May 1968?[44] A parable of colonial collapse? A lesbian revision of the gender/genre dynamic? An existential

Figure 8.7 The *duel d'actrices*.

refusal of constraint by outlaw women that anticipates *Thelma & Louise* (Ridley Scott, 1991)? These interpretations, however, find unsure footing in the film's flimsy narrative and generic logic: 'Bardot's class and insolence, the health and spirit of Cardinale, strain to cover for the insignificance of this western parody.'[45] The film's governing coherence and interest remain anchored in the stars themselves.

Whether a distraction or a redeeming feature, Bardot's star image is nonetheless cannily transposed in the film to accommodate a more mature screen presence. The photographer Terry O'Neill, on the set, remarked: 'Most of the English photographers had an image of Brigitte Bardot as a petite and sexy young French girl, but there she was, a 5-foot 10-inch woman, stunning-looking and very confident.'[46] O'Neill's widely reproduced image of Bardot dressed in Frenchie's shirt and bandana, smoking a cigar while long hair blows across her face, captures the revised persona featured in the film. Where the younger Bardot melded an insolent gamine and unfiltered sexual drives, in *Les Pétroleuses* she sheds both adolescent and 'dumb blonde' traits to join an adult masculinised figure with that of a resourceful and authoritative woman: surrounded by the younger members of the gang she commands, it is now Bardot who represents the older generation, and unlike the older women her characters previously challenged, in *Les Pétroleuses* she remains firmly in charge. She retains the option to ravish with her beauty at will, but does so strategically.

In addition to the cross-dressed sequences she makes an entrance in an elaborate gown, hat and parasol, winning Pollard's bashful admiration, but within minutes, still in pink frills, she is riding a bucking horse and firing a pistol. She also twice frolics nude in bathing sequences for transfixed male voyeurs. Throughout, dressed as a man, a woman, or not at all, she remains sexualised and uninhibited, and is unequivocally the hunter and not the prey when, holding the four naked Sarrazin brothers at gunpoint, she assesses them from both front and back with an appreciative smile before the film cuts to a suggestive ellipsis.

As noted in the preceding chapter, the manipulation of language is also a constitutive element of a star's persona. Star vehicles create a distinct experience for spectators who recognise a familiar mode of line delivery from prior performances on stage, screen, radio and sound recordings. The reception of *Shalako* vividly illustrated the consequences of disrupting expectations in this arena. However, language schemes that allow French stars in westerns to speak their native language may also mire a film in contrivance, ambiguity and contradiction. *The Legend of Frenchie King* implements a pre-emptive alibi of linguistic verisimilitude to justify Bardot's line delivery in French. Early in the film an establishing shot lingers on a sign to anchor the conceit: 'State of Texas/Bougival Junction/Ville fondée par des français en 1858/Soyez le bienvenu (Howdie)/English Spoken if Necessary'; a banner over the town's street reads 'Joyeux Christmas'. English, French or any mix thereof finds justification, however ludic or far-fetched the premise. This suggestion of bilingualism, however, belies the *de facto* language regime. In this western town of plank sidewalks, covered wagons and swinging saloon doors populated by French immigrants who drink Beaujolais instead of whisky and wear the traditional dress of their province of origin, the inhabitants talk almost exclusively in French. English is all but confined to Pollard's running gags, and even he learns enough French to court Cardinale's Maria. Rife incongruities (not to mention the historical record) roundly vitiate the scheme for instituting French as the lingua franca on the circa 1880 Texas frontier, but these concessions of realist logic yield an expedient return: by avoiding the ambiguity of French-for-English translation or leaving the star 'stranded on the screen' in a language she does not adequately speak, Bardot is allowed to speak freely in French with her familiar voice and signature affectless delivery, without the presumed filter of translation (Cardinale also delivers her lines in French, her accent justified by the character's Corsican heritage).

When numbers are adjusted as a proportion of total ticket sales for the year, *The Legend of Frenchie King* joins *Viva Maria!* as one of Bardot's greatest box-office successes among French spectators. In terms of commercial viability these two films constitute bright points in her later career, and their relative success prompts a revision of characterisations of an unremitting downward slide. Both films owe a good measure of their success (to believe the critics) to a self-conscious foregrounding and framing of the Bardot star image. Whether in a dancehall number or a garment-shredding fistfight, Bardot performs her 'dance' *en abyme* while both diegetic onlookers and cinema audiences contemplate the famed but more mature star, familiar but refashioned, who holds her own in these staged encounters. In his review of *The Legend of Frenchie King* Baroncelli observes: 'The boyish allure suits Cardinale better than Bardot, but the latter is without equal as soon as she returns to the finery of her own sex.'[47] In the hands of a director who had previously studied it, Bardot's star image, though forged in adolescence, is pliable enough to remain viable into her later film career.

The unsung importance of these films for the western genre, however, is less evident. *Viva Maria!* defied clear classification as a western or any other genre, while *Shalako* fell flat in no small measure because of Bardot's clash with its retro-western orthodoxy. *The Legend of Frenchie King* is explicitly set in the familiar frontier West, but its parodic impulse tightly swaddles the genre's conventions in a giddy irony that demobilises familiar narratives in favour of the spectacle of two European stars chewing up the scenery. The sight and sound of Bardot and Cardinale provide the main attraction and the focus of Christian-Jaque's directorial purpose. Despite the differences, however, in each of the three films, for better or for worse, intentionally or not, Bardot's presence runs roughshod over genre conventions, and none of these films represents a smooth alignment of her star image and the western genre – unless, that is, 'western' here refers specifically to the French iteration of the genre in which, were one to venture a generalisation about this disparate archive of film, the lack of such integration represents a rare consistent trait.

Viva Maria! and *The Legend of Frenchie King* present playful irreverence towards the integrity of the western while self-consciously surcharging it with Bardot, the face of French cinema for a generation, who flaunts a familiar star image that includes her distinctive French speech. However, these two films are not simply parodic derivatives whose star tramples Hollywood convention underfoot; they draw energy from the friction between their French star and the familiar genre as they enact a renegotiation of both. Even in *Shalako*, though it could be called neither playful nor French, Bardot's performance resembles the other films in the following respect: the assertions of French cinema and the western genre operate as distinct modes of address whose enunciations echo with dissonant tones. As Lloyd and Dmytryk heavy-handedly impose the western conventions, what may we read in the charcoal-rimmed eyes that gaze into the camera as Bardot mutilates the English language? Is it defiance? Indifference? Incomprehension? Bardot's performance simultaneously draws on and disturbs her star image forged in earlier years, along with the frames of French cinema and of the western genre that would contain it.

Notes

1. Vincendeau's study stands out for its more comprehensive account of Bardot's film career. Ginette Vincendeau, *Brigitte Bardot* (London: BFI), 2013.
2. Dyer, *Stars*, 52.
3. Tudor's 'empiricist's dilemma'. See Chapter 1.
4. Pauline Kael, '"Brooding", They Said', *New York Times*, 21 February 1965, 43–4.
5. Antoine de Baecque, *La Nouvelle Vague: portrait d'une jeunesse* (Flammarion: Paris), 2009.
6. Vincendeau catalogues these distinct phases in Bardot's film career in *Brigitte Bardot*.
7. Vanessa Schwartz, *It's So French: Hollywood, Paris, and the Making of Cosmopolitan Film Culture* (Chicago: University of Chicago Press, 2007), 104.
8. See, for example, Linda Williams, 'Film Bodies: Gender, Genre, and Excess', in *The Film Genre Reader III*, ed. Barry Keith Grant (Austin: University of Texas Press, 2003), 141–59.
9. A recent anthology brings to light some of the range of this diversity. See Sue Matheson, ed., *Women in Westerns* (Edinburgh: Edinburgh University Press, 2018).
10. Tompkins, *West of Everything*, 43–4.
11. Florence Jacobowitz, 'The Dietrich Westerns: Destry Rides Again and Rancho Notorious', in *The Book of Westerns*, ed. Ian Cameron and Douglas Pye (New York: Continuum, 1996), 88–9.
12. V. F. Perkins, 'Johnny Guitar', in *The Book of Westerns*, ed. Ian Cameron and Douglas Pye (New York: Continuum, 1996), 221–8.
13. Simone de Beauvoir, 'Brigitte Bardot and the Lolita Syndrome', *Esquire*, August 1959, 36.
14. 'The most overt confrontations always take place between her and older women.' Vincendeau, 'The Old and the New', 82.
15. 'Je fais un rôle d'homme, presque.' Arte Online. 'Perle rare: le tournage de "Viva Maria" de Louis Malle.' Available at <http://sites.arte.tv/pnb/fr/perle-rare-le-tournage-de-viva-maria-de-louis-malle-063046–000> (accessed 17 March 2016).
16. 'L'amour, je ne sais pas ce que c'est.'
17. Vincendeau, *Brigitte Bardot*, 110.
18. 'un pastiche d'un film d'aventures, une sorte de "Zazie" tropicale à gros budget.' Louis Malle, *Louis Malle par Louis Malle* (Paris: Éditions de l'Athanor, 1978), 20.

19. Joanne Stang, 'Vive "Les Marias" From Paris Down Mexico Way', *New York Times*, 21 February 1965, 9.
20. Henri Chapier, '"Viva Maria" de Louis Malle: un opéra tendre et baroque, somptueux et burlesque, où la férocité du regard s'abrite derrière une apparente liberté', *Combat*, 12 October 1965, 10.
21. Film attendance was in decline after the 1950s, complicating the comparison of box-office data over time.
22. 'Baader war ein rührender Verlierer', Taz.de. (15 February 2002). Available at <http://www.taz.de/1/archiv/?dig=2002/02/15/a0198> (accessed 2 August 2016).
23. Detlef Siegfried, *Time is on my Side: Konsum und Politik in der westdeutschen Jugendkultur der 60er Jahre* (Göttingen: Wallstein Verlag), 2006. See also Pierre Billard, *Louis Malle: le rebelle solitaire* (Paris: Plon, 2003), 255–6.
24. The suit was brought by exhibitors against the censorship of local authorities in Texas. *Justia*, 'Interstate Circuit, Inc. v. City of Dallas 390 U.S. 676'. Available at <https://supreme.justia.com/cases/federal/us/390/676/case.html> (accessed 3 August 2022).
25. Pierre Billard, 'Ave Maria y Maria', *L'Express*, 12 December 1965, 69.
26. Anonymous, 'Carnival in Brio', *Time*, 31 December 1965, 77. Quoted in Marie-Dominique Lelièvre, *Brigitte Bardot: plein la vue* (Paris: Flammarion, 2012), 212.
27. Mac McSharry and Terry Hine, 'Euan Lloyd: The Ties that Bond Part 2: The Way West', *Cinema Retro* 2 (May 2005): 38.
28. Ibid., 38–40.
29. Christopher Bray, *Sean Connery: A Biography* (New York: Pegasus, 2012), 147.
30. Pauline Kael, 'The Missing West', *The New Yorker*, 16 November 1968, 127.
31. Anonymous, '"Shalako" d'Edward Dmytryk', *Les Lettres Françaises*, 11 December 1968, 20.
32. 'Elle s'est complètement trompée de scenario.' Jean de Baroncelli, '"Shalako"', *Le Monde*, 10 December 1968, 18.
33. Anonymous, 'Biggest British Western', *Times of London*, 16 December 1968, 6.
34. Renata Adler, 'Connery and Bardot in a Good Old Western: "Shalako" Begins Run at Theaters Here', *New York Times*, 6 November 1968, 32.
35. Henri Chapier, '"Shalako" d'Edward Dmytryk: amateurisme désinvolte…', *Combat*, 9 December 1968, 13.
36. 'J'écoutais en pensant à autre chose; je disais "yes, yes" en fumant une cigarette.' Brigitte Bardot, *Initiales B.B.* (Bernard Grasset: Paris, 1996), 433.
37. 'Le cinéma est mort.' Cited in Karim Ghiyati, 'Christian-Jaque et la Comédie-Française', *1895* 28 (October 1999): 170.
38. Philippe Roger, 'L'Étagement de la mise en scène dans le diptyque *Les Disparus de Saint-Agil* et *L'Enfer des anges*', *1895* 28 (October 1999): 69.
39. 'le cinéaste n'intéressait plus personne, les histoires du cinéma le négligeaient complètement, la presse spécialisée et les cinéphiles l'ignoraient purement et simplement'. Olivier Barrot, 'Christian-Jaque tel que je l'ai connu', *1895* 28 (October, 1999): 7.
40. 'homme de métier qui sait l'efficacité de ses procédés et ne cherche qu'à se concilier, sans complaisance coupable, un large public'. *Télérama* (2 February 1972).
41. 'Un film réalisé à la manière d'un méchant feuilleton de télévision: photo affreuse, aucun soin des cadrages, mise en scène provinciale, musique à gogo soulignant le vide des répliques, absences d'idées à tous les niveaux.' Henri Chapier, '"Les Pétroleuses" de Christian-Jaque: un tas de boue', *Combat*, 20 December 1971, 13.

42. 'Pour oser présenter pareil affront à la notion même de spectacle, on devrait payer des amendes!' Henri Chapier, '"Les Pétroleuses,"' 13.
43. Louis Chauvet, '"Les Pétroleuses" à l'eau de rose', *Le Figaro*, 21 December 1971, 22.
44. In addition to the oilfield that drives the plot, the title also references the notorious arsonists of the Paris Commune.
45. 'La classe et l'insolence de Bardot, la santé et la fougue de Cardinale tendent d'escamoter l'insignifiance de cette parodie de Western.' Gilles Jacob, *L'Express*, 12 February 1972, 5.
46. Quoted in Joanna Pitman, 'Brigitte Bardot as a Gunslinger', *The Times of London* magazine, 18 June 2005, 6.
47. 'L'allure garçonnière convient mieux à Claudia Cardinale qu'à Brigitte Bardot, mais celle-ci est inégalable dès qu'elle retrouve les atours de son sexe.' Jean de Baroncelli, '"Les Pétroleuses" de Christian-Jaque', *Le Monde*, 21 December 1971, 18.

IV
The Baguette Western

9

Spaghetti and camembert

In 1967 film critic Pauline Kael, exasperated by a spate of recent Hollywood releases, proclaimed 'the new western is a joke'.[1] In *El Dorado* (Howard Hawks, 1966), the remake of *Stagecoach* (Gordon Douglas, 1966), *The Way West* (Andrew V. McLaglen, 1967), and *The War Wagon* (Burt Kennedy, 1967), Kael saw the agony of a Hollywood genre whose tired conventions and ageing stars had lost relevance in the social climate of the late 1960s: 'The code of the old western heroes probably wouldn't have much to say to audiences today.'[2] At the time, the civil rights movement, the feminist movement and anti-war protests were challenging the ideology of narratives that celebrate a violent Anglo-Saxon masculinity and register the weakness, irrelevance and often destruction of women and characters of other ethnicities. The standardised studio production that favoured genres was also coming to an end, and television had superannuated the production of 'B' westerns and serials. Statistics bear out Kael's assertion. In 1958 the Hollywood studios released westerns at a rate of more than one per week, but by 1962 the rate would fall to only eleven for the entire year.[3] A few years later Kael struck a more definitive elegiac note: 'a few more westerns may straggle in, but the western is dead'.[4]

Kael falls into a long line of critics who have been announcing the western's demise since the early 1910s, and with hindsight her obituary, too, seems premature. True, Michael Cimino's *Heaven's Gate* (1980) flopped on an unprecedented scale, leading to devastating losses for United Artists and skittishness among producers towards the genre. However, in the following decade *Dances with Wolves* (Kevin Costner, 1990) and Clint Eastwood's *Unforgiven* (1992) each reaped multiple Oscars, in both cases including the best picture and best director awards. Subsequent releases include, among others, the auteurist turns *Dead Man* (Jim Jarmusch, 1996) and *No Country for Old Men* (Ethan and Joel Coen, 2007), well-received remakes of *3:10 to Yuma* (James Mangold, 2007) and *True Grit* (Ethan and Joel Coen, 2010), vehicles for major stars like *The Assassination of Jesse James by the Coward Robert Ford* (Andrew Dominik, 2007) and *The Revenant* (Alejandro Iñárritu, 2015), and revisions of the genre's representation of race, gender and sexuality in *Posse* (Mario Van Peebles, 1993), *The Ballad of Little Jo* (Maggie Greenwald Mansfield, 1993), *Brokeback Mountain* (Ang Lee, 2005), *Django Unchained* (Quentin Tarantino, 2012), and *The Power of the Dog* (Jane Campion, 2021). The longstanding tradition of western parodies continues, from *Blazing Saddles* (Mel Brooks, 1974) through *City Slickers* (Ron Underwood, 1991) and *Cowboys and Aliens* (Jon Favreau, 2011). Certainly, in numbers the continued production represents a trickle compared to the volume that previously flowed out of Hollywood. Nonetheless, although these nostalgic, revisionist or satirical iterations often announce the genre's passing even as they rework it, the American western has remained timely beyond the end of the studio era.[5]

A more contemporaneous challenge to Kael's death proclamation issues from the 'international' western films that were being released in increasing numbers as she was writing. These films are often designated by a national dish of the country in which they were produced: spaghetti (Italian) westerns, sauerkraut (German) westerns, kim-chi (Korean) westerns, and roast beef (English) westerns, among others. Often dismissive and derogatory, these 'culinary epithets' collectively represent a corpus that has nonetheless repurposed the western for new generations of spectators worldwide.[6] The uncontested main course on this buffet, with the most consistent and concentrated flavour, is the cycle of nearly 500 Italian westerns produced between 1962 and 1979. In the late 1960s this *filone* (as such cycles are known in Italian) was reaching its peak, and between 1966 and 1968 the spaghetti westerns were being released at a rate of more than one per week. They were also beginning to reach American audiences: in 1967 nine of these films had an American release, the following year there would be fifteen, and a total of ninety-five would have American distribution before the cycle ran its course.[7] The 'spaghettis' proved popular among spectators, if not critics, and could be enormously profitable: Sergio Leone's *A Fistful of Dollars*, made for $200,000, would gross over 14 million in the United States alone.

Far from moribund, the western genre would appear reinvigorated by this prolific and popular supplement to diminished American production. However, whether the Italian films represent a renewal of the genre will depend on the terms under which they are considered westerns. It was not only the structure of the industry that had changed; so, too, had the films. Their dismissive reception in the American press thematises key differences between the Italian imports and their Hollywood predecessors. Westerns had always traded in violence, but in Leone's films dismayed critics saw something different. The violence appeared gratuitous and cynical, amoral and sadistic, and newly graphic for American spectators as the end of the Production Code led to the institution of a more permissive ratings system. In a study of the American reception of Leone's 'Dollars Trilogy' (*A Fistful of Dollars*; *For a Few Dollars More*; *The Good, the Bad, and the Ugly*), William McClain observes the 'almost venomous hostility' of Kael and other mainstream critics to this strain of film.[8] The critics held to the assumption that

> [the] western is, and should be, a historical morality play based on the questions of the frontier, the role of the individual in society, the (dis)continuity of contemporary American society with its past, and of course the morals, meaning, and consequences of just versus unjust violence.[9]

Leone may have magnified the tropes and situations of the western – a lone gunman emerging from the wilderness, dusty streets, six-guns and saloons, sweat and horses – but he also refashioned them, often dismantling the moral, social, historical and mythic scaffolding that was, in the esteem of the mainstream critics, constitutive of the genre's 'syntax' in its American iteration. Measured against studio-era Hollywood westerns Kael found them lacking, at the *New York Times* Bosley Crowther deemed them outright dangerous, and the two join a chorus who condemned the Italian films as debased eviscerations of the very genre they exploit.

The American critics were 'attempting to defend the genre as both an aesthetic and a social institution',[10] but they were also championing a mode of production that by the late 1960s no longer existed. They did so, moreover, by rehearsing a well-trodden opposition between benchmark Hollywood genres and 'foreign' derivatives that have historically been overshadowed in film scholarship and criticism. However, unlike Soviet musicals, German horror films and other strains of European cinema that invite 'rescue from oblivion',[11] the spaghetti *filone* was prolific, profitable and in the 1960s had, in numbers, displaced Hollywood production as the western's centre of gravity. Some of the films achieved cult status, and Leone's trilogy made Clint Eastwood an international star. Before the last spaghetti western was produced in Italy the cycle was already garnering theoretically informed critical attention, and it has left what may be the widest (and still expanding) wake of commentary in the study of European popular cinema.[12] These films do not need 'recovering'; they were never forgotten by either the public or the critics.

Commentary on the Italian westerns reveals that the cinematic junk food dismissed by the mainstream American critics may also have nutritional value, so to speak, as a site of serious political and social critique. Christopher Frayling's *Spaghetti Westerns: Cowboys and Europeans from Karl May to Sergio Leone* (1981) remains a seminal point of reference in studies of the cycle. Frayling shifts focus away from comparisons with Hollywood to illuminate other influences, purposes and modes of production that shape these films. For example, the films are tied to the business model of the massive *Cinecittà* studios, which favoured the rapid production of inexpensive films; the prolific burst of westerns follows similarly intensive runs of 'weepy' melodramas and the muscle-bound 'sword-and-sandal' epics of the ancient world. Furthermore, where for the American critics the Italian westerns fail to conform to the narrative syntax of Hollywood production, Frayling locates the deficiency not in the films but in a definition of the genre derived from American cultural myths. He identifies alternative narrative structures, noting how the success of German adaptations of Karl May's *Winnetou* novels, in the early 1960s, revealed the viability of a European western that was more than an imitation or parody of American films.[13] He also identifies the distinct Italian variant of the western narrative in films that allegorise revolutionary politics and contemporary Italian society, an inquiry Austin Fisher further develops in *Radical Frontiers in the Spaghetti Westerns: Politics, Violence, and Popular Italian Cinema*. For both critics, the Italian films relocate the frontier between East and West, a key structural component in many American westerns, to the divide between the prosperous industrial north of Italy and the agrarian, impoverished south. These hot, dusty villages are similarly distant from the seat of legal and administrative powers whose emissaries may be corrupt and brutal villains, but here recourse to outlaw violence becomes a mode of resistance to northern power and an industrialised modernity that was destroying a traditional way of life without providing much in return. Fisher maps these alternative strains of the western narrative onto the post-war Marxist thought of Gramsci, Althusser and Marcuse, and onto the debate in the militant left over legitimate uses of violence for revolutionary causes.

These studies expand the discussion of the 'international' western beyond measures of deficiency compared to Hollywood production. Nonetheless, the allegory of contemporary Italy also constricts the perspective on these films. The resonances loaded into the more political 'spaghettis' (most often cited are films by Sergio Sollima, Damiano Damiani and Sergio Corbucci) are not always generalisable to the broader *filone*, and commentary rooted in the politics of Italian society will not similarly explain the films' appeal and reception outside Italy. Furthermore, the distinct mode of production in the Italian studios does not account for 'international' western films made elsewhere. Cautioning against an 'essential Italian-ness' in characterisations of these films, Dimitris Eleftheriotis observes how even the more political 'spaghettis' tend to erase the protagonist's nationality (the man 'from nowhere', or 'with no name'), and that multinational co-production agreements and international casts further act to 'weaken the "national" as its referent'.[14] Furthermore, even the more overtly political films blunt the thrust of the leftist critique by conjoining politics to familiar and marketable cinematic pleasures: attractive stars, flashy style, high emotional pitch, playful irony and spectacular violence. The 'revolutionary' plots unfold in films that in many respects resemble their less political contemporaries, are distributed in the same cinematic marketplace and are consumed by the same audiences. The more political spaghettis may offer more than jejune exploitations of violence, but the anti-capitalist overtones remain embedded in an industrial product destined for mass exploitation in a capitalist culture industry.

The contradictions that condition the production, distribution and reception of the spaghetti westerns provide a lens for considering contemporaries that may (with ample qualification) be called French, or more precisely, that position the enunciation of a French national referent alongside that of the western genre. Among the vectors of this enunciation is a watershed moment in French political and cultural history. Social unrest roiled many countries in the late 1960s, including the United States and Italy, but the events of May 1968 disrupted French society with singular and concentrated force. The occupation of government buildings, universities, factories and theatres, along with national strikes and daily demonstrations and riots, shook the institutional pillars of French society for five turbulent weeks. The disruption ended in a conservative reaction, and the aftermath led newly radicalised and (often) disillusioned intellectuals and artists fundamentally to question their role, and that of their work, in a system steered by a state apparatus, both repressive and ideological, that served entrenched interests and power.

The institution of cinema, the role of the filmmaker and the practice of filmmaking were not exempt from the reconsideration that followed May '68, and the western genre provided a canvas, intended or not, for the reckoning. A comparison of two films vividly opens a perspective on the consequences of the moment for cinema, from different and in many respects opposite angles. In *Cemetery Without Crosses* (*Une corde, un colt*), director Robert Hossein intentionally positions his film in the vein of Italian productions. Hossein shot his film just before the events of May '68 but it was released afterwards, and the film's mode of a timeless 'westernness' found diminished relevance in the aftermath. *Cemetery Without Crosses* contrasts with an audacious experiment, examined in the following chapter, that is explicitly positioned as a response to May '68. *Wind from the East*, a co-production filmed in Italy by the Dziga Vertov Group and a multinational cast, constitutes a post-'68 assault not only on the western genre but on cinema itself. Although the first film embraces the genre and the second pillories it, they nonetheless present commonalities: both emphatically reference the western genre in its Italian declension, each has been called a 'baguette' or 'camembert' variant on the spaghetti *filone*, and each, in its way, exposes a discordance between its enunciation of the western genre and the historical moment of May '68 in France. A fundamental difference nonetheless pushes the films to opposite ends of a cinematic spectrum. One bespeaks an effort to reconcile French and western in a tragic mode, a gesture that will ultimately diminish the film's timeliness; in the other, a radical post-1968 politics and the western genre are intentionally positioned as antagonists, but the dissonances wrought by the measure of a specifically French enunciation also add dimension to the critique in this paradigmatic work of political cinema.

A stale baguette?

Cemetery Without Crosses is, paradoxically, both conventional and singular in its reworking of the western genre. Ginette Vincendeau characterises the film as 'at once loving tribute, pastiche, and deconstruction of the American western', while observing 'the Italian legacy in Hossein's fetishising of the western' and also asserting that it is 'in many ways a very French film'.[15] In an April 1968 interview Hossein states that his purpose was not to imitate American or Italian production, but to invest something 'personal' into the myth of the West: in doing so, he claims the mantle of the 'first French Western'.[16] However, history was moving very fast in the spring of 1968, and *Cemetery Without Crosses* less sits at the intersection of these national vectors – American, Italian, French – than cuts across them, landing apart from all three.

The plot turns on a blood feud. Ben Caine, the husband of Maria (Michèle Mercier), has stolen several bags of gold and killed the foreman of the powerful Rogers family, who have been trying to drive the Caines off their land. The Rogers men pursue Ben to his home and summarily hang him in front of his wife. This opening act launches a chain of violent retaliations. A determined Maria visits Manuel (Hossein), a mysterious gunman who lives alone in a nearby ghost town. It will later be revealed that Maria and Manuel were once lovers, but that she married Ben in Manuel's absence, believing he would never return. Maria hires Manuel to exact vengeance, and he reluctantly accepts the charge with a premonition that it will end badly. His strategy is to ingratiate himself with the Rogers clan, and he is hired as the new foreman on their ranch. Through a ruse Manuel kidnaps the Rogers's daughter Diana, whom Maria's brothers-in-law brutally assault. In exchange for the daughter's return Maria demands that the Rogers give her dead husband a public funeral and burial, digging the grave themselves with the entire town as witnesses. They comply, but use the hostage exchange to avenge their shaming, leading to the violent deaths of Maria and both remaining Caine brothers. In the final sequence the Rogers men come to the ghost town to kill Manuel, who prevails over all four in a showdown shootout. However, Diana Rogers has followed, and she executes Manuel with a rifle shot to end the film.

Cemetery Without Crosses is a French–Italian co-production, and despite Hossein's expressed aim to create something different his film has a foot planted squarely in the spaghetti *filone*. Hossein had lived and worked in Italy for several years. Sergio Leone had cast him in *Once Upon a Time in the West* (1968), though contractual obligations elsewhere kept him from participating. Hossein dedicated his film to Leone, who directed (uncredited) one of its most memorable sequences: a dinner scene where the Rogers play a practical joke on Manuel. Leone's ludic contributions stand out against the film's otherwise earnest tone.

Mood aside, other traits typical of the Italian films are pervasive. Vincendeau notes the extreme close-up on a boot that introduces Hossein's character as an example of typical Italian-style framing, likens Manuel's mysterious origins to Leone's 'man with no name' (Manuel says simply 'I come from elsewhere'), and remarks how the editing of the final shootout, as in many Italian westerns, constitutes the excitement of the sequence more than the filmed action itself.[17] There are other similarities: Manuel's signature cigarillo, indexed by a puff of smoke from behind a door jamb, further references Eastwood's 'no name' persona. *Cemetery Without Crosses* also shares the backdrop of the Almeria hills of southern Spain with many Italian films, and the music – twanging guitars, a grunting male chorus, Iberian/Mexican motifs – resembles the scores Ennio Morricone wrote for Leone and other Italian directors.[18] In significant measure the film looks and sounds like a spaghetti western.

Nonetheless, the treatment of the western genre in *Cemetery Without Crosses* also diverges from its Italian contemporaries. It does not, for example, conform to the narrative structures typical of the Italian films. Frayling identifies an 'Italian plot' whose foundational structure derives from a hero who serves two 'masters' but cynically plays them off each other, eschewing both sentiment and moral/ethical values in his ploy for personal gain. Periodising the narrative structures of the Italian *filone*, Frayling proposes a variant that after 1967 leads to the more political

Figure 9.1 Spaghetti-style framing.

'Zapata-Spaghettis' in which the pair of protagonists, one European, one Mexican, become involved in a revolutionary movement: the European may in some cases remain cynical, but in others he joins the cause.[19] Parsing the more radical post-1967 westerns, Fisher identifies (after Louis Althusser) an 'RSA' ('repressive state apparatus') plot variation in which law, justice and civilising forces are revealed to be oppressive, driven by greed and irredeemably corrupt. He identifies an 'insurgency plot', a variation on the 'Zapata' narrative that transfers agency to the Mexican sidekick character.[20] Again, both critics caution that these narrative structures must be situated in a broader social, political and economic context of contemporary Italy. Frayling places focus on the Italian film industry's distinct mode of production and exhibition, while Fisher examines the films' resonance with the political and social unrest of the time.

These narrative structures and political impulses are not easily generalisable to *Cemetery Without Crosses*. Hossein's film is instead a morality play about the destructive consequences of violence and revenge. The stolen gold is only the latest chapter in a long feud, and rather than constituting an end in itself (as in the *Dollars* trilogy) it serves as an instrument for advancing the purpose of characters bound by family honour. The characters often exhibit indifference to the gold itself; their obsession lies elsewhere. In her share Maria sees the means towards vengeful satisfaction in the public recognition of her husband's murder and a proper civic burial. As for serving two masters, Manuel might feign to ally with the Rogers but the longing glances he exchanges with Maria leave little doubt where his loyalty lies. With the prescience of a Greek chorus he foresees the plot's disastrous outcome when Maria comes to hire him, and he voices a premonition: 'They'll kill you.'[21] The dubbing of the line in the Italian release delivers an aphorism that summarises the moral of this story: '*La vendetta è una brutta pianta che da frutti amari…per tanti quanti*' ('revenge is an ugly plant that bears bitter fruit…for everyone').[22] In this cautionary tale everyone suffers and there is no escape from the cycle of retaliations. The film is less a celebration or justification for violence than the illustration of its inexorable outcome, namely, the bloody annihilation of the narrative agents. The universal morsel of wisdom transcends time and place. Revenge doesn't pay. *On ne badine pas avec la vengeance.*

The film further asserts the timelessness of its narrative logic through evocations of tragic dramatic mode. The most obvious instance is Maria's resemblance to Antigone in her single-minded insistence that her murdered husband receive a civic burial in a hostile town, but other resonances abound. The implacable feud recalls the strife in the house of Atreus, as does the return of a man who finds that the woman he loved has married another. Manuel is also, effectively, a Trojan horse: a cunning and insidious 'gift' to the Rogers clan who is allowed within their compound's walls, after which he abducts the daughter of this rival 'city'. Internecine violence is also a tragic trope, and Maria commits symbolic fratricide when she shoots her treacherous brother-in-law in the ghost town's saloon. There is no escape for the unhappy mortals trapped in this cycle of violence. The two sides are doomed to a chain of reprisals that culminates in a climactic bloodbath and leaves the screen littered with bodies. There are no winners, nor, despite the portrayal of the Rogers family as corrupt bullies, is there an unequivocal 'right side' to the dispute: the characters on both sides have their reasons and their flaws, and the Caines are also criminal and violent.

Moreover, unlike the looser episodic structure of some Italian westerns, the actions of the clockwork plot follow each other with the strict probability and necessity Aristotle admired in tragedy, and make a bid to inspire both fear (the spectators see the violence coming) and pity (clearly established motivation allows them to relate to why the characters act in this manner). In the final moments the Rogers daughter, up to this point a pawn in the conflict, appears out of nowhere like an avenging goddess on horseback, Diana *ex machina* with a rifle instead of a bow, to end the feud and the narrative with a lead-filled full stop. There will be peace at last, if not redemption or reconciliation, but only because there is a single woman standing with no one left to kill. In a filmed reportage taken on the production location, Hossein explicitly aligns his film with the tragic mode: 'it is possible to transpose the full range of passions and emotions, exactly as in a Shakespeare tragedy, through a western'.[23] The passions and emotions remain the same, he implies, whether they play out in ancient Greece, Elsinore in 1600 or Dodge City in 1880 – or, one may add, western Europe in early 1968.

The emphasis on universal human emotions permits a nearly abstract representation of the society in which the plot of *Cemetery Without Crosses* unfolds. The weak sheriff under the thumb of the powerful Rogers clan faintly represents the corrupt authority found in some Italian westerns, but the town and its inhabitants are here a backdrop. The warring families most often pitch battle from their remote ranches and the ghost town, islands of action and speech set in the *tabula rasa* of an arid and inhospitable desert.[24] The strife, ending in death tallies that rival those of

Hamlet and *King Lear*, does not specifically resonate with Italian demographic tensions or third-world revolutions, nor does it evoke American frontier myths of expansion and regeneration. Hossein is a self-identified humanist, and the bid for a universal and timeless depiction of a shared human experience acts to neutralise precise allegories of post-war French society: the fallout of post-war industrial modernisation, the struggles of decolonisation, or other sites of tension in the turbulent years of the late 1960s. Vincendeau considers *Cemetery Without Crosses* an example of a typically European pessimism whose tragic element 'mostly borders on nihilism'.[25] This pessimism, however, derives from a human condition that transcends an historical moment and disables a more dialectical inquiry, through cinema as both practice and product, into the contradictions of the material, social and political conditions of a specific historical time and place, be it frontier-era America, post-war Italy or 1960s France. The cautionary lesson that violence doesn't pay, moreover, does little to stoke revolutionary fervour.

Cemetery Without Crosses is not the first western set in a tragic mode, nor is it singular in positioning a female character as the agent of the central act of revenge in a spaghetti-style film.[26] Jane Tompkins argued that Western narratives frequently celebrate a masculinity released from the power women hold in the advancing 'Eastern' civilisation and its institutions, but the full range of women's roles remains unexamined when the focus lies on the genre's ritual rehearsal of their inexorable defeat.[27] 'She is essential,' asserts Sue Matheson in the opening of an anthology that reveals the diversity of female characters in the genre, including substantial roles in the Italian westerns: the Electra allegory in *Forgotten Pistolero* (*Il pistolero dell'Ave Maria*, Ferdinando Baldi, 1969), the title character of *The Belle Starr Story* (*Il mio corpo per un poker*, Piero Cristofani and Lina Wertmüller, 1968) and Claudia Cardinale's character in Leone's *Once Upon a Time in the West*.[28] Nonetheless, these characters remain exceptional among their spaghetti contemporaries, which often relegate women to super-numerary roles whose purpose is 'merely to establish masculinity as heterosexual'[29] or that betray a 'pernicious misogyny which the narrative singularly fails to reject'.[30] The Italian westerns are often glib in their representation of violence towards female characters, who are routinely objectified, expendable and, for long stretches of screen time, absent.

In *Cemetery Without Crosses* the cast remains primarily male, and both Maria and the Rogers daughter suffer violence at the hands of these men. However, these violent acts are not shrugged off as inconsequential, nor do they unequivocally bespeak a ritual disempowerment of women. Maria's predicament as a widow seeking closure is not a mere opening pretext to set in motion a fight among men whose masculinity is on the line. She remains an active agent driving the plot throughout, present and engaged. Mercier's determined face – whether her character is cutting a deal, digging a grave, shooting a rifle or dispassionately butchering a rabbit – is a recurring visual motif: she is unyielding, resourceful and capable of achieving her goal. Both Maria and Diana Rogers are unafraid to resort to violence, and each will have decisively exacted her revenge by the end of the film.

Beyond instances of women doing 'what a man's gotta do', the co-equal heft of Mercier's and Hossein's roles further strays from the spaghetti narratives by placing a heterosexual couple at the heart of the drama. The casting of Hossein and Mercier as co-conspirators and lovers in a period setting was, in 1968, a familiar and bankable bet. In *Angélique marquise des Anges* (Bernard Borderie, 1964) Mercier played a young woman forced into marriage with a disfigured older nobleman (Hossein) whom she initially loathes, but with whom she eventually falls in love. *Angélique marquise des Anges* is the first film in a cycle of romanticised dramas set in the seventeenth century, three of which feature Hossein.[31] The role of Angélique made Mercier a star, and *Cemetery Without Crosses* draws on 'continuities in the Hossein-Mercier couple'.[32] Certainly, there are marked

Figure 9.2 The determined widow.

differences between the films: the western's austere setting, spaghetti-like framing, restraint and sparseness of dialogue sharply contrast with the chatty and frilled *Angélique* cycle. However, in its emotional climax *Cemetery Without Crosses* pulls closer to the earlier Mercier-Hossein pairings in both tone and filming style. Ben's death reawakens Manuel's hope for a future together with Maria, and her successful revenge mission frees her from lingering bonds to her husband's legacy. She has done a widow's due diligence: her husband is dead and buried, properly, in a manner that exposes and shames his killers. Manuel proposes they leave together, but it is too late: Maria is dying. With perfectly applied eye liner and a trickle of blood to signify her agony, Maria delivers a tearful dying explanation and request for forgiveness in close-up while Manuel, her avenger, former lover and final consoler, having just ridden up on a white horse, cradles her in a *pietà*-like pose and gazes upon her tenderly. The shot-reverse shot editing, the thick emotion and teary close-ups, the sudden verbalisation of repressed feelings, the dashed dreams of running away together, the deathbed absolution, the tight narrative closure, and the triumph of love over money or thirst for vengeance as the deepest bond between these characters decisively wrench their motivation away from nihilist violence and plant it on the threshold of melodramatic romance. What might have initially appeared to be a business relationship is confirmed to be rooted in sentimentality: the man from nowhere is, in fact, from here. The justification for Manuel's final acts of violence, in the following sequence, is consequently diverted from cynical economic gain, struggle against corrupt power or even professionalism ('finishing the job'). It is instead rooted in the psychology of buried emotions, star-crossed love, marital legitimacy and a bruised heart. To understand the compass that steers Hossein's mysterious character, *cherchez la femme*.[33]

Cemetery Without Crosses taps established dramatic forms in its framing of well-known stars in a western setting, but it is not a parody in the mode of the vehicles featuring Raynaud, Mariano, and Fernandel a few years earlier. It is neither comic nor overtly ironic: on the contrary, Leone's playful turn notwithstanding, *Cemetery Without Crosses* is a taciturn and brooding film. However, if the film is a sum of diverse parts, it remains challenging to characterise precisely what this 'whole' is. To generalise Hossein's treatment as representative of a broader French offshoot of the Italian *filone* – a 'baguette' or 'camembert' western made by a French director with a pair of French stars – may be meaningless, for by this measure it may be the only film that falls into the category. It is

Figure 9.3 *Pietà*: Maria's dying disclosures.

perhaps easier to identify what the film is not. *Cemetery Without Crosses* stands apart from the narrative structures, the political allegories, the gratuitous violence and the gendered dynamic identified as central to its Italian contemporaries.

Box-office statistics would indicate that these differences were infelicitous for the reception of *Cemetery Without Crosses*. Released in January, 1969, the film drew fewer than a million French spectators over the course of the year; by comparison, in the same year Leone's *Once Upon a Time in the West* drew nearly 15 million spectators in France alone. Despite his support and participation, Leone's exceptional appeal to the paying public did not transfer to Hossein's film. Furthermore, the timing of the film's release also mitigated its success, at least according to Hossein, who later lamented that the film was eclipsed as the aftermath of May '68 consumed the French public and the press: despite good reviews 'it didn't even have the chance to be a success or not' due to the 'absolutely terrible [*terrible*]' strikes and social climate.[34] The distinction drawn between the space the film would have commanded in the public sphere and the events roiling French society is telling: namely, the inference that the film and its reception were not part of the conversation about the radicalisation, the revolutionary imagination and the reaction in the aftermath. On the contrary, Hossein suggests that the interest and discourse (presumably positive) the film would have generated was displaced by these polemics. The bid for timelessness proved untimely, and in the newly urgent interrogation of what cinema as both a practice and an institution should be in a post-1968 world, *Cemetery Without Crosses* had little to say.

Notes

1. Pauline Kael, 'Saddle Sore', *The New Republic* (5 August 1967), 39.
2. Ibid., 41.
3. Frayling, *Spaghetti Westerns*, 50.
4. Quoted in William McClain, 'Westerns Go Home! Sergio Leone and the "Death of the Western" in American Film Criticism', *Journal of Film and Video* 62, nos. 1–2 (2010): 61.
5. To characterise continued production Pete Falconer favours the term 'afterlife' in 'Spaghetti Westerns and the "Afterlife"' of a Hollywood Genre', in Austin Fisher, ed. *Radical Frontiers in the Spaghetti Western: Politics, Violence and Popular Italian Cinema* (London and New York: I. B. Tauris and Company, 2011), 262–78. In a less elegiac mode Lee Clark Mitchell prefers the term 'late western' in *Late Westerns: The Persistence of a Genre* (University of Nebraska Press, 2018).
6. Tim Bergfelder, *International Adventures: German Popular Cinema and European Co-Productions in the 1960s* (New York and Oxford: Berghahn, 2005), 172.
7. Fisher, *Radical Frontiers*, 226. The 1970s also saw a significant uptick in the production of American westerns, some of them inspired by the style of the Italian films whose success abroad had drawn the attention of American producers. See Frayling, *Spaghetti Westerns*, 50.
8. McClain, 'Westerns Go Home!', 52.
9. Ibid., 60–1.
10. Ibid., 63.
11. Richard Dyer and Ginette Vincendeau outline this project in *Popular European Cinema* (London and New York: Routledge, 1992).
12. In addition to Frayling's *Spaghetti Westerns*, see Laurence Staig and Tony Williams, *Italian Westerns: The Opera of Violence* (London: Lorimer, 1975) for another early account. Subsequent monographs include Fisher's *Radical Frontiers* and Bert Fridlund's *The Spaghetti Western: A Thematic Analysis* (Jefferson, NC: McFarland, 2006).
13. The purview of Frayling's 'European western' comprises primarily German and Italian films, but he mentions Joë Hamman's films as a French inflection of the genre.
14. Dimitris Eleftheriotis, 'Spaghetti Western, Genre Criticism, and National Cinema: Re-Defining the Frame of Reference', in *Action and Adventure Cinema*, ed. Yvonne Tasker (New York and London: Routledge, 2004), 321. In a similar line of critique, Christopher Robé seeks to 'complicate the more monolithic theorisations' with a more fluid and multidirectional transnational circulation than a characterisation that derives primarily from exchange between distinct Italian and American industries. Christopher Robé, 'When Cultures Collide: Third Cinema Meets the Spaghetti Western', *Journal of Popular Film and Television* 42, no. 3 (2014): 173.
15. Ginette Vincendeau, 'Western Without Americans', liner notes for *Cemetery Without Crosses* (DVD, restored edition), directed by Robert Hossein (Arrow Films, 2015): 6.

16. Interview with Robert Hossein, *Côte d'Azur Actualités*, broadcast 17 April 1968. Supplementary material for *Cemetery Without Crosses* (DVD, restored edition), directed by Robert Hossein (Arrow Films, 2015).
17. Ibid., passim.
18. The music was composed by Hossein's father André.
19. Frayling, *Spaghetti Westerns*, 52.
20. See the chapter 'Violent Mexico: "Crossing the Border" into Armed Insurgency'. Fisher, *Radical Frontiers*, 117–60. Fridlund further elaborates variants on these narrative structures in *The Spaghetti Western*.
21. 'Je t'ai dit de laisser tomber, ça ne m'intéresse pas. . .Ni pour lui, ni pour toi, je ne veux plus d'histoires. . .Ils te tueront.' ('I told you to drop it. / I'm not interested. / Neither for him [Ben] nor for you, I'm through with it. / They'll kill you.)
22. The English version is less poetic: 'You believe in revenge, but I don't. It never ends.'
23. 'on peut transposer toutes les passions et les sentiments exactement comme dans une tragédie de Shakespeare à travers un western' ('one can transpose all the passions and feelings exactly as in a Shakespeare tragedy through a Western'). Interview with Robert Hossein, *Cemetery Without Crosses* (DVD, restored edition), directed by Robert Hossein (Arrow Films, 2015).
24. Here the film also evokes the spatial configuration of tragedy in a Racinian mode, as described by Roland Barthes. Roland Barthes, *On Racine*, trans. Richard Howard (Berkeley: University of California Press, 1992), 5.
25. Vincendeau, 'Western Without Americans', 11.
26. Martin M. Winkler analyses the allegories of Greek tragic heroines in Anthony Mann's *The Furies* (1950) and *The Forgotten Pistolero* (*Il pistolero dell'Ave Maria*, 1969) in 'Clytemnestra and Electra Under Western Skies', in *Women in the Western*, ed. Sue Matheson (Edinburgh: Edinburgh University Press, 2020). See also Martin M. Winkler, 'Classical Mythology and the Western Film', *Comparative Literature Studies* 22, no. 4 (Winter 1985): 516–40.
27. See, again, Tompkins, *West of Everything*.
28. Matheson, *Women in the Western*, 1.
29. Maggie Günsberg, *Italian Cinema: Gender and Genre* (New York: Palgrave Macmillan, 2005), 187.
30. Fisher, *Radical Frontiers*, 113.
31. The other two, both directed by Bernard Borderie, are *L'Indomptable Angélique* (*Untamable Angélique*, 1967) and *Angélique et le Sultan* (*Angélique and the Sultan*, 1968).
32. Vincendeau, 'Western Without Americans', 15.
33. Mercier characterised the film as a 'love story' as well a vengeance narrative. Interview in supplementary material, *Cemetery Without Crosses* (DVD, restored edition), directed by Robert Hossein (Arrow Films, 2015).
34. 'Il n'avait même pas l'occasion de pouvoir marcher ou pas marcher.' 'Remembering Sergio' (interview with Robert Hossein), Arrow Films, 2015.

10

East meets west(ern)

From its conception, *Wind from the East* was positioned as both a response to the events of May 1968 and an enunciation of the western genre. Daniel Cohn-Bendit, the co-author of the film's original pitch who was exiled for his role in the May uprising, attributes the project's genesis to profit-hungry producers eager to work with a newly notorious public figure:

> It was after May, I was in Italy, Bertolucci was there and I see his producer, who asks 'Don't you want to make a film?' They were telling themselves: 'We'll make a film with Cohn-Bendit, it will make money.' People are simpleminded, sometimes.[1]

Cohn-Bendit pitched an idea: 'I want to make a western with Godard.' Jean-Luc Godard agreed to participate and the two prepared a sketch for a story about striking mine workers in Dodge City. The Cineriz distribution company generously funded the project, and Gian Maria Volonté, the left-leaning actor who had played opposite Clint Eastwood in Sergio Leone's *A Fistful of Dollars* and other western roles, signed on. A 'western in colour written by Cohn-Bendit, directed by Jean-Luc Godard and featuring Volonté'[2] promised an appealing blend of youthful and radical post-1968 politics, New Wave style and the spaghetti-style western at the height of the Italian cycle's popularity.

It would not be Cohn-Bendit with whom Godard ultimately shaped *Wind from the East*, nor was the film that resulted clearly a western, Hollywood, spaghetti or otherwise. By accounts, it is surprising that a complete film ever came of the initial arrangement. Godard's circle of filmmaking collaborators was joined in Italy by members of Cohn-Bendit's radicalised student cohort from the university at Nanterre, along with a number of leftist Italian militants; few of these participants, Godard later remarked, 'gave a damn' about the film. 'Collective creation' and 'auto-gestion' were the rule of the day, and the *assemblée générale* (general assembly) that preceded a day's filming could devolve into chaotic and contentious discussions. Due to the film's generous financing the set was flush with cash, much of it rumoured to have been funnelled towards the purchase of Ferraris, vacations in Sicily and the opening of a drag bar. Meanwhile, the footage, only a small fraction of which would be used, began to pile up. In Cohn-Bendit's word, the production site was a *bordel* (a 'mess') and he later confessed to being too swept up in the 'collective frenzy' (*délire collectif*) to tell Godard to 'let them all go to the beach and we'll think about the film'.³

It was not only *délire* on the set that threatened the film's completion. The two collaborators had divergent conceptions of what the film would entail. Cohn-Bendit had admired Louis Malle's playful *Viva Maria!* (his 'cinematic ideal'⁴) and a number of the more overtly political Spaghetti westerns had recently been released, but whatever its politics a western parody or a spaghetti *à thèse* does not necessarily constitute a revolutionary reexamination of cinema practice. Cohn-Bendit's vision remained ill defined ('it was all very vague', Anne Wiazemsky recalls), and he later concedes that he and his Nanterre cohort 'were a group who really had nothing to say about the cinema. We wanted to have fun. It was a little unfair to Godard.'⁵

Godard, on the other hand, had plenty to say, including the assertion that he never had any intention of making a western. The genre nonetheless remains richly invoked as both a practice and a critical trope. In its American and Italian iterations, the western furnishes the foremost emblem of the cinema whose destruction *Wind from the East* demands and, in its way, enacts. The film is also framed as a cinematic response to May 1968 by notable participants in the events, and the western genre in the film is enunciated alongside precise references to the events in France. If the rejection of existing filmmaking practices finds a lightning rod in the familiarity of American and Italian westerns, which other dimension does the far less familiar conjunction of the western and a French referent lend to the blistering critique?

The death of the auteur

Godard had been advocating new modes of filmmaking since his years as a critic at the *Cahiers du cinéma*, a goal he realised, to an extent, with the production of *Breathless*, *Contempt* and other 'classics' of New Wave cinema. By the mid-1960s he was a star director, studied and imitated around the world. However, instead of continuing in the vein of his New Wave successes Godard was increasingly engaged in a sweeping interrogation of the institution of cinema, including his own prior work. After 1965 his thought took a sharp left turn as he espoused a radical cinematic practice openly informed by a Marxist-Leninist (Maoist) critique and the representational strategies of the Marxist playwright and stage director Bertolt Brecht. *La Chinoise* (1967) follows a group of university students who self-critically, if not always effectively, work through the terms of their political commitment. The style – disconnected tableaux, droning Maoist discourse – exposes the fragmented nature of cinema that is smoothly concealed by classical continuity, but unlike the foregrounded discontinuity in Godard's earlier films it is yoked to a didactic political critique. *Weekend* (1967) further undoes continuity in narration, character and dialogue while thematising the necessity of violent acts and roasting the French bourgeoisie (literally, in the cannibalistic conclusion). The film ends with a blunt declaration on a title card, a warning shot for what would follow: *Fin du cinéma*, 'end of cinema', at least as it had previously been known and practised.

Where in *Weekend* Godard challenges the spectator to conceptualise the end of cinema, *The Joy of Learning* (*Le Gai Savoir*, 1969) pushes cinema onto the brink of this precipice. Dazzling *tour de force* filmmaking (the eight-minute travelling shot in *Weekend*, for example) is notably absent in this spare film depicting two figures who methodically work through a Maoist-inspired education and auto-critique. The episodic form, non-integration of elements, bare stage-like setting and educational purpose draw from Brecht's playbook.[6] By breaking the illusion of consistency in time, space, narrative logic and character psychology, the established relations between these elements come under scrutiny, raising the question of what the world – and cinema – can be like if they are undone, and prompting reflection on how to enact their undoing. As with Brecht's metaphorical brass seller, who sees in a trumpet only a chunk of scrap metal with potential to be reshaped for purposes other than producing musical sounds (as a weapon, perhaps), cinema here is reduced to a sparse foregrounding of its basic elements – sound and image – whose relationship, no longer cohering as an integrated unit, may subsequently be examined, critiqued, re-imagined and redeployed as something different from familiar practices, and to different ends: 'Zero constitutes the integral part of *Le gai savoir*. It justifies, situates, and symbolises the film.'[7] Brecht quipped that the institution of theatre was so wholly compromised by bourgeois aesthetics that he needed a new word for his reconceived practice, proposing to call it 'tha-ëter' instead. For Godard, 'cinema' similarly became the epithet for an entrenched institution and practice.

With cinema degree zero at hand, where does one go next? The events of May '68 amplified the question's urgency. In an interview with Argentine filmmaker Fernando Solanas given shortly after the unrest, Godard hails May '68 for decisively revealing both the necessity of wiping the slate clean and the freedom to do so:

> 'May '68' was a fantastic liberation for many of us. 'May '68' imposed its truth on us, it forced us to speak and consider problems from another perspective. Before that 'May,' here in France, all intellectuals had alibis that enabled them to live well, to have a car, an apartment, etc. But 'May' created a very simple problem: the problem of having to change your lifestyle, to break with the system.[8]

The break is not an end in itself, but a challenge that Godard and others had already begun to answer with an exploration of what a new mode of filmmaking (a 'cé-ni-ma?') might entail.[9] He is unsparing in his condemnation of existing practice:

> there is no European cinema, it's just American cinema everywhere. Just like there is no English film industry, only an American industry that works in England; in the same way that you said there is no Argentinian culture, just a European-American culture that operates through Argentinian intermediaries. There's no European cinema either, only American cinema.[10]

Even self-identifying leftist cinemas are 'absorbed' into this system. Godard imagines Hollywood-style bio-pics about Che Guevara or Mao Tse-Tung as grotesque examples of a new flavour poured into familiar cinematic packaging for sale in the service of bourgeois profit. However, the sweeping denegation also encompasses European art cinema, along with Solanas's politically committed filmmaking. Naming a number of his contemporaries, Godard indicts the figure of the auteur itself as a 'category of bourgeois cinema' and the 'ally of reaction'. No matter how radical a director's politics, this new 'scientific cinema' also demands a theoretically informed Marxist critique of the function of authorship.

The denegation soon encompassed Godard himself as an auteur figure: he stopped making films as 'Jean-Luc Godard' and began working as a collective with at least one other contributor, and often more. In 1969 a number of these collaborators began calling themselves the Dziga Vertov Group, named after the early Soviet filmmaker who called for a 'fresh perception of the world'. The three-year experiment unfolded through projects that include a documentary of the Rolling Stones in rehearsal (*One Plus One*), a farcical re-enactment of the Chicago Seven trial (*Vladimir and Rosa*), an interrogation of truth and meaning in images (*Pravda*) and a star vehicle meditation on the contradictions of bourgeois political commitment (*Tout va bien*). The group's constellation of contributors varied, but Godard most consistently worked with the journalist and political theorist Jean-Pierre Gorin. Godard's celebrity helped to secure financing for these ventures, though disappointed producers baulked at distributing much of what the collective produced. The failure to meet conventional measures of a film's success – a theatrical release resulting in box-office receipts, wide spectatorship, mainstream critical acclaim – advanced the group's critique of the institution of cinema: the *salle de cinéma* (movie theatre) itself was, in Godard's pun, a *sale lieu* (a filthy place) where pleasure is bought and sold. An examined indifference to profitability and conventional filmgoing pleasures was part of the group's ethos.

On the set of *Wind from the East* Godard's dogmatic and methodical practice clashed with the rudderless shoot, not to mention with the commission for a 'political western'.[11] After a couple of months Godard was ready to abandon the project, and he sent an ultimatum to Gorin in Paris: 'either you come or I stop the film'.[12] Gorin showed up, Cohn-Bendit left, and after finishing the shooting Gorin and Godard returned to Paris where, far from the *bordel*, they edited the footage into a feature-length film that had begun, nominally at least, as a western.

An anti-cinema

The opening of *Wind from the East* announces the coming provocation. Two stationary shots of over three minutes each, separated briefly by footage of a cavalry officer (Volonté) pacing with a rifle, show a young couple lying handcuffed in the grass while non-diegetic voices speak on a soundtrack. One voice begins narrating the schematic story of a western town ('Dodge City'), a mine, a strike and an uprising. This narrative is swiftly interrupted by other voices labelling the description with terms that constitute the true outline of *Wind from the East*, and that will later appear on title cards to mark its successive sections: 'strike', 'the union delegate', 'active minorities', 'general assembly', 'repression', 'the active strike' and 'the police state'. As the image cuts to Volonté, a more assertive voice enters to dismiss the narrative about a western mine as a 'lie', and names the succession of terms, which characterise both the western-themed plot and the events of May '68 it allegorises, as only a 'stutter' towards a more examined critique.[13] The lack of action, the nearly still images, and the overlapping and often indistinct voiceovers withhold the establishment of character motivation and plot parameters expected in a conventional narrative film's exposition. The image remains decontextualised and disconnected from the voices, and its static nature contrasts with the flourishes of the film's spaghetti western contemporaries, which amplified suspense and dramatic tension through canted frames, extreme close-ups, spectacular violence, rapid editing and overwrought music.

In reading this sequence, James McBean imagines the thoughts of frustrated spectators:

> We are impatient to get into the movie, we are impatient to get on with plot. We wonder why the young couple are lying on the ground and why they are chained together. We wish they would at least regain consciousness enough to start talking to each other so that we could find out, from their dialogue, what is happening – that is, what is happening *to them*. As usual, in the cinema we don't ask ourselves what is happening *to us*. We don't ask ourselves why a film addresses *us* in a particular way. In fact, we rarely think of a film as addressing us, or, for that matter, anyone at all. We sit back and accept the tacit understanding that a film is a 'reflection of reality' captured in the mirror of that magical 'eye of God' that is a movie camera.[14]

However, the nearly still images and the commentary are already nudging these discomfited spectators towards awareness that something is, in fact, being done to them. The missing dialogue, music, character development and appeal to emotion expose the lack of (and desire for) the 'magic's' sleight of hand. So, too, does the disjoined relation of image to sound, as the layered commentary does not collude with the images to create a story or lend a compellingly cohesive 'reality' to the fiction; on the contrary, the voices question the 'eye of God' of the camera. The gesture emphasises the disjuncture of sound and image, emotions and identification with the characters are placed on hold, and, if this Brechtian ploy works, rational inquiry kicks in: what are we seeing and hearing?

The film that follows defies nutshell description. Throughout, the western-themed footage presents situations and characters in episodic vignettes (Volonté's cavalry rider, a well-dressed union representative and others in period clothing, an 'Indian'), with intermittent references to the storyline about a mine, a strike, the 'Nixon hotel' and a kidnapped boss. These fragments are discontinuous and decontextualised and, as the opening announced, there will be virtually none of the character motivation and causal development that hold conventional dramatic representation together. Even in shots with costumed actors it can be difficult to call the setting a diegesis; they are as much actors in costume and make-up on a shooting location as characters in a period piece, and it is not always clear when they are 'in character' and when it is documentary footage of people making a film. Much of the film has no explicit connection to the thinly sketched story. Alongside the schematic western-themed episodes, shots reveal the production personnel, cameras, the clapperboard, sound recording equipment and an *assemblée générale* where, off screen, Godard can be heard arguing while the cast and crew listen, interact and relax inattentively. The moving images of the film's first half are intercut with stills and the hand-lettered title cards, while the second half launches a critique of what has already been shown. Dialogue is discontinuous and relatively scant, and a significant part of the soundtrack consists of the emotionally flat voiceovers. Editing is often in abrupt cuts, actors wander in front of the lens and block the view, and Godard can be heard feeding the actors lines. These 'mistakes' (by conventional measures) put into relief other shots that, in contrast, present a carefully composed *mise-en-scène* and self-conscious camera movement. Near its end, the film shows repetitions of still images, scratched and fragmented footage, instructions on how to construct a home-made bomb and stretches of blank red or black screens. At the close, the film stock appears simply to run out. Meanwhile, over the disjointed image track, the voiceover intones the repetitive Marxist-Leninist critique of the filmmaking process.

The mash of images, title cards and layered speech quickly thickens to the point of opacity. Nonetheless, *Wind from the East* presents a highly structured and methodical analysis of filmmaking practice followed by a systematic auto-critique. Within minutes the project is plainly stated. Unbelievable things have been happening in the world. What to do? Make a film. How? What does it mean to be a *cinéaste militant* at this juncture in history? The questions are first asked of the schematic plotline and western-themed fragments: how can they constitute a political film? They've already been labelled a lie. The events that the strikes, kidnapped boss and union delegate allegorise are soon evoked without the filter of a western narrative, and by the time the 'general assembly' begins (the fourth 'chapter') the footage shows the film's crew and cast, not western characters in a fictive Dodge City, engaged in heated debate about how to move forward with film production in the wake of May '68.

The aim of making a political western is now openly driving a broader inquiry: namely, how to make any film politically, western or otherwise, without rethinking the fundamental relation of sound and image in cinema.[15] An image of Stalin and Mao on the familiar western trope of a 'wanted' poster sparks a contentious discussion over the adequacy of the image as a stable assertion of meaning. As communist leaders, Stalin and Mao are 'wanted' by the capitalist system. However, Stalin's face also references the 'revisionist' politics of the Brezhnev regime, which had recently invaded Czechoslovakia, and of the official French Communist Party, which aligned with Soviet policy and did not support the student/worker coalition during the May '68 strikes. The images on the poster cannot 'speak for themselves'. Their truth exists in the system of relations in which they become visible: the images must be situated in the class struggle with all its contradictions, and in the filmic text with its plural strands. For whom and against whom are the images being wielded? A task is taking shape: these relations must be identified and understood before a new practice may be theorised. The debate over the 'wanted' poster elicits an epigram that has become the signal assertion of the film: *Ce n'est pas une image juste, c'est juste une image* ('This is not a just [correct] image, it's just an image'). The aphorism is directed not only at the poster, but at all the images produced in *Wind from the East*. The indissociable arenas of politics and of cinematic image-making – the complicity with a bourgeois system of representation of even the so-called 'revolutionary' images of a political western, or of its film crew holding a general assembly – comes under systematic questioning.

The failure of existing practices to expose these relations launches a critique of known political cinemas, and even before the *assemblée générale* sequence Godard and Gorin begin slaughtering some sacred cows. Sergei Eisenstein is the first to be dispatched: despite the events it represents, *The Battleship Potemkin* was inspired by the same 'fascist' storytelling devices deployed by D. W. Griffith in Hollywood. Eisenstein is cast as a 'revisionist' betrayal of the early Soviet cinema exemplified by Dziga Vertov, after whom the group was named: where Eisenstein drew on Hollywood-style seduction, Dziga Vertov interrogated the relation between the cinematic image and the class struggle. In turn, Dziga Vertov is dismissed for *Eleventh Year*, a celebration of Stalin's achievements that in *Wind from the East* is labelled the 'death of the Revolutionary film'. The criticism is then directed at contemporary 'White Christians' from the developed world whose cameras convey purportedly true stories about African populations. Claims to a you-are-there documentary truth in a neo-realist or a *cinéma-vérité* mode are suspect for not rising out of an emotionally charged perception of events into a rational and theoretical understanding: the same images of strikes, rebellion or squalid conditions might, after all, also appear on state-run television news, or in the pages of *Paris-Match* or *Newsweek*. Without adequate examination they remain 'bourgeois sociology'.[16] The critique also targets the efforts of 'third cinema' filmmakers from outside Europe and America. Brazilian director Glauber Rocha appears in the film, standing at a crossroads. A woman approaches and asks him which is the way to political cinema; he offers two alternatives, but they are cryptic and provide scant discernment.[17] She begins to follow one of the paths, but changes her mind and heads off through the grass: Godard would reproach Rocha's spontaneity and mysticism, as well as a 'producer's mentality' that underlies a wish to establish, rather than undo, a Brazilian cinema.[18] Underground cinema and its celebration of drugs and sex is summarily dismissed as 'a cinema for which nothing is taboo, except the class struggle'.[19] *Wind from the East* reserves especially barbed contempt for the cinemas sanctioned by Soviet leaders: 'Brezhnev-Mosfilm says it is attacking Nixon-Paramount, but, in fact, it supports it.'[20] Soviet socialist realism emblematises how a 'revisionist' filmmaking practice, even in a political mode, merely cuts different shapes from the same stuff as Hollywood film, television and, among other manifestations of bourgeois culture targeted in the film, Monet's paintings and the writings of Marcel Proust. This culture, its consciousness, and the cinemas it fosters, even when they are oppositional, must be distanced, negated and stripped to zero.

Wind from the East is scorched-earth cinema, and left few spectators indifferent. The film struck some as artless, preachy, elitist and, in a widely repeated criticism, excruciatingly boring. During its limited release in the United States, disappointed critics wrote that it is 'impossible to sit through' and 'it's strictly home movie time'.[21] After asking 'how, one wonders, can he [Godard] hope to change the world by risking putting it to sleep?' the *L.A. Times* critic calls the film 'a hate letter' to cinema.[22] In the *New York Times* Vincent Canby finds the dialectical critique intriguing, but concludes that 'the content, however, is almost pure junk'.[23] Joan Mellen takes Godard to task for the 'mechanical' and 'stubborn reassertion of the rightness of his conception', pointing out the irony of an auto-critique that is uncritical of the Maoist discourse it relentlessly intones, or the situation on the ground in China under the cultural revolution.[24] She notes a 'pathetically inadequate imagery' and condemns Godard's layering of voices over blank screens as 'abandoning the pretense of making a film at all'.[25] Glauber Rocha's own remarks further raise the question of whether *Wind from the East* constitutes a 'film': he recounts attending a screening for the producers who, dismayed and in a panic (sobbing, praying), consider suing Godard for not delivering a 'film' by existing understandings of the term. A more pointed thrust of Rocha's criticism derives from the fact that the call for a *fin du cinéma* looks starkly different from the perspective of a filmmaker working in a country where there is not yet a cinema to destroy, only imitations of Hollywood or of European art cinema auteurs like Godard. Rocha reserves choice words for Godard's show of contempt for capitalist representation while, at the same time, he spends the funds from Fiat and Rizzoli that his fame and prior success helped to procure:

> There he is, calling the merry May leftist club for help, using production money to pay for a nice holiday in Sicily, leaving Cohn-Bendit and his hysterical Mao-Spontec discussions behind and rushing to Paris to show some excerpts of his film on Czechoslovakia [*Pravda*], coming back to Rome out of breath to declare that he doesn't want to make money with the film, criticising me of having a producer's mentality. Then he asks me to help him destroy cinema.[26]

He concludes: 'I have seen from up close the corpse of Godard, having committed suicide, up there on the screen, projected in 16mm. It was the dead image of colonisation.'[27]

The charges of boredom find justification in the film's didacticism, which, as in the schoolroom, has other purposes than to entertain.[28] The charge of colonialist privilege also resonates with critiques of 'zero degree' approaches to revolutionary cultural production: in literary and anthropological studies of the 1960s, structuralism was evacuating the ideological myth of 'man' at the very moment when, as colonial empires were breaking up, 'people in struggle, oblivious to the embarrassment of structuralists, seemed to fight all the harder to be recognised as men'.[29] Nevertheless, the charges of a 'hate letter to cinema', of not producing a 'film' at all, or even of auteurist 'suicide' do not squarely land their punch, for one may easily imagine Godard and Gorin disarming these indictments with an unapologetic 'precisely!' *Wind from the East* is, in fact, a diatribe against cinema (as it exists), does not resemble a film (by 'Hollywood-Mosfilm' measures) and, alongside other modes of filmmaking, autopsies the cinema that earned Godard fame as an auteur-genius.

Where some critics saw an artless and pleasureless screed, others hailed *Wind from the East* as an emblematic alternative to the mode of filmmaking that dominated cinema from its earliest years.[30] In an influential article published after the film's American screenings, Peter Wollen enumerates, point by point, how the film delivers a decisive repudiation of the bourgeois system of representation, 'slice of life' realism, and the *image juste*.'[31] Situating *Wind from the East* under the sign of Brecht, Wollen names it 'a pioneering film, an avant-garde film, an extremely important film', and the exemplar of a counter-cinema whose purpose is 'writing in images, rather than representing the world.'[32] In the pages of the *Cahiers du cinéma* the same year, *Wind from the East* is named 'the most accomplished film' in Gorin's and Godard's collaboration,[33] and in a riposte to Rocha's elegiac criticism Marc Cerisuelo later asserts that 'the real "creative suicide" for Godard would have been *not to work with Gorin*'.[34] An irony nonetheless hovers over this praise: among the very few who saw this paradigmatic work of 'counter-cinema', a significant quotient rejected it as a crushing bore. Wollen concedes that Godard, however much he owed to Brecht, disregarded a prime tenet, namely, that the experience at the theatre must first and foremost be fun.[35] Although singular and pivotal in theory, *Wind from the East* remained widely unwatched, and those who saw it often deemed it unwatchable.

In the polarised reception of *Wind from the East* there is consensus on one point: a spaghetti-style western was not the outcome. The narrative about a Dodge City mine strike lies in shards from the opening sequence, and the realisation of a political western is framed not as a goal but as a conundrum through which to launch a sweeping critique and theorisation of cinema practice. The voiceover is candid: 'the principal task is the theory', not to tell a story about the old West.

The western prism

The western nonetheless remains richly invoked in *Wind from the East*. Its enunciation is fragmented, however, and refracts into plural national referents. At its most explicit, the western acts as the synecdoche for the American-dominated cinema with which Gorin and Godard seek a decisive break. In the second part of the film, the voiceover directly denounces the genre in the castigation of 'Brezhnev-Mosfilm' as the 'lackey' of 'Nixon-Paramount': 'You forget that this boss has been demanding the same film from you for fifty years. You forget that this film has a name – the western – and that it is not by chance.'[36] The *Cahiers du cinéma*, in its 1972 presentation of the Dziga-Vertov group, characterises the film's evocation of the western as the 'emblem and structure of the cinema practiced and distributed by imperialism' and a 'symbol of dominant ideology in cinematographic practice'.[37] For both the filmmakers and critics the western acts as shorthand for the 'bourgeois mode of representation' and the 'dream in which you have to pay to enter'.

To illustrate this dream's power, Godard and Gorin offer a taste of the heretofore withheld Hollywood magic. In an exceptional sequence, sounds and images conventionally collude as vigorous western-style music, complete with a male chorus, accompanies a shot of Volonté's cavalry officer, on horseback, pulling his 'Indian' captive with a rope. Christopher Frayling characterises the sequence as 'filmed in a stylised way which is intended to draw attention to the form which such a scene would normally take, if the director wanted the audience to consider the scene as "realistic" [...] to identify emotionally with the oppressed'.[38] However, the artifice of this integrated cinematic moment, which would normally be obscured by the pall of narrative suspense and emotional involvement, is foregrounded and held to scrutiny as the voiceover continues: 'This dream, Hollywood makes you believe it is real, that it is more real than nature. Hollywood. Hollywood makes believe.'[39] The voiceover enumerates how familiar western tropes act as vehicles for the illusion:

> Hollywood makes believe that this reflection of a horse is really a horse and that this reflection of a horse is even more real than a horse, which it not even is. Hollywood makes believe that this movie Indian is more real than an Indian and that on the horse the extra is more real than a Union soldier. This extra is called an actor.

This actor is called a character. The adventures of these characters are called a film and the making of this film is called *mise en scène*.⁴⁰

This cinema promises an *image juste* even as it rehashes the hackneyed semantics of a genre whose Hollywood manifestation, by 1969, was widely deemed exhausted and outdated. Indeed, the western imagery's oversaturated familiarity allows it efficiently to emblematise the unexamined illusion of reality. Obviously contrived but 'more real than nature': the moment exposes the triumph of fabricated verisimilitude over truth that has gripped not only cinema but much western dramatic representation since Aristotle theorised *mimesis* as an imitation of life that is superior, dramatically speaking, to life itself. The 'American cinema par excellence' acts once again as the paradigm of Hollywood and its mode of representation.

However, the butt of the film's criticism is not solely the western, nor only the American cinema it emblematises. The voiceover continues: 'Every year Hollywood decorates and rewards the best directors in the entire world, and there you are. The imperialist representation of reality

Figure 10.1 'I am General Motors!'

passes for reality itself.'[41] A key term in this assertion is 'the whole world': the voiceover names the festivals of Leipzig, Moscow and Pesaro where alternatives to Hollywood production are shown, hailed and given awards. Each, however, represents a cinema already repudiated in *Wind from the East* as inadequate and 'revisionist'. The sequence exposes the fallacy of an oppositional cinematic practice within the 'bourgeois mode of representation'. As he is pulled, the 'Indian' identifies himself in English as a member of various oppressed groups in the contemporary world: 'I am Black! I am Indian! I am Vietnamese! I am Peruvian! I am Czechoslovakian!' To each Volonté answers the same: '*Io sono* [I am] General Motors!' Multiple geo-political conflicts may be allegorised in this image of a subaltern oppressed by an armed avatar of American capitalism, but they are merely a substitution of terms within an unshaken system of representation: it's the same film, over and over. Whether the hero is the nation-building cavalry officer or his subaltern captive, whether produced by Hollywood or Mosfilm, this mode of cinema perpetuates the preponderance of 'American cinema everywhere'.

The western genre has no proprietary hold on Hollywood's weaponised dream, and a second sequence in *Wind from the East* illustrates the seductive power of Hollywood-style imagery more generally. The film cuts to a film crew setting up a shoot, while the voiceover intones: 'He's a character from a western, from a psychological drama, from a police film or from a historical picture, it doesn't matter, in short, he's always a seducer.'[42] In the carefully framed shot that results, a young man looks into the camera and describes (in Italian, which the voiceover translates into French) the movie theatre into which he ostensibly is peering. He expresses his wish to have sex with a spectator, inviting her into his idealised world. As he seduces his audience, so, too, does the moving image as the camera tracks back to reveal a lush landscape surrounding a waterfall that spills into a lake; actors dive off a cliff, timed precisely to be framed in this long take. The smooth *mise-en-scène* is swiftly interrupted by the voiceover, which reminds the viewer that 'this dream at the same time for Hollywood is a weapon'.[43] The seduction and 'magic' are also a subjugation and a lie, whatever the genre. There is nothing specifically 'western' about this sequence, which represents more generally the 'bourgeois screen'.

Nonetheless, although familiar tropes of the western genre in *Wind from the East* are just images alongside others, they are not just any images. '*Ce n'est pas par hasard*': it is not by chance that this genre was chosen. The western's longevity, familiarity and strong assertion of American dominance, both within its narratives and in its mode of production, positions the genre to serve as the emblematic expression of both Hollywood and, more broadly, of cinema in general. The genre also lends force to the implication of Godard's prior activities as a critic and filmmaker. Despite emphatic professions of distaste, Godard's contributions to the *Cahiers du cinéma* in the late 1950s present unabashed admiration for westerns directed by Anthony Mann, Samuel Fuller and Nicholas Ray. These films inform his vision of what cinema could (or should) be as he was preparing to make his first films. He was so taken with Mann's *Man of the West* that he dubbed the western 'cinema's most cinematographic genre', and he would soon quote gestures from the favoured westerns in *Breathless*: Jean Seberg's gaze through a rolled poster reproduces the shot he admired in his review of Fuller's *Forty Guns*,[44] Belmondo's final stumble closely resembles the shots of *Man of the West* that Godard singled out in his account (Michel Marie calls it a 'magnificent rewriting' of Mann's sequence)[45] and Michel Poiccard's character aligns with Godard's description of the title role of Ray's *The True Story of Jesse James*.[46]

'Cinema's most cinematographic genre' provides *Wind from the East* with a superlative vehicle for sharpening the contrast between existing cinematic practices and the new ones being demanded. Consider, for example, how the framing of the western genre as the signature emblem of 'Hollywood-Mosfilm' constitutes a rejection of the films Godard and others had earlier praised, theorised and in some cases imitated. In a 1969 interview given before *Wind from the East* was completed, Godard corrects his prior interest in the genre: 'I'm always amazed that so many of the militants are so fond of westerns, which I hate. They are not bothered by the fact that it's a fascist form. They don't care. They enjoy it.'[47] The choice of the western in *Wind from the East* lends the strike on 'Nixon-Paramount' a force that a genre less prolific, less identified with Hollywood and less admired by the earlier Godard would not similarly deliver.

In addition to the assault on Hollywood, references to the western in an Italian mode trace a second vector for critique. In 1969 Hollywood could no longer claim to be the undisputed centre of western film production, and the positioning of the genre in *Wind from the East* also indexes Italian production in multiple modalities. Filmed in Italy with Italian funding, the western-themed sequences in the film include a multinational and multilingual cast who occasionally speak in Italian, and in Volonté they feature a foremost star of the spaghetti cycle.[48] The political allegory embedded in the Dodge City plotline further resonates with the Italian releases that invest left-leaning politics into the western frame. These films frequently deploy imagery similar to, for example, the sequence with the white-clad captive, who evokes less Hollywood's befeathered 'Indians' than similarly dressed (and mistreated) Central American insurgent figures in a number of Italian westerns.[49]

The positioning of *Wind from the East* in relation to the Italian westerns is contested. Frayling and Fisher include a discussion of *Wind from the East* in their studies on the spaghetti cycle, with divergent conclusions. Frayling situates the 'fallacious application' of the western genre, even in a spaghetti mode, squarely in the sights of the film's broader critique. He quotes Godard: 'Hollywood is more powerful than ever before: they don't even need to make movies themselves anymore, they have found slaves everywhere to make the movies they want'; political allegories notwithstanding, the Italian spaghetti westerns 'epitomise this process'.[50] Fisher, on the other hand, situates *Wind from the East* on a continuum with the more openly political Italian films and reads *Wind from the East* as a 'divergent', not oppositional, mode of leftist cinema: gestures in the Italian westerns that more subtly preclude 'passive acceptance of the realist illusion' are taken to an 'erudite extreme' by Godard, who had licence to work with indifference to the demands of producers and the marketplace.[51] However, the continuum argument is qualified by a concession that many spectators might view a Sollima or Damiani film no differently from less political contemporaries, with which they share a mode of representation that *Wind from the East* categorically thwarts.[52] Furthermore, the political parables in the Italian films are delivered in narrative structures, charted in detail by Frayling and Fisher alike, with causal chains of events, coherent characters, and beginnings, middles and ends: variations on Hollywood's playbook whose systematic undoing is foregrounded in *Wind from the East*.

Just an image

Wind from the East references the American and Italian westerns roundly to reject them. However, there is a third national referent enunciated in the film, and the critical edge honed by its meeting with the western genre cuts on a different angle. Though no more decisively a French film than a western, *Wind from the East* indexes a French referent in multiple registers. Key participants of the production team are French, as are many of the players in the film.⁵³ Although the film is multilingual, the spoken language is primarily French, which dominates especially in the register of the voiceovers: the commentary, for example, addresses a French-speaking spectator specifically when it translates Italian dialogue into French (the inverse is not the case).

More generally, *Wind from the East* is explicitly framed as a response to May '68. During the *assemblée générale* sequence, the voiceover invokes a collective 'we' as participants in the events who are seeking an adequate cinematic practice in their wake:

> It was about discussing something we experienced in May '68. In the factories, in the universities, in the offices, in the neighbourhood meetings, comrades gathered and formed groups. In the confusion of the discussions they nonetheless progressed. How, today, can we account for this? How can we find truth in this confused progress? And what is the true way to find it? Very quickly a number of comrades took up filmmaking [...]⁵⁴

Certainly, France had no monopoly on insurgency and unrest in the late 1960s and to a degree the references to uprisings are generalisable to a broader political context, notably contemporaneous events in Italy.⁵⁵ On the set, 'we' includes a significant cohort of Italians, and there are references to Italian society in the film. Prague, Madrid and other sites of protests are also listed. However, they garner little more than a mention, while the events in France are invoked at length and in precise detail.⁵⁶ The *assemblée générale* sequence, for example, is followed immediately by the lengthy reading, in French, of an exchange of letters between a worker in a French factory during the May strikes and a supporter outside. The letters, like numerous other passages in the film, are replete with specific references to the French uprising. Punctuating the images and the soundtrack, the appearances of Wiezamsky and Cohn-Bendit, as well as the sound of Godard's voice, locate visible participants from the events on the streets of Paris in the filmic text itself. The voiceover then takes up the account, listing precise dates, places and events: the Citroën and Peugeot factories, the CGT labour union, the Sorbonne, the Odéon theater, the occupation of the National Institute of Astronomy and Geophysics on Saturday the 17th, and the closing of the Lycée Bergson in Paris on Friday the 23rd, among others.

The positioning of Cohn-Bendit in the *assemblée générale* footage further binds the film's theorisation of a new cinematic practice to the events in France. The voiceover identifies the purpose of the meeting as

> asking the question of our time, the question of the history of imperialism, the question of the history of revisionism. And to ask the question about the real history of revisionism, means truly asking what we have agreed to call the 'Stalin question', that is to say, no longer to get stuck over the image of Stalin.[57]

In place of the 'wanted' poster of Stalin, the image that accompanies this assertion shows instead the leader of the Nanterre student movement reclining in the grass, grinning and waving at the camera. This gesture effectively displaces ('unsticks') the film's questioning critique from the image of Stalin and trains it instead onto the same smiling face that, just a few months prior, had itself been printed on a poster and was plastered on the walls of Paris streets; this widely circulating image of a smiling Cohn-Bendit confronting a helmeted police officer became 'one of the most iconic images associated with May 1968'.[58] The reproduction of this image, and its relation to language, were publicly contested in a debate that anticipates the discussion at the *assemblée générale* shown in the film. The artists who printed the poster initially used the caption 'We are all German Jews', a reference to the anti-Semitic denunciation of Cohn-Bendit as 'Jewish and German' in the pages of the right-wing *Minute*, and also to the French Communist Party leader Georges Marchais' xenophobic remarks the following day. However, the wording was amended to the less pointed 'We are all undesirables', effectively soft-pedalling the anti-Semitism and the complicity between the right and left establishments exposed in the first caption.[59] For whom and against whom is this image being shown? How does its meaning emerge from a relation to language? The face of the exiled student leader, no less than Stalin's, is 'just an image' and begs examination of its position in the contradictions of May 1968 in Paris, and in relation to the language and other images in the film being made in the aftermath. At this precise juncture in *Wind from the East*, the 'stuttering' efforts to produce a political western, including the discussion among the cast and crew about how to proceed, are falling subject to the film's more systematic critique. The poster boy of May '68 appears as the debate over the cinematic image, examined by the voiceover, is steering cinematic

Figure 10.2 Just an image: Cohn-Bendit at the *assemblée générale*.

practice away from a spoof western about Dodge City and towards Cohn-Bendit's departure from the project.

Wind from the East opens an arena where enunciations of 'French' and 'western' meet, and the energies released by this encounter push in multiple directions. On the one hand, the critique of the western as a dominant 'bourgeois' mode of cinema, in both its Hollywood and Italian modes, would seem generalisable to any French declension of the genre. Consider the films examined in the previous chapters of this study: if Godard's own prior work is implicated along with Rocha's *Antonio das mortes* and other political cinemas, wouldn't the critique plainly attain the serials, star vehicles, comedies and musicals that are intentionally conceived as commercial entertainment produced within the conventions of an established industry? Would these films not exemplify the servility of Nixon-Paramount's acolytes, thereby sharing the metaphor with the 'slavish' imitations bemoaned by critics who characterise French westerns as deficient knock-offs of American production? Whether French, Italian or otherwise, the emblematic 'fascist' genre of the western would, from this perspective, seem to represent the 'American cinema everywhere' from which a post-68 practice must be liberated.

However, *Wind from the East* also sharpens its critical edge by distancing the French assertion from the emblematic genre. Positioned as a perspective liberated by the events of May '68, the voiceover's commentary, delivered in French, is distinct from the horses, riders, 'Indians', wanted poster and other semantic remnants of westernness on which it works its critique. The consistently French commentary of the prosecuting voiceover contrasts with the speech in the western-themed footage and other episodic vignettes, which may be in Italian and English. The western-themed images and the synchronised speech are repeatedly judged inadequate on their own, while the French voiceover systematically intones the analysis, the auto-critique and the theorisation of a new practice. Indeed, towards the end of the film the images themselves degrade and disappear: in the reprise of the *assemblée générale* sequence the footage is mutilated, the diegetic discussion is cacophonous, and the images are intercut with the blank red screens over which the unrelenting voiceover delivers a decisive rejection of efforts at 'auto-gestion' and worker-led production. The opposition between the voiceover's didactic clarity and the muddled debates maps onto the constitutive antagonism that structures the film: on the one hand a hegemonic 'bourgeois mode of representation' with global dominance that includes 'revisionist' efforts (a political spaghetti-style western, for example), and on the other an original theorisation in the making that leads cinematic practice far from anything that could be called a western or, for some, even a film.

There is therefore a vantage from which the enunciation of the genre positioned as French lends dimension and force to the methodical evisceration of existing cinema practice. In its Hollywood and Italian iterations the western readily emblematises the seductive cinema that promises a 'just image' and that Godard and Gorin reject, but when has the meeting of French and western ever credibly acceded to the *image juste*? Unlike the American and Italian expressions of the genre, the associated enunciation of a French referent and the western genre has no comparable claim to seductive familiarity. On the contrary, since the silent era, French westerns have exposed, foundered on, and at times exploited the 'un-justness' in this conjunction of a film genre and a national referent. The meeting of 'French' and 'western' has persistently presented what Wollen identifies as key counter-cinematic devices operative in *Wind from the East*: disjuncture over synthesis, openness over closure, unsteadiness over stability and alienation over familiarity. Julia Lesage has submitted that the use of a female voice to intone the Marxist-Leninist critique, a discourse dominated in the post-1968 discussions by men, enacts a Brechtian distancing of the opening images: 'The directors, in adding the post-sync sound tract, may just have been banking on the absence of women in leadership positions in radical organizations, so that the sound of women's voices giving the radical rap was an estrangement effect.'[60] It is not only the voice's gender, however, that unseats the familiarity of the images. The assertive voice also delivers its critique in French, and explicitly speaks for a collective 'we' who experienced the events in France the previous May and who are seeking a post-1968 cinematic practice in the aftermath. The dissonance between the western genre and a critical perspective positioned as French amplifies the dialogic encounter of cinema's competing elements staged in the film, and from the first frames adds relief to the estrangement of the cinema that the western emblematises.

Nonetheless, *Wind from the East* remains a fundamentally reactive film. After observing the implementation of alienating tropes and asserting their importance, Wollen cautions that '[Godard] is mistaken if he thinks that such a counter-cinema can have an absolute existence. It can only exist in relation to the rest of cinema', in other words, in relation to what it seeks to destroy. Dismantling existing cinema to its zero degree – revealing it to be 'just an image' – remains a primary purpose, and a constitutive antagonism towards existing cinema thwarts liberation from the status quo to which this critique remains tethered. Zero-degrees of representation, Roland Barthes warned, are both a utopia and, insofar as they are unattainable, a tragedy. *Wind from the East* does not end in the triumph of a new cinema over the old, or *a fortiori* of French over western. Instead, the spectators are left with a ticking explosive device (complete with instructions on how to make their own), the images degrade and disappear, and the film runs out. They are left with neither a 'just image' nor 'just an image', but with no image at all.

The 'internationalisation' of the western in the 1960s did not relax or resolve the tensions that attend French western films; *Cemetery Without Crosses* and *Wind from the East*, each in its way, put these tensions on display. The bid for greater integration in the first film collided with the aftermath of a watershed event in French political and cultural history, and the film met middling critical and commercial success: well made, perhaps, but out of step with its historical moment. In the second film, an unfamiliar encounter of 'French' and 'western' lends dimension to the film's systematic interrogation of the cinematic image from a position distinct from the critique of both Hollywood and Italian iterations of the genre. For both films, the term 'baguette western' is misleading insofar as it implies the exploitable conformity of a genre or cycle, aligned with a stable assertion of a national cinema. Each stages the encounter of multiple cinematic modes and national referents, and each does so in a singular manner. Multivalence, variegation and singularity are not the stuff that classificatory regimes are made of, be they film genres or national cinemas. The French western fails to present a distinct, recognisable and generalisable savour – baguette, camembert or otherwise – and once again stages the failure of this conjunction to come into focus as the *image juste* of a recognisable corpus. With or without intention, it exposes instead the labours of imagination that such recognition would demand.

Notes

1. 'C'était après mai, j'étais en Italie, il y avait Bertolucci et je vois son producteur, qui me dit: *"Tu veux pas faire un film?"* Ils se disaient: *"On va faire un film avec Cohn-Bendit, ça va rapporter."* Les gens sont simples d'esprit, parfois.' Thierry Lounas and Jean Narboni, 'Cohn-Bendit: Godard, Bardot, & moi', *Sofilm* (19 June 2017), no page number. Available at <https://sofilm.fr/cohn-bendit-godard-bardot-moi> (accessed 10 August 2021).
2. Quoted in Glauber Rocha, 'Godard's Latest Scandal', trans. Stoffel Debuysere, *Diagonal Thoughts*. Available at <https://www.diagonalthoughts.com/?p=2020> (accessed 10 August 2021).
3. 'On était dans un délire collectif et je n'ai pas pu me sortir de ce délire pour dire à Godard : 'Bon. . . Maintenant, qu'ils aillent tous à la plage, et nous, on réfléchit au film.' Quoted in Thierry Lounas and Jean Narboni, 'Cohn-Bendit: Godard, Bardot, & moi'.
4. See Chapter 7.
5. Richard Brody, *Everything is Cinema: The Working Life of Jean-Luc Godard* (New York: Picador, 2009), 347. Cohn-Bendit would later call the project 'a completely wacky story' (*'une histoire complètement dingue'*) and 'a befuddling idea' (*'une idée abracadabrante'*). Daniel Cohn-Bendit, 'Mon ami Godard', *Le Monde*, 27 December 2010. Available at <https://www.lemonde.fr/idees/article/2010/12/25/mon-ami-godard_1457343_3232.html> (accessed 10 August 2021).
6. Jean-Pierre Léaud and Juliet Berto deploy an emblematic 'estrangement' effect of Brecht's practice when they look into the camera and say 'he said' or 'she said' after delivering their character's lines.
7. Marc Cerisuelo, 'Jean-Luc, Community, and Communication', in *A Companion to Jean-Luc Godard*, ed. Tom Conley and T. Jefferson Kline (Malden and Oxford, 2014), 298.
8. Jean-Luc Godard and Fernando Solanas, 'Godard by Solanas. Solanas by Godard', *Cinema Comparat/ive Cinema* 4, no. 9 (2016): 16. On the divergent interpretations of how this dust did eventually settle, see Kirsten Ross, *May '68 and its Afterlives* (Chicago: University of Chicago Press, 2002).

9. Godard's experimentation unfolded with the events of May 1968, as he (alongside Alain Resnais, Chris Marker and others) made 'cinétracts' in the streets of Paris during the uprising. In 1967 Marker's *Service de lancement des oeuvres nouvelles* (SLON) filmed the strikes at the Rhodiaceta factory in Besançon that anticipated the events of May '68. On Marker's projects, and how Godard's post-1968 cinema may be understood as both an extension and a critique of them, see Trevor Stark, 'Cinema in the Hands of the People: Chris Marker, the Medvedkin Group, and the Potential of Militant Film', *October* 139 (winter 2021): 117–50.
10. Godard and Solanas, 17.
11. A similar tension is frequently invoked to characterise two strains of the May '68 student movement: the free-love anarchists vs. the orthodox, theoretically informed Maoists. Kristen Ross defines, and challenges, the polarised stereotypes of the 'Maoist practicing militant discipline' and the 'purely hedonist anarcho-libertarian "thrill seeker"'. Ross, *May '68*, 99.
12. Quoted in Brody, *Everything is Cinema*, 347.
13. The narration references '*les voix qui bégaient*'. The cited text of *Le Vent d'est* is drawn from the scenario reprinted in the *Cahiers du cinéma* 240 (July–August 1972): 31–50. Available at <https://archive.org/stream/CahiersDuCinma/Cahiers%20du%20Cin%C3%A9ma/240_djvu.txt> (accessed 7 July 2023). The translations of this script are the author's.
14. James Roy McBean, *Film and Revolution* (Bloomington: Indiana University Press, 1975). Online edition. Available at <https://muse.jhu.edu/pub/3/oa_monograph/chapter/2964075> (accessed 11 September 2021).
15. The Dziga Vertov group's *Pravda*, a meditation on the truth in the cinematic image filmed in Czechoslovakia after the 1968 uprising, was being edited by Godard and Gorin during the production of *Wind from the East*.
16. Gillo Pontecorvo is named, and his 1966 *Bataille d'Algers* is implicitly targeted as 'imperialism creeping back via the camera'. Also implied is Chris Marker's 'credulous faith in cinema as a putatively unmediated technique that could simply be transferred from the bourgeoisie to the working class'. Stark, 'Cinema in the Hands of the People', 146.
17. Cerisuelo characterises Rocha's advice as the utterance of a filmmaker who is 'quite simply unable to describe the future for political film'. Marc Cerisuelo, 'Jean-Luc, Community, and Communication', 308.
18. Quoted in McBean, *Film and Revolution*. The litany of rejections in *Wind from the East* may be supplemented by filmmakers Godard names elsewhere: Fellini, Antonioni, Dreyer, Pasolini, Bergman and, among others, himself for making films 'for the ruling class' (albeit of high quality). See his interview with Fernando Solanas 'Godard by Solanas, Solanas by Godard', *Cinema Comparat/ive Cinema*, 4, no. 9 (2016): 17.
19. 'un cinéma pour qui rien n'est tabou, sauf la lutte des classes'.
20. 'BREJNEV-MOSSFILM dit qu'il attaque NIXON-PARAMOUNT, mais, dans les faits, il lui vient en aide.'
21. Gary Arnold, 'Godard's "East Wind"', *The Washington Post*, 10 November 1970, D 7.
22. Kevin Thomas, 'Godard's "Wind" Opens Run', *The Los Angeles Times*, 25 February 1972, H 13.
23. Vincent Canby, 'Godard Film in Festival: "Wind from the East" in Alice Tully Hall', *New York Times*, 12 September 1970, 31.

24. Serge Daney develops this line of critique in his assessment of the Dziga-Vertov group's rehearsal of unquestioned discourse that, effectively, bullies the spectator: 'There is still a big unknown in his [Godard's] pedagogy, the nature of the relationship that he upholds with the "good" discourses (those that he defends) is undecidable [...] not a discourse in power but a discourse that has power: violent, assertive, already constituted, provocative.' ['Il y a toujours une grande inconnue dans sa pédagogie, c'est que la nature du rapport qu'il entretient avec ses "bons" discours (ceux qu'il défend) est indécidable [...] pas un discours au pouvoir mais c'est un discours qui a *du* pouvoir: violent, assertif, déjà constitué.'] Serge Daney, 'Le thérrorisé: (pédagogie godardienne)', *Cahiers du cinéma* 262–3 (January 1976): 34.
25. Joan Mellen, 'Wind from the East', *Film Comment* 7, no. 3 (Fall 1971): 66.
26. Glauber Rocha, 'Godard's Latest Scandal'. Unlike Godard's repudiation of existing cinemas, Rocha's evocation of the Western genre in *Antonio das mortes* has been read as a 'way to recover the revolutionary potential of the western in a global context'. Chelsea Wessels, 'A Third Western(?): Genre and the Popular/Political in Latin America', *Frames* 4 (January 2013). Available at <https://framescinemajournal.com/article/a-third-western-genre-and-the-popularpolitical-in-latin-america> (accessed 20 March 2022).
27. Rocha, 'Godard's Latest Scandal', Ibid.
28. See, again, Daney, 'Le thérrorisé'. This didactic format distinguishes *Wind from the East* from two other post-1968 films that deploy the Western in a more playful mode. *A Girl is a Gun* (1971), made on a shoestring budget by Luc Moullet, presents an absurdist spoof of Western tropes. Marco Ferreri's *Touche pas la femme blanche!* (1974) offers, perhaps, a glimpse of what *Wind from the East* might have looked like if Cohn-Bendit's initial idea were followed, had not footage of the destruction of the old market district of Les Halles lent this heavy-handed farce a poignant documentary dimension (Ferreri also participated in filming *Wind from the East*). Moullet's film was not initially distributed in French (it was later released in a dubbed English-language version), and Ferreri's was a box-office bomb despite the participation of Marcello Mastroianni, Michel Piccoli, Catherine Deneuve and Serge Reggiani.
29. Kristin Ross, *Fast Cars, Clean Bodies*, 163.
30. The two assessments are not mutually exclusive. After judging it 'self-indulgent to the point of being masturbatory and politically jejune', Julia Lesage continues: 'In terms of the film's immediate political usefulness as an organizing tool, I still consider the above evaluation valid. But I've discovered there is much more to be said, not so much about the film in and of itself, but the film in the context of the issues it raises. *Wind from the East* is a remarkable film.' Julia Lesage, 'Godard and Gorin's *Wind from the East*: Looking at a Film Politically', *Jump Cut* 4 (1974): online version, no page number. Available at <https://www.ejumpcut.org/archive/onlinessays/JC04folder/WindfromEast.html> (accessed 10 August 2022).
31. Peter Wollen, 'Godard and Counter-Cinema: Vent d'Est', *AfterImage* 4 (Autumn 1972): 6–17.
32. Ibid., 10. 'Writing' is a charged word. In *Writing Degree Zero* (1953) Roland Barthes (one of the leading advocates of Brecht in France) exposed literature as a mode of 'writing' (*écriture*) generated by a bourgeois class structure, and envisioned its end. One could draw an analogy with Godard's critique of 'cinema' as a class-based mode of writing with images – but cautiously: the two figures' response to 1968 led in opposite directions. Barthes eschewed militant dogmatism as 'hysteria' and by 1969

was already exploring a textual hedonism that would culminate in *The Pleasure of the Text* (1973).
33. 'le film le plus abouti'. 'Le Groupe Dziga Vertov', *Cahiers du cinéma* 238–9 (May–June 1972): 38.
34. Cerisuelo, too, calls the film a '"watershed" in film production: in its content, its form, but especially [...] in a *new set of relationships* between the film and the spectator, between image and sound, and between the very form and content of the work'. Marc Cerisuelo,' Jean-Luc, Community, and Communication', in Conley and Kline, *A Companion*, 303.
35. '[theatre] needs no other passport than fun, but this it has got to have. We should not by any means be giving it a higher status if we were to turn it e.g. into a purveyor of morality; it would on the contrary run the risk of being debased, and this would occur at once if it failed to make its moral lesson enjoyable [...] Nothing needs less justification than pleasure.' Bertolt Brecht, 'A Short Organum for the Theatre', in *Brecht on Theatre*, trans. John Willett (New York: Hill & Wang, 1964), 180–1.
36. 'Tu oublies que ce patron te commande depuis 50 ans le même film, tu oublies que ce film a un nom, le western, et que ce n'est pas par hasard.'
37. 'emblème et structure du cinéma pratiqué et diffusé par l'impérialisme'; 'symbole de l'idéologie dominante dans la pratique cinématographique'.
38. Frayling, *Spaghetti Westerns*, 229.
39. 'ce rêve Hollywood fait croire qu'il est réel, est plus vrai que nature, Hollywood, Hollywood fait croire'.
40. 'Hollywood fait croire d'abord que ce reflet du cheval est un cheval, et ensuite que ce reflet du cheval est encore plus vrai qu'un cheval. Ce qu'il n'est même pas. Hollywood fait croire que cet indien de cinéma est plus vrai qu'un indien et que sur le cheval le figurant est plus vrai qu'un soldat nordiste. On appelle ce figurant un acteur. Cet acteur on l'appelle un personnage, et les aventures de ces personnages, on les appelle un film, et la fabrication du film on l'appelle mise en scène.'
41. 'Chaque année, Hollywood décore et récompense des meilleurs metteurs en scène du monde entier. Le tour est joué, l'idée impérialiste du réel passe pour la réalité elle-même.'
42. C'est un personnage de Western, de drame psychologique, de film policier ou de film historique, peu importe, enfin c'est toujours un séducteur.'
43. 'ce rêve en même temps pour Hollywood c'est une arme'.
44. 'Eve sells rifles. Gene aims one at her for fun. The camera takes his place and Eve is seen through the rifle's barrel. Track forward until the opening of the barrel frames her in a close up. Next shot: she and he are kissing.' ('Eve vend des fusils. Gene la vise pour s'amuser. La caméra prend sa place et l'on voit Eve à travers le canon du fusil. Travelling avant jusqu'à ce que la bouche du canon la cadre en gros plan. Plan suivant: elle et lui en train de s'embrasser.') Jean-Luc Godard, 'Signal', *Cahiers du cinéma* 76 (November 1957): 41.
45. Michel Marie, *Comprendre Godard: Travelling avant sur A bout de souffle et Le Mépris* (Paris: Armand Colin, 2006), 137. See also Jean-Luc Godard, 'Super Mann', *Cahiers du cinéma* 92 (February 1959): 48–50.
46. Jean-Luc Godard, 'Le cinéaste bien-aimé', *Cahiers du cinéma* 74 (August–September 1957), 51–3. Other western references in the film include Patricia's wish to see a western, and the poster for Budd Boetticher's recently released *Westbound* (1959) above the marquee. Godard's film is also dedicated to Monogram studios, a gesture

whose motivation is often attributed to the studio's production of 'B' gangster films. What generally eludes comment is that Monogram was founded on the niche exploitation of the western, and although it later diversified its catalogue it continued to churn out serial westerns. On the studio's founding and history, see Kyle Dawson Edwards, '"Monogram Means Business": B-film Marketing and Series Filmmaking at Monogram Pictures', *Film History* 23 (2011): 386–400.

47. Jonathan Cott, 'Jean-Luc Godard: The Rolling Stone Interview', *Rolling Stone*, 14 June 1969. Available at <https://www.rollingstone.com/movies/movie-news/jean-luc-godard-the-rolling-stone-interview-183636> (accessed 31 October 2021). In the same interview, Godard questions the very possibility of making this film: 'We're trying to find a script by Cohn-Bendit to make a film that I don't really think is possible – a western, a political western, one that will not be absorbed by the establishment.'
48. Volonté's westerns include roles in Sergio Leone's *Fistful of Dollars* and *For a Few Dollars More*, Sergio Sollima's *Face to Face* (*Faccia a faccia*, 1967) and Damiano Damiani's *A Bullet for the General* (*Quién sabe?*, 1967).
49. Tomas Milian notably played a similarly clad character in Sollima's *The Big Gundown* (*La resa dei conti* 1966), *Face to Face* and *Run Man Run* (*Corri uomo corri*, 1968), and also in *Tepepa* (Giulio Petroni, 1969).
50. Frayling, *Spaghetti Westerns*, 230.
51. Fisher, *Transnational Frontiers*, 209.
52. Christopher Robé cautions: 'the political Spaghetti western often precariously teeters between the twin desires of addressing ethical values and simply putting on a good show'. Christopher Robé, 'When Cultures Collide: Third Cinema Meets the Spaghetti Western', *Journal of Popular Film and Television* 42, no. 3 (2014): 166.
53. To be clear, Godard was Franco-Swiss, and Cohn-Bendit held joint French and German citizenship.
54. 'Il s'agissait de parler de quelque chose que nous avons connu en mai 68. Dans les usines, dans les universités, dans les bureaux, dans les réunions de quartier, des camarades se sont assemblés, se sont groupés. Dans la confusion des discussions, ils ont quand même avancé. Comment, aujourd'hui, en rendre compte? Comment trouver la vérité de cette progression confuse? Et comment la trouver de manière vraie? En fait, très vite, plusieurs camarades ont pris en main la fabrication du film [...]'
55. The 'auto-critique' that opens the second half of the film identifies what was seen in the first: 'D'un mouvement réel, mai 68 France, 68–69 Italie, tu as fait un film' ['you have made a film about a real movement: May '68 in France, '68–'69 in Italy'].
56. Godard and Gorin would explore the Italian context in a subsequent film, *Lotte in Italia* (1971).
57. 'Toute assemblée générale pose aujourd'hui la question de notre époque: la question de l'histoire de l'impérialisme, la question de l'histoire du révisionnisme. Et, poser la question d'une histoire réelle du révisionnisme, c'est poser réellement ce qu'on a convenu d'appeler "la question de Staline" c'est-à-dire ne plus se bloquer sur l'image de Staline.'
58. Liam Considine, 'Screen Politics: Pop Art and the Atelier Populaire', *Tate Papers* no. 24, Autumn 2015. Available at <https://www.tate.org.uk/research/tate-papers/24/screen-politics-pop-art-and-the-atelier-populaire> (accessed 7 July 2023).
59. Ibid. MacCabe also includes reproductions of the various iterations of the poster images. MacCabe, *Godard*, 208.
60. Lesage, 'Godard and Gorin's *Wind from the East*'.

Epilogue

In the summer of 1993, a cycle of five westerns directed by Anthony Mann played at the Arlequin cinema in Paris. I trace my interest in westerns to this time and place, although the rendezvous with the genre nearly didn't happen. I had no abiding interest in Hollywood westerns, and the few I had seen struck me as corny relics relegated to late-night television re-broadcasts. I was in France to study theatre, and any serious interest in cinema was fuelled primarily by 'foreign' films I'd seen at campus film society screenings or in art houses. Nevertheless, I indulged a friend who wanted to see an old American western called *Winchester '73*. I was surprised to find a long queue of spectators snaking down the sidewalk at two o'clock in the afternoon, and even more so by the film. It was strange and edgy, visually stunning, and emotionally pitched as high as opera. Certain characterisations fulfilled sceptical expectations (Rock Hudson in red-face speaking 'Hollywood Injun' English), but the film's moral universe was more complex than I had anticipated: the 'hero' is revealed to be a neurotic and anxious figure obsessed with killing his brother, and by the end the fetishised title firearm, photographed as if it were the star, had led the narrative far from a ritual celebration of violence. I returned to see the film a second time, along with the rest of the cycle. Nicholas Ray's *Johnny Guitar* was playing nearby; I saw it, too. I was hooked, and joined the ranks of cinephiles who discovered the 'genius' of Hollywood in the left-bank cinemas of Paris.

The crowded screening on the rue de Rennes was not simply a symptom of Hollywood's relentless invasion of French screens. The experience of an American spectator discovering the Hollywood western in a Paris screening of film by an auteur admired by generations of French filmmakers, critics and audiences vividly evinces a transnational sphere of cinematic practices: it is neither an antagonistic French affront to its Hollywood rival, nor a hegemonic cinema experienced in the same manner the world over. Nor, however, does it enact a new transnational synthesis that supersedes local audiences and practices. The irony that an American had to go to Paris to discover the American cinema *par excellence* was not lost on me: there remained something distinctly French (or at least Parisian) in watching a 'classic' Hollywood film by a revered auteur in a packed art cinema in the middle of the afternoon.

It is less clear when my awareness of French western films was sparked, but I may place it around the time of the American theatrical release of Manuel Poirier's *Western* (1997). By then I was teaching a course on Hollywood cinema and had seen many westerns, good, bad and ugly. An iteration of the genre set in contemporary France was intriguing. However, the expectations were thwarted by what appeared more to be a road film, a buddy film, or a romantic comedy about two men in search of love on a stretch of highway in small-town Brittany. Poirier's film strongly invokes national referents, French and otherwise (the protagonists are immigrants in a remote corner of rural France), but the western element is oblique. Had the film been given a different title, the nod towards the genre would easily be lost on a spectator. I was looking for a French western, but instead experienced the genre's evacuation as the title played its ruse on the audience.

Around the same time, during a visit to the George Eastman Museum I discovered one of the silent western-tinged Camargue films. As I began to take note of other French western films, sitting in plain sight but marginalised in discussions of either French cinema or the western genre, a trickle of new releases seemed only to confirm the prevailing characterisations of these films as *faux-westerns* and *curiosités*.[1] The conceit of *Big City* (Djamel Bensalah, 2007), a story of children who assume the professions of the missing adults who are away fighting the 'Indians', enacts a burlesque of western clichés that may initially appear to target a family audience, but the parody is jarred by less child-friendly imagery: the whipping of a child, kiddie klansmen riders, a twelve-year-old prostitute peddling her charms, and a deep draw on stereotypes that American westerns had, at this point, been revising for decades. Despite the ostensible lessons embedded in the narrative (corruption exposed, the racists defeated, a Rousseau-ist view of youngsters cutting through adult nonsense, a possible allegory of the multicultural Paris suburbs), the film's unusual address met a dismal return on investment. In a different vein, *Les Colts de l'or noir*

(Pierre Romanello, 2008), made the following year on a budget reputed to be 8,000 euros, candidly exhibited the consequences of its limited resources. Commenting on *La Loi des maudits* (2013), the film's sequel reportedly produced for even less money, a critic marvels that a film 'impossible to make' was being shown at all, and locates the film's 'never-seen-before' interest in the spectacle of extreme budgetary constraint.[2]

Screen adaptations of the French and Belgian *bande dessinée* (*BD*) offer a more mainstream encounter of French cinema and the western genre. The illustrated stories of the *BD*, often published in large format albums, enjoy popularity and cultural legitimacy in the Franco-Belgian context, where the *BD* is known as the 'ninth art', its promotion and curation receive government subsidies and support (including the *Cité Internationale de la Bande Dessinée*) and the form is celebrated annually at the *Festival International de la Bande Dessinée* in Angoulême. The *BD* matured in both style and content, and includes volumes for both adults and children. A vast catalogue of these albums draws on the character types and situations of western film and literature, including some of the most well-known titles of the form. The *Lucky Luke* series alone comprises at least 72 volumes published between 1949 and 2002, with an estimated 300 million copies sold. The protagonists of other series include Jack Diamond, Jerry Spring, Alexis McCoy and Lieutenant Mike Blueberry, whose exploits are recounted in a 28-volume series inaugurated in 1963.[3]

The *BD* developed alongside cinema, and since the Lumières' earliest films the comic strip and the cinema have shared narratives and visual style.[4] The western *BD* strongly references Hollywood films: beyond style, themes and visual framing, the *Lucky Luke* corpus includes numerous 'cameos' with caricatures of American movie actors and their western characters.[5] Hollywood features could be transposed wholesale into a French *BD* issue.[6] Inversely, film producers saw potential in characters and situations that were already richly developed and had enduring appeal to a broad fan base. However, despite star treatment, the fate of two twenty-first-century screen adaptations of well-known *BD* series suggests that the western genre's longstanding success on the illustrated page does not readily transfer to screen.

The first, Jean Kounen's 2004 *Blueberry: l'expérience secrète* (released in English as *Renegade*), cast Vincent Cassel as the title character whose adventures culminate in a lengthy drug trip, filmed with CGI, that has earned the film the moniker 'acid western'. This re-positioning of the popular western character in a tale of psychedelic shamanism and high-tech hallucinations strays from the source *BD* material in both style and narrative. *Blueberry* baffled critics, spectators and fans of the *BD* series, and the film performed poorly at the French box office. The live-action *Lucky Luke* (James Huth, 2009), starring Jean Dujardin, also met with a tepid reception. The humorous comic book hero had found some prior success in animated films and a television cartoon series, which could more faithfully reproduce the familiar imagery and accommodate, among other elements, his anthropomorphised chess-playing horse. The 2009 film was a critical and commercial disappointment, and the terms of the criticism – *douloureux, laborieux* – echo the dismissive criticism of French western production in the 1950s and 1960s.[7]

The French western's contested existence is as long as the history of cinema itself. Throughout this study, the focus has lain on the point of contact where a national cinematic referent and a film genre work on each other both as stumbling block and vehicle, as rival and accomplice, and as agent of disarray and generator of possibilities. This encounter has not been a reliable formula for commercial or critical success. However, under the current emphasis on transnational flows and dialogic hybridity, where a prevailing assertion is that 'the western is not only transgeneric, but also transnational, despite its national origins',[8] could the long disparaged and dismissed French western, precisely by virtue of the tensions and pressures that hold it under erasure as a category of film, find new relevance and timeliness? Could this mode of cinema be considered less a marginal curiosity than a revealing illumination of the constitutive and productive instability of both genres and national assertions in cinematic practice?

The arguments put forth in the preceding pages would support an affirmative response to these questions. However, a simple 'yes' is inadequate, as two films released during the preparation of this book vividly evince. Both may be considered enunciations of a French cinematic referent and the western genre in what could appear to be a more consonant modality. Both also continue to harbour tensions in this persistently unstable conjunction.

Jacques Audiard's *The Sisters Brothers* (*Les Frères Sisters*, 2018), a tale of fraternal bounty hunters in Oregon during the gold rush, presents a harmonious integration of the elements that sowed discordance in previous French westerns. Filmed in English with an English-speaking cast playing English-speaking roles, there are none of the dissonances wrought by the incursion of French language, French stars or French characters on the American frontier. Exterior footage shot in Romania and Spain passes plausibly as the Oregon frontier. The film blends humour and irony into its narrative, but it is not a parody. The sometimes glib violence may seem to resonate with the cynicism of the Italian spaghetti cycle, but as the narrative unfolds the protagonists' actions are revealed to be rooted in sentimentality, psychological motivation, and family melodrama that build to a culminating sequence where the physically and emotionally battered 'good bad men' seek out their estranged mother. The shot framing the doorway as they re-enter their childhood home evokes the ending of John Ford's *The Searchers*, but unlike John Wayne's Uncle Ethan, who is shut out of the domestic space, they cross the threshold to find a measure of peace, reconciliation and home after wandering for years as killers. The positioning of the western genre in *The Sisters Brothers* rings neither cheap, nor *faux*, nor, despite some quirkiness, *curieux*. Nor was the film overlooked or a critical failure: among numerous accolades *The Sisters Brothers* was nominated for nine César awards and won four, including the awards for best director and best cinematography; it also took the Lumière awards for best film, best direction and best cinematography.

The French production team and the western diegesis co-exist harmoniously and, by some commercial and critical measures, successfully in *The Sisters Brothers*. But does the film integrate 'French' and 'western' into a new synthesis when these enunciations remain separated in distinct, if no longer rival, spheres? The French film industry is amply represented and recognised behind the camera, but in front of it explicit French referents do not trouble the consonance of setting, language, character and performer. An oblique reference to Fourier aside (the utopist is not named), the narrative itself does not openly stage the contact of 'Frenchness', either antagonistic or complicit, with the western genre, and one may ask if the tensions between 'French' and 'western' are less resolved than untested. The harvest of Lumière and César nominations is in this respect telling: all went to the French production personnel, but none went to the A-list Hollywood actors John C. Reilly, Joaquin Phoenix and Jake Gyllenhaal. As English-speaking performers in an English-language film, they were not considered for the French film industry's most visible awards.[9]

The second film richly registers French referents in the filmic text itself, and does so along many of the vectors identified in this study. *Savage State* (*L'État sauvage*, David Perrault, 2019) is a Civil War story about a wealthy expatriate French family tainted with southern sympathies. After Union soldiers begin terrorising their Missouri town, the parents fear for their family's safety and decide to return to France. The way east is closed by the ongoing war and the only viable escape route is westward across the frontier. The family father hires a rugged westerner and a small crew to lead him, his wife, his three grown daughters and a black servant (who is also the father's mistress) on the journey. Once in the wilderness the Civil War fades into the background, and as in numerous other westerns the narrative follows the transformation of this microcosm of society after it leaves 'civilisation' behind. In *Savage State* the men on the journey consistently prove to be feckless, greedy or cowardly, and all end up dead, while the newly uncorseted (literally and figuratively) women find and assert themselves: one daughter professes her lesbianism, another acts on her desire for the guide, the servant refuses to serve, and the mother is forced to confront her prejudices and the hollowness of her Christian convictions. At the end, taking matters (and rifles) into their own hands, the women, on their own, fight and prevail over the group of bandits who were stalking them.

Savage State is, plainly, not a western from the 'classic' Hollywood mould. The content is revisionist, notably in terms of gender roles, and the mannered visual style casts an expressionist gloss on the mountains, ghost towns, horses and guns. The use of slow motion and manipulated sound lends the film a dream-like atmosphere. For example, at one point an eerie green light, whose source is not disclosed, illuminates an orgiastic dance by the unhinged leader of the ghoulish gang of outlaws. At times the film approaches gothic horror: murder by voodoo doll, a ruined church full of burning candles and an attack by the speechless and faceless zombie-like bandits. Ponderous symbolism is foregrounded: a large cross in the street of the snowy ghost town fills the left side of the frame (it is later dynamited), or white garments falling in slow motion as the women cross over a treacherously narrow precipice, a figurative rebirth that precipitates their respective transformations. In melodramatic fashion, these charged images tap a moral universe churning under the surface of a linear narrative grounded in historical events.[10]

Multiple genres and national referents may be registered in a film, and *Savage State* also presents an ample array of familiar western tropes. The journey over the frontier enacts a progressive degradation of 'eastern' social hierarchies in a land where power and authority are rooted in survival-of-the-fittest mettle, and where the individual may no longer rely on social structures for protection; the use of shifting dinner-table mores to reveal this transformation takes a lesson from John Ford. The coming of the railroad is invoked as the harbinger of the end of the frontier, and the guide Victor, looking like the Marlboro Man with his broad-brimmed hat and shearling coat as he smokes a cigarette, voices the plight of the 'good bad man' in elegiac words that any number of Hollywood's western gunmen might have uttered: 'no need for people like myself anymore' (the twist in *Savage State* is that Victor will reveal himself to be just another 'bad bad man'). The culminating shootout shows a familiar rank of threatening adversaries advancing down the street of a deserted ghost town, to be picked off one by one.

Nonetheless, *Savage State* stands out in its manner of integrating familiar genre markers with a rich and multivalent enunciation of French national referents. Unlike the bids to exploit the irony of French language, stars and characters in a western film, in this film the mimetic logic of the conjunction of 'French' and 'western' is carefully established and sustained. The negotiation of language, for example, hews to a studied verisimilitude that the inconsistent francophone frontiers of earlier films openly undermined or couched in implausible conceits. In *Savage State* French speech is French, English is English, and there is no recourse to schemes that allow one language to signify the other. The number of bilingual characters, who speak with their respective accents in the non-native language, facilitates this coherence, yet the ploy is not far-fetched; it is hardly surprising that the members of the expatriate family speak English after living many years in the United States, that the servant Layla speaks Creole as well as French and English or that the guide Victor has learned French from his travels. The challenges of conveying indigenous speech are skirted by the absence of Native American characters. Also absent is a bid to generate comedy from the ironic sight of a French performer intentionally 'playing cowboy' against type. The leading actors inhabit their roles with a tense and restrained acting style, and histrionics are relegated to secondary characters who are neither French nor francophone: a maniacal bandit, a drunk soldier, a *buffa* chanteuse. *Savage State* was also partly filmed in North America (the snow and visible breath in the cold air are real), and the other landscapes, photographed with pictorialist care, are plausible stand-ins for the American West.

The cultivated consonance of performers, landscapes, language, characters and narrative advance a conjunction of French and western whose logic is further buttressed with a precise historical alibi. Title cards provide a propaedeutic explanation for the presence of a French family in Missouri, and the cause of their plight is prepared in the opening sequences: the Mississippi river connects the state to Louisiana where French soldiers have intervened on behalf of the population being terrorised by the Union army. The established fact that the servant Layla is free (France abolished slavery in 1848) does not exempt the family from the presumption of southern leanings newly associated with French nationality, hence the urgency of their flight. This evocation of Saint Charles, Missouri, 1863, is not a blank-canvas 'West' where the precise year and geographical location is often irrelevant, nor is the French presence on the American frontier a flimsy pretext for silliness, song and schtick; there is nothing random (surprise inheritances, stolen deeds) about it. The experience of the five women as they undergo their respective self-discoveries is anchored in a consistent and carefully constructed *mimesis* that lends causal narrative logic to their liberation from the roles assigned by the legacy of colonialism, slavery, Catholicism, marriage and presumed heterosexuality. The film closes with the victorious women riding on an idyllic and deserted beach: the French mother and the Creole Layla, formerly mistress and servant and rivals in love, now placidly share a horse. The five women have, effectively, ridden into the sunset beyond the plains and mountains of the inland West, and the experience has transformed and freed them from the societal constraints and political strife back East.

Savage State stages a tense encounter between a French family and the people and landscapes of the American West, but does not exploit discordance between 'French' and 'western' to fracture the diegesis or stoke parody. The film works methodically to lower the raised eyebrows, to mute the laughter and to disarm the surprise that have historically greeted an expression of the western genre also positioned as French. The dramatic narrative depends on the spectators' acceptance of this conjunction, and assiduously courts their consent. As wartime refugee migrants these French characters, in the end, may not have found a home on this range, but integrated into a narrative and justified as its agents they find a carefully prepared home in this western film.

It would nonetheless be premature to conclude that *Savage State* stabilises and legitimises the French western film. By taming the surprise delivered by other French westerns *Savage State* becomes, ironically, surprising nonetheless, and among French westerns the film remains an outlier, *curieux*, an oddity in its own right. In this respect, the more careful and consonant integration of the French and western referents does not represent a more perfect or more evolved realisation of the conjunction, an arrival or end point, but instead one more site of contact, one more instance of proliferation outward towards an ever-receding horizon. Furthermore, as in some of the earlier French westerns, the characters ride into an unimagined future: an eventual return to Napoléon III's France hardly promises freedom from social and political constraint, and the film's end leaves the outcome of the narrative's careful logic, like the five newly liberated women, stranded on a deserted beach. Finally, if *Savage State* demonstrates what a film stands to gain in a bid for greater consonance, what is lost in smoothing the edge that other films have wielded in the service of parody, stardom, political critique and surplus visual interest? Though often scorned or overlooked, the French western has found purpose and possibility in the irresolution, illogic and dissonance that results from the encounter of its two constitutive terms. The implied quotation remarks remain in place around this contested category of film.

Notes

1. See, again, Chapter 1 for a discussion of these terms.
2. 'Du jamais-vu'. 'Cow-boys landais, Western gascon', *Le Sud-Ouest*, 7 September 2013. Available at <https://www.sudouest.fr/2013/09/07/cow-boys-landais-western-gascon-1161503-3307.php?nic> (accessed 13 February 2022).
3. For an overview of western characters and settings in the Franco-Belgian *BD*, see Tangi Villerbu, *BD Western: Histoire d'un genre* (Paris: Karthala, 2015).
4. Lance Rickman, 'Bande dessinée and the Cinematograph: Visual Narrative in 1895', *European Comic Art* no. 1 (Spring 2008): 1–19.
5. Pierre Lagayette notes the *BD*'s caricatures of Jack Palance, Lee Van Cleef, John Carradine and other Hollywood and spaghetti western performers in 'Visions of the West in *Lucky Luke* Comics: From Cliché to Critique', in Miller and Van Riper, *International Westerns*, 94.
6. *Escape from Fort Bravo* (John Sturges, 1953) was adapted in Issue 330 of the *Tintin Journal* series as *Fort Bravo*, featuring a stylised likeness of William Holden in the leading role.
7. For a representative taste of this criticism, see Gérard Lefort and Bruno Icher, '*Lucky Luke*. Très rantanplan'. *Libération*, 20 October 2009. Online edition. Available at <https://www.liberation.fr/cinema/2009/10/21/lucky-luke-tres-rantanplan_588945> (accessed 25 July 2022). See also Isabelle Regnier, 'Le Cow-boy restera seul', *Le Monde*, 20 October 2009. Online edition. Available at <https://www.lemonde.fr/cinema/article/2009/10/20/lucky-luke-le-cowboy-restera-seul_1256116_3476.html> (accessed 25 July 2022). An earlier live-action effort that places focus on Lucky Luke's antagonists, *Les Dalton/The Daltons* (Phillipe Haïm, 2004), fared even worse among critics and filmgoers.
8. Marek Paryz, 'Introduction', in Paryz and Leo, *The Post-2000 Film Western*', 9.
9. Both Reilly and Phoenix received nominations from other award-granting organisations.
10. Peter Brooks uses the term 'moral occult' to refer to melodrama's characteristic assurance that 'the universe is morally legible'. Peter Brooks, *The Melodramatic Imagination* (New York: Columbia University Press, 1976), 43.

Bibliography

Abel, Richard. *Americanizing the Movie and 'Movie-Mad' Audiences, 1910–1914*. Berkeley: University of California Press, 2006.
Abel, Richard. *The Red Rooster Scare: Making Cinema American*. Berkeley: University of California Press, 1999.
Abel, Richard, Giorgio Bertellini and Rob King, eds. *Early Cinema and the 'National'*. New Barnet: John Libbey, 2008.
Adler, Renata. 'Connery and Bardot in a Good Old Western: "Shalako" Begins Run at Theaters Here'. *New York Times*, 6 November 1968.
Alison, Joan, and Murray Burnett. *Everybody Comes to Rick's*. Unpublished script. Available at <vincasa.com/Screenplay-Everybody_Comes_to_Rick%27s.pdf> (accessed 8 January 2019).
Altman, Rick. *The American Film Musical*. Bloomington: Indiana University Press, 1987.
Altman, Rick. *Film/Genre*. London: BFI, 1999.
Altman, Rick. 'A Semantic/Syntactic Approach to Film Genre'. *Cinema Journal* 23, no. 3 (Spring 1984): 6–18.
Altman, Rick. *Sound Theory, Sound Practice*. New York and London: Routledge, 1992.
Anderson, Benedict. *Imagined Communities: Reflections on the Origin and Spread of Nationalism*. Revised edition. London and New York: Verso, 2006.
Anonymous. 'Le "Groupe Dziga Vertov"'. *Cahiers du Cinéma* 238–9 (May–June 1972): 37.
Arnold, Gary. 'Godard's "East Wind"', *The Washington Post*. 10 November 1970, D 7.
Arte Online. 'Perle rare: le tournage de "Viva Maria" de Louis Malle'. Available at <http://sites.arte.tv/pnb/fr/perle-rare-le-tournage-de-viva-maria-de-louis-malle-063046-000> (accessed 17 March 2016).
Astre, Georges-Albert, and Albert-Patrick Hoarau. *Univers du Western*. Paris: Cinéma Club/Editions Seghers, 1973.
'Baader war ein rührender Verlierer'. *Taz.de*. 15 February 2002. Available at <http://www.taz.de/1/archiv/?dig=2002/02/15/a0198> (accessed 2 August 2016).
Baecque, Antoine de. *La Nouvelle Vague: portrait d'une jeunesse*. Paris: Flammarion, 1998.
Baecque, Antoine de. *Truffaut: A Biography*. Berkeley: University of California Press, 2000.
Bardot, Brigitte. *Initiales B.B.* Paris: Bernard Grasset, 1998.
Baroncelli, Jean de. '"Les Pétroleuses" de Christian-Jaque'. *Le Monde*, 21 December 1971.
Baroncelli, Jean de. '"Shalako"'. *Le Monde*, 10 December 1968.

Barrot, Olivier. 'Christian-Jaque tel que je l'ai connu'. *1895* 28 (October 1999): 7–10.
Barthes, Roland. *Mythologies*. Translated by Annette Lavers. New York: Hill and Wang, 1972.
Barthes, Roland. *On Racine*. Translated by Richard Howard. Berkeley: University of California Press, 1992.
Bastide, Bernard. *Aux sources du cinéma en Camargue: Joë Hamman et Folco de Baroncelli*. Avignon: Palais du Roure, 2018.
Bastide, Bernard. 'Jacques de Baroncelli, chantre de la Camargue'. Available at <http://www.cineressources.net/ressources/JacquesdeBaroncelli_ChantredelaCamargue.pdf> (accessed 22 February 2022).
Baudry, Leon, and Marshall Cohen, eds. *Film Theory and Criticism*. 6th edition. New York and Oxford: Oxford University Press, 2004.
Bazin, André, 'Beauty of a Western'. Translated by Liz Heron. In *Cahiers du Cinéma, the 1950s: Neo-realism, Hollywood, the New Wave*, edited by Jim Hillier, 165–8. Cambridge, MA: Harvard University Press, 1985.
Bazin, André. 'The Evolution of the Western'. Translated by Hugh Gray. In *What is Cinema?* Volume 2, 149–57. Berkeley: University of California Press, 1971.
Bazin, André. 'An Exemplary Western'. 1957. Translated by Philip Drummond. In *Cahiers du Cinéma, the 1950s: Neo-realism, Hollywood, the New Wave*, edited by Jim Hillier, 169–72. Cambridge, MA: Harvard University Press, 1985.
Bazin, André. 'On the *Politique des Auteurs*'. Translated by Peter Graham. In *Cahiers du Cinéma, the 1950s: Neo-realism, Hollywood, the New Wave*, edited by Jim Hillier, 248–59. Cambridge, MA: Harvard University Press, 1985.
Bazin, André, et al. 'Six Characters in Search of Auteurs: A Discussion about the French Cinema'. Translated by Liz Heron. In *Cahiers du Cinéma, the 1950s: Neo-realism, Hollywood, the New Wave*, edited by Jim Hillier, 31–46. Cambridge, MA: Harvard University Press, 1985.
Bazin, André. *What is Cinema?* Volume 2. Translated by Hugh Gray. Berkeley: University of California Press, 1971.
Beauvoir, Simone de. 'Brigitte Bardot and the Lolita Syndrome'. *Esquire*, August 1959, 33–8.
Bell, Allan, and Andy Gibson. 'Staging Language: An Introduction to the Sociolinguistics of Performance'. *Journal of Sociolinguistics* 15, no. 5 (November 2011): 555–72.
Bellour, Raymond, ed. *Le Western*. Paris: Gallimard, 1993.
Berger, Verena, and Miya Komori, eds. *Polyglot Cinema: Migration and Transcultural Narration in France, Italy, Portugal, and Spain*. Vienna: LIT Verlag, 2010.
Bergfelder, Tim. *International Adventures: German Popular Cinema Co-Productions in the 1960s*. New York and Oxford: Bergahn, 2005.
Bergfelder, Tim. 'Transnational Genre Hybridity: Between Vernacular Modernism and Postmodern Parody'. In *Genre Hybridisation*, edited by Ivo Ritzer and Peter W. Schulze, 39–55. Marburg: Schüren, 2013.
Bergman, Ingrid, and Alan Burgess. *My Story*. New York: Delacorte, 1980.
Betz, Mark. *Beyond the Subtitle: Remapping European Art Cinema*. Third edition. Minneapolis: University of Minnesota Press, 2009.
'Biggest British Western'. *Times of London*, 16 December 1968.
Billard, Pierre. 'Ave Maria y Maria'. *L'Express*, 12 December 1965.
Billard, Pierre. *Louis Malle: le rebelle solitaire*. Paris: Plon, 2003.
Bleton, Paul. *Western, France: la place de l'Ouest dans l'imaginaire français*. Paris: Les Belles Lettres, 2002.

'Blind Date with Nitrate'. Program for *The 3rd Nitrate Picture Show*, 2017: 14. Available at <https://drive.google.com/file/d/0B0TTVsrv1oMQcmRacTMyU1VfYzQ/view> (accessed 8 January 2019).

Bloom, Peter. 'Beyond the Western Frontier: Reappropriation of the "Good Badman" in France, the French Colonies, and Contemporary Algeria'. In *Westerns: Films Through History*, edited by Janet Walker, 197–216. New York: Routledge, 2001.

Bonneau, Albert. 'Le Far-West en France'. *Cinémagazine*, 8 May 1925.

Bourdieu, Pierre. *Distinction: A Social Critique of the Judgment of Taste*. Translated by Richard Nice. Cambridge, MA: Harvard University Press, 1984.

Bourton, William. *Le Western, conscience du nouveau monde*. Paris: Campion, 2016.

Bowser, Eileen. *The Transformation of Cinema 1907–1915*. Berkeley: University of California Press, 1990.

Bray, Christopher. *Sean Connery: A Biography*. New York: Pegasus, 2012.

Brecht, Bertolt. *Brecht on Theatre*. Translated by John Willett. New York: Hill & Wang, 1964.

Brody, Richard. *Everything is Cinema: The Working Life of Jean-Luc Godard*. New York: Metropolitan Books, 2008.

Brooks, Peter. *The Melodramatic Imagination*. New York: Columbia University Press, 1976.

Broughton, Lee. 'Emancipation *all'Italiana*: Giuseppe Colizzi and the Representation of African Americans in Italian Westerns'. In *Radical Frontiers in the Spaghetti Western: Politics, Violence and Popular Italian Cinema*, edited by Austin Fisher, 103–24. London and New York: I. B. Tauris and Company, 2011.

Brown, Royal S., ed. *Focus on Godard*. New York: Prentice Hall, 1972.

'Buffalo Bill's Wild West and Congress of Rough Riders of the World in the Grandest of Illuminated Arenas, 2 Electric Plants, 250,000 Candle Power'. Library of Congress digital file. Available at <https://www.loc.gov/resource/ds.08325> (accessed 6 July 2019).

Bucholtz, Mary, and Quiana Lopez. 'Performing Blackness, Forming Whiteness: Linguistic Minstrelsy in Hollywood Film'. *Journal of Sociolinguistics* 15, no. 5 (2011): 680–706.

Bucholtz, Mary. 'Race and the Re-embodied Voice in Hollywood Film'. *Language & Communication* 31 (July 2011): 255–65.

Burns, Emily. 'Taming a "Savage" Paris: The Masculine Visual Culture of Buffalo Bill's Wild West and France as a New American Frontier'. *The Popular Frontier: Buffalo Bill's Wild West and Transnational Masculine Culture*, edited by Frank Christensen, 129–54. University of Oklahoma Press, 2017.

Burns, Emily. *Transnational Frontiers: The American West in France*. Norman: University of Oklahoma Press, 2018.

Buscombe, Edward, and Roberta E. Pearson, eds. *Back in the Saddle Again: New Essays on the Western*. London: BFI, 1998.

Cameron, Ian, and Douglas Pye, eds. *The Book of Westerns*. New York: Continuum, 1996.

Campbell, Neil. *Post-Westerns: Cinema, Region, West*. Lincoln: University of Nebraska Press, 2013.

Campbell, Neil. *The Rhizomatic West: Representing the American West in a Transnational, Global Media Age*. Lincoln: University of Nebraska Press, 2008.

Camy, Gérard, ed. *Western: que reste-t-il de nos amours? CinémAction* 86 (first trimester, 1998).

Canby, Vincent. 'Godard Film in Festival: "Wind from the East" at Alice Tully Hall'. *New York Times*, 12 September 1970, 31.
'Carnival in Brio'. *Time*, 31 December 1965, 77.
Cawelti, John G. *The Six-Gun Mystique*. Bowling Green, OH: Bowling Green University Popular Press, 1970.
Cerisuelo, Marc. 'Jean-Luc, Community, and Communication'. In *A Companion to Jean-Luc Godard*, edited by Tom Conley and T. Jefferson Kline, 298–317. Malden, MA and Oxford, 2014.
Chabrol, Claude. 'The Evolution of the Thriller'. Translated by Liz Heron. In *Cahiers du Cinéma, the 1950s: Neo-realism, Hollywood, the New Wave*, edited by Jim Hillier, 158–63. Cambridge, MA: Harvard University Press, 1985.
Chabrol, Claude. 'Petits poisons deviendront grands'. *Cahiers du cinéma* 45 (March 1955): 45–6.
Chapier, Henri. '"Les Pétroleuses" de Christian-Jaque: un tas de boue'. *Combat*, 20 December 1971.
Chapier, Henri. '"Shalako" d'Edward Dmytryk: amateurisme désinvolte. . .'. *Combat*, 9 December 1968.
Chapier, Henri. '"Viva Maria" de Louis Malle: un opéra tendre et baroque, somptueux et burlesque, où la férocité du regard s'abrite derrière une apparente liberté'. *Combat*, 12 October 1965.
Charney, Leo, and Vanessa Schwartz, eds. *Cinema and the Invention of Modern Life*. Berkeley: University of California Press, 1995.
Chauvet, Louis. '"Les Pétroleuses" (à l'eau de rose)'. *Le Figaro*, 21 December 1971.
Cherchi-Usai, Paolo. *Silent Cinema: a Guide to Study, Research, and Curatorship*. Third edition. London: BFI, 2019.
Chion, Michel. *La Comédie musicale*. Paris: Cahiers du cinéma, 2002.
Chion, Michel. *Le Complexe de Cyrano: la langue parlée dans les films français*. Paris: Cahiers du cinéma, 2008.
Chion, Michel. *Words on Screen*. Translated by Claudia Gorbman. New York: Columbia University Press, 2017.
Chion, Michel. *The Voice in Cinema*. Translated by Claudia Gorbman. New York: Columbia University Press, 1999.
Christensen, Frank, ed. *The Popular Frontier: Buffalo Bill's Wild West and Transnational Masculine Culture*. Norman: University of Oklahoma Press, 2017.
'Le Cinéma et l'art dramatique'. *Le Courrier cinématographique* 3, no. 27 (5 July 1913): 4–6.
'Les Clientèles touristiques de la Camargue'. 2013. Available at <https://en.calameo.com/read/001239688ebf5e4cf111f> (accessed 19 August 2021).
Cohl, Emile, Jean Durand, Pierre Phillipe et al., dirs. *Le Cinéma premier. Volume 2. 1907–1916*. Neuilly-sur-Seine: Gaumont Vidéo, 2009. DVD.
Cohn-Bendit, Daniel, 'Mon ami Godard'. *Le Monde*, 27 December 2010. Available at <https://www.lemonde.fr/idees/article/2010/12/25/mon-ami-godard_1457343_3232.html> (accessed 10 August 2021).
Collet, Jean. 'No Questions Asked: A Conversation with Jean-Luc Godard'. In *Focus on Godard*, edited by Royal S. Brown, 40–5. New York: Prentice Hall, 1972.
Conley, Tom. 'Louis Aragon, "Elsa je t'aime"'. In *Twentieth-Century French Poetry: A Critical Anthology*, edited by Huges Azérad and Peter Collier, 105–15. Cambridge: Cambridge University Press, 2010.

Conley, Tom, and T. Jefferson Kline, eds. *A Companion to Jean-Luc Godard*. Chichester: Wiley Blackwell, 2014.
Considine, Liam. 'Screen Politics: Pop Art and the Atelier Populaire'. *Tate Papers* no. 24, Autumn 2015. Available at https://www.tate.org.uk/research/tate-papers/24/screen-politics-pop-art-and-the-atelier-populaire (accessed 7 July 2023).
Cott, Jonathan. 'Jean-Luc Godard: The Rolling Stone Interview'. *Rolling Stone*, 14 June 1969. Available at <https://www.rollingstone.com/movies/movie-news/jean-luc-godard-the-rolling-stone-interview-183636> (accessed 31 October 2021).
'Cow-boys landais, Western gascon'. *Le Sud-Ouest*, 7 September 2013. Available at <https://www.sudouest.fr/2013/09/07/cow-boys-landais-western-gascon-1161503-3307.php?nic> (accessed 13 February 2022).
Le Courrier cinématographique 4, no. 15 (11 April 1914): 44–5.
Crépeau, Michel. 'Avant-propos'. In *Les Indiens de Buffalo Bill et la Camargue*, edited by Thierry Lefrançois, 7. Paris: Editions de La Martinière, 1994.
Crisp, Colin. *The Classic French Cinema 1930–1960*. Indiana University Press, 1997.
Crisp, Colin. *Genre, Myth, and Convention in the French Cinema 1929–1939*. Indiana University Press, 2002.
Cronin, Michael. *Translation Goes to the Movies*. London and New York: Routledge, 2008.
Daney, Serge. 'Le Thérrorisé: (pédagogie godardienne)'. *Cahiers du cinéma* 262–3 (January 1976): 32–40.
Datta, Venita. 'Buffalo Bill Goes to France: French-American Encounters at the Wild West Show 1889–1905'. *French Historical Studies* 41, no. 3 (August 2018): 525–55.
De la Bretèque, François. 'Images of Provence: ethnotypes and stereotypes of the south in French cinema'. In *Popular European Cinema*, edited by Richard Dyer and Ginette Vincendeau, 58–71. London & New York: Routledge, 1992.
De la Bretèque, François Amy. 'Le Paysage de la Camargue dans les westerns français: un rôle discret'. In *Western Camarguais*, edited by Estelle Rouquette and Sam Stourdzé, 110–12. Arles: Actes Sud, 2016.
Delafosse, Maurice. *Vocabulaires comparitifs de plus de 60 langues ou dialectes parlés à la Côte d'Ivoire et dans les régions limitrophes*. Paris: Ernest Leroux, 1904.
Derrida, Jacques. 'The Law of Genre'. In *Acts of Literature*, edited by Derek Attridge, 221–52. New York and London: Routledge, 1992.
Derrida, Jacques. 'The Theater of Cruelty and the Closure of Representation'. In *Writing and Difference*. Translated by Alan Bass. Chicago: University of Chicago Press, 1978.
Devaivre, Jean. *Action: mémoires 1930–1970*. Paris: Nicolas Philippe, 2002.
Devaivre, Jean, and René Mejean. *Miss Cow-boy* (shooting script). Paris: Archives of the Cinémathèque Française, 1949.
Dibon, Henriette. *Folco de Baroncelli*. Nîmes: Bene, 1982.
Doane, Mary Anne. 'The Voice in Cinema: The Articulation of Body and Space'. *Yale French Studies* 60 (1980): 33–50.
Dupuis, Jean-Jacques. *Le Western*. Paris: J'ai lu, 1990.
Durand, Jacques. 'Lost Paradise. In *Western Camarguais*, edited by Estelle Rouquette and Sam Stourdzé, 136–7. Arles: Actes Sud, 2016.
Ďurovičová, Nataša. 'Vector, Flow, Zone: Towards a History of Cinematic Translation'. In *World Cinemas, Transnational Perspectives*, edited by Nataša Ďurovičová and Kathleen Newman, 90–120. London and New York: Routledge, 2010.
Dyer, Richard. *Stars*. London: BFI, 2008.

Dyer, Richard, and Ginette Vincendeau, eds. *Popular European Cinema*. London and New York: Routledge, 1992.
Edwards, Kyle Dawson. '"Monogram Means Business": B-film Marketing and Series Filmmaking at Monogram Pictures'. *Film History* 23 (2011): 386–400.
Eleftheriotis, Dimitris. *Popular Cinemas of Europe: Studies of Texts, Contexts and Frameworks*. New York & London: Continuum: 2001.
Eleftheriotis, Dimitris. 'Spaghetti Western, Genre Criticism, and National Cinema: Re-Defining the Frame of Reference'. In *Action and Adventure Cinema*, edited by Yvonne Tasker, 309–27. London and New York: Routledge, 2004.
Elsaesser, Thomas, and Adam Barker, eds. *Early Cinema: Space Frame Narrative*. London: BFI, 1990.
Ezra, Elizabeth. *Georges Méliès*. Manchester and New York: Manchester University Press, 2000.
Fabe, Marilyn. *Closely Watched Films*. Berkeley: University of California Press, 2004.
Falconer, Pete. 'Spaghetti Westerns and the "Afterlife" of a Hollywood Genre'. In *Radical Frontiers in the Spaghetti Western: Politics, Violence and Popular Italian Cinema*, edited by Austin Fisher, 262–78. London and New York: I. B. Tauris and Company, 2011.
Fanon, Franz. *Black Skin, White Masks*. Translated by Richard Philcox. New York: Grove Press, 2008.
Fisher, Austin. *Radical Frontiers in the Spaghetti Western: Politics, Violence and Popular Italian Cinema*. London and New York: I. B. Tauris and Company, 2011.
Fisher, Austin, ed. *Spaghetti Westerns at the Crossroads: Studies in Relocation, Transition, and Appropriation*. Edinburgh: Edinburgh University Press, 2016.
Forestier, François. 'Dynamite Jack: le western-bouillabaisse de Fernandel'. *Le Nouvel observateur*, 27 April 2013. Available at <https://www.nouvelobs.com/cinema/20130427.CIN4029/dynamite-jack-le-western-bouillabaisse-de-fernandel.html> (accessed 21 June 2016).
Frayling, Christopher. *Spaghetti Westerns: Cowboys and Europeans from Karl May to Sergio Leone*. London and New York: I. B. Tauris and Company, 2006.
Fridlund, Bert. *The Spaghetti Western: A Thematic Analysis*. Jefferson, NC: McFarland, 2006.
Gemünden, Gerd. 'Between Karl May and Karl Marx: The DEFA Indianerfilme (1965–1983)', *Film History* 10, no. 3 (1988): 399–407.
Ghiyati, Karim. 'Christian-Jaque et la Comédie-Française'. *1895* 28 (October 1999): 159–72.
Giré, Jean-François. *Il était une fois. . .le western européen: 1901–2008*. Paris: Bazaar & Co., 2008.
Giré, Jean-François. *Il était une fois. . .le western européen, volume 2: Les dernières chevauchées du western*. Paris: Bazaar & Co., 2012.
Gledhill, Christine, ed. *Stardom: Industry of Desire*. London and New York: Routledge, 1991.
Godard, Jean-Luc, and Fernando Solanas. 'Godard by Solanas, Solanas by Godard'. *Cinema Comparat/ive Cinema* 4, no. 9 (2016): 15–19.
Godard, Jean-Luc. *Introduction à une histoire véritable du cinéma*. Albatros: Paris, 1980.
Godard, Jean-Luc. 'Saut dans le vide'. *Cahiers du cinéma* 83 (May 1958): 56–7.
Godard, Jean-Luc. 'Signal'. *Cahiers du cinéma* 76 (November 1957): 41.
Godard, Jean-Luc. 'Super Mann'. *Cahiers du cinéma* 92 (February 1959): 48–50.

Godard, Jean-Luc, and Jean-Pierre Gorin. 'Le Vent d'est (bandes paroles)'. *Cahiers du cinéma* 240 (July–August, 1972): 31–50.
Grant, Barry Keith. *The Film Genre Reader*. Austin: University of Texas Press, 1986.
Grey, Zane. (1912). *Riders of the Purple Sage*. Paperback edition. New York: Pocket Books, 1980.
Günsberg, Maggie. *Italian Cinema: Gender and Genre*. New York: Palgrave Macmillan, 2005.
Gunning, Tom. 'An Aesthetic of Astonishment: Early Film and the (In)Credulous Spectator'. In *Film Theory and Criticism*, sixth edition, edited by Leon Baudry and Marshall Cohen, 872–76. New York and Oxford: Oxford University Press, 2004.
Gunning, Tom. *D. W. Griffith & the Origins of American Narrative Film: The Early Years at Biograph*. Urbana: University of Illinois Press, 1994.
Gunning, Tom. 'Early Cinema as Global Cinema: The Encyclopedic Ambition'. In *Early Cinema and the 'National'*, edited by Richard Abel, Giorgio Bertellini and Rob King, 11–16. New Barnet: John Libbey, 2008.
Gunning, Tom. 'Systematizing the Electric Message: Narrative Form, Gender, and Modernity in *The Lonedale Operator*'. In *American Cinema's Transitional Era*, edited by Charlie Keil and Shelly Stamp, 15–50. Berkeley: University of California Press, 2004.
Hamman, Joë. *Du Far-West à Montmartre: un demi-siècle d'aventures*. Paris: les Editeurs Français Réunis, 1962.
Hamman, Joë. 'Mon cheval'. *Film*, 15 January 1920.
Hammond, Paul. *Marvellous Méliès*. London: Gordon Fraser, 1974.
Harmetz, Aljean. *Round Up the Usual Suspects: The Making of Casablanca*. Hyperion, 1992.
Hansen, Miriam Bratu. 'Fallen Women, Rising Stars, New Horizons: Shanghai Silent Film as Vernacular Modernism'. *Film Quarterly* 54, no. 1 (Autumn 2000): 10–22.
Hansen, Miriam Bratu. 'The Mass Production of the Senses: Classical Cinema as Vernacular Modernism'. *Modernism/Modernity* 6, no. 2 (April 1999): 59–77.
Hayward, Susan. *French Costume Drama of the 1950s: Fashioning Politics in Film*. Chicago: University of Chicago Press, 2010.
Hayward, Susan. *French National Cinema*. Second edition. London & New York: Routledge, 1993.
Heath, Stephen, and Patricia Mellencamp, eds. *Cinema and Language*. Bethesda, MD: University Publications of America, 1983.
Heumann, Joseph, and Robin L. Murray. *Gunfight at the Eco-Corral: Western Cinema and the Environment*. Norman: University of Oklahoma Press, 2012.
Higbee, Will, and Sarah Leahy, eds. *Studies in French Cinema: UK Perspectives 1985–2010*. Bristol and Chicago: Intellect, 2011.
Hillier, Jim, ed. *Cahiers du Cinéma, the 1950s: Neo-realism, Hollywood, the New Wave*. Cambridge, MA: Harvard University Press, 1985.
Hjort, Mette, and Duncan Petrie, eds. *The Cinema of Small Nations*. Edinburgh University Press, 2007.
Hjort, Mette. 'On the Plurality of Cinematic Transnationalism'. In *World Cinemas, Transnational Perspectives*, edited by Nataša Ďurovičová and Kathleen Newman, 12–33. New York and London: Routledge, 2010.
Hofstede, David. 'The French John Wayne'. *Cowboys & Indians* 15, no. 5 (July 2007): 175–8.
Jacob, Gilles. 'Les Pétroleuses'. *L'Express* (2 January 1972), 5.

Jacobowitz, Florence. 'The Dietrich Westerns: Destry Rides Again and Rancho Notorious'. In *The Book of Westerns*, edited by Ian Cameron and Douglas Pye, 88–98. New York: Continuum, 1996.
Johnstone, Barbara. 'Dialect Enregisterment in Performance'. *Journal of Sociolinguistics* 15, no. 5 (November 2011): 657–79.
Justia. 'Interstate Circuit, Inc. v. City of Dallas 390 U.S. 676'. Available at <https://supreme.justia.com/cases/federal/us/390/676/case.html> (accessed 10 August 2017).
Kael, Pauline. '"Brooding", They Said'. *New York Times*, 21 February 1965.
Kael, Pauline. 'The Missing West'. *The New Yorker*, 16 November, 1968, 127.
Kael, Pauline. 'Saddle Sore'. *The New Republic*, 5 August 1967, 38–41.
Kael, Pauline. 'The Street Western'. *The New Yorker*, 25 February 1974, 100.
Keil, Charlie. *Early American Cinema in Transition: Story, Style, and Filmmaking 1907–1913*. Madison: The University of Wisconsin Press, 2001.
Keil, Charlie. 'From Here to Modernity: Style, Historiography, and Transitional Cinema'. In *American Cinema's Transitional Era*, edited by Charlie Keil and Shelly Stamp, 51–65. Berkeley: University of California Press, 2004.
Keil, Charlie, and Shelly Stamp, eds. *American Cinema's Transitional Era*. Berkeley: University of California Press, 2004.
Kersztesi, Rita et al., eds. *The Western in the Global South*. New York and London: Routledge, 2015.
Kilpatrick, Jaquelyn. *Celluloid Indians: Native Americans and Film*. Lincoln: University of Nebraska Press: 1999.
Kitses, Jim. *Horizons West: Directing the Western from John Ford to Clint Eastwood*. London: BFI, 2004.
Kitses, Jim, and Gregg Rickman, eds. *The Western Reader*. New York: Limelight, 1998.
Kozloff, Sarah. *Overhearing Film Dialogue*. Berkeley: University of California Press, 2000.
Kuisel, Richard. 'The Fernandel Factor: The Rivalry between French and American Cinema in the 1950s'. *Yale French Studies* 98 (2000): 119–34.
Lacassin, Francis. *Pour une contre-histoire du cinéma*. Arles: Actes Sud, 1994.
Lagayette, Pierre. 'Visions of the West in Lucky Luke Comics: From Cliché to Critique'. In *International Westerns: Re-locating the Frontier*, edited by Cynthia Miller and A. Bowdoin Van Riper, 83–103. Lanham, MD: Scarecrow Press 2014.
Langford, Barry. *Film Genre: Hollywood and Beyond*. Edinburgh: Edinburgh University Press, 2005.
'The Last Minute'. *Moving Picture World* 18, no. 4 (25 October 1913).
Lawrence, Amy. *Echo and Narcissus: Women's Voices in Classical Hollywood Cinema*. University of California Press, 1991.
Layerle, Sébastien, and Raphaëlle Moine, eds. *Voyez comme on chante! Films musicaux et cinéphilies populaires en France (1945–1958)*. Théorème 20 (Paris: Presses Sorbonne Nouvelle, 2014).
Lee, Daryl. 'Robida's Mormons'. *Transatlantica* 2 (2017). Available at <http://journals.openedition.org/transatlantica/10869> (accessed February 20, 2021).
Lefort, Gérard, and Bruno Icher. '*Lucky Luke*. Très rantanplan'. *Libération*, 20 October 2009. Online edition. Available at <https://www.liberation.fr/cinema/2009/10/21/lucky-luke-tres-rantanplan_588945> (accessed 25 July 2022).
Lefrançois, Thierry, ed. *Les Indiens de Buffalo Bill et la Camargue*. Paris: Editions de La Martinière, 1994.
Le Gras, Gwénaëlle and Delphine Chedaleux, eds. *Genres et acteurs du cinéma français*. Rennes: Presses universitaires de Rennes, 2012.

Leguèbe, Eric. *L'Histoire universelle du Western*. Paris: Editions France-Empire, 1989.
Lelièvre, Marie-Dominique. *Brigitte Bardot: plein la vue*. Paris: Flammarion, 2012.
Lesage, Julia. 'Godard and Gorin's *Wind from the East*: Looking at a Film Politically'. *Jump Cut* 4 (1974): 18–23. Available at <https://www.ejumpcut.org/archive/onlinessays/JC04folder/WindfromEast.html> (accessed 10 August 2022).
Leutrat, Jean-Louis, and Suzanne Liandrat-Guigues. *Western(s)*. Paris: Klincksieck, 2007.
'Le Roi du lasso: le premier cow-boy du cinéma mondial'. *Franc-tireur* (14 June 1950).
Limerick, Patricia Nelson. *Legacy of Conquest: The Unbroken Past of the American West*. New York: Norton, 1987.
Lippi-Green, Rosina. *English with an Accent: Language, Ideology, and Discrimination in the United States*. London and New York: Routledge, 1997.
Looseley, David. 'Fabricating Johnny: French Popular Music and National Culture'. *French Cultural Studies* 16, no. 2 (2005): 191–203.
Looseley, David. 'Une passion française: The Mourning of Johnny Hallyday'. *French Cultural Studies* 29, no. 4 (October 2018): 378–88.
Lounas, Thierry, and Jean Narboni. 'Cohn-Bendit: Godard, Bardot, & moi'. *Sofilm* (19 June 2017). Available at <https://sofilm.fr/cohn-bendit-godard-bardot-moi> (accessed 10 August 2021).
'Lucy Meets Charles Boyer'. *I Love Lucy*, Season 5, Episode 19. Directed by James V. Kern. Written by Jess Oppenheimer et al. Aired 5 March 1956.
Lunn, David. 'The Eloquent Language: Hindustani in 1940s Indian Cinema'. *BioScope* 6, no. 1 (September 2015): 1–26.
MacCabe, Colin. *Godard: A Portrait of the Artist*. New York: Farrar, Straus & Giroux, 2003.
Malle, Louis. *Louis Malle par Louis Malle*. Paris: Éditions de l'Athanor, 1978.
Malthête-Méliès, Madeleine. *Méliès l'enchanteur*. Paris: Editions Ramsey, 1983.
Manessy, Gabriel. *Le Français en Afrique Noire: mythes, stratégies, pratiques*. Paris: L'Harmattan, 1994.
Marhis-Mouren, Laure, and Estelle Rouquette. 'Wild South Camargue'. In *Western Camarguais*, edited by Estelle Rouquette and Sam Stourdzé, 16–19. Arles: Actes Sud, 2016.
Marie, Michel. *Comprendre Godard: Travelling avant sur A bout de souffle et Le Mépris*. Paris: Armand Colin, 2006.
Marie, Michel. *The French New Wave: An Artistic School*. Translated by Richard Neupert. Malden, MA and Oxford: Blackwell, 2003.
Martel, Philippe, 'Le Félibrige: un incertain nationalisme linguistique'. *Mots: Les langages du politique* 74 (2003): 43–57.
Martin, Marcel. 'Safari chez les Apaches: "Shalako" d'Edward Dmytryk'. *Les Lettres Françaises* (11 December 1968): 20.
Matheson, Sue, ed. *A Fistful of Icons: Essays on Frontier Fixtures of the American Western*. Jefferson, NC: McFarland, 2017.
Matheson, Sue, ed. *Women in the Western*. Edinburgh: Edinburgh University Press, 2020.
McBean, James Roy. *Film and Revolution*. Bloomington: Indiana University Press, 1975. Online edition. Available at <https://publish.iupress.indiana.edu/read/film-and-revolution/section/30295a76-98bb-4003-befb-ca010d78817a> (accessed 11 September 2021).
McClain, William. 'Westerns Go Home! Sergio Leone and the "Death of the Western" in American Film Criticism'. *Journal of Film and Video* 62, nos. 1–2 (2010): 52–66.

McQuade, James S. 'The Red Man's Honor'. *Moving Picture World* 14, no. 11 (14 December 1912): 1064.
McQuade, James S. 'The Subterranean City'. *Moving Picture World* 18, no. 7 (15 November 1913): 717.
McSharry, Mac, and Terry Hine. 2005. 'Euan Lloyd: The Ties that Bond Part 2: The Way West'. *Cinema Retro 2* (May 2005): 38–45.
Meek, Barbra. 'And the Injun Goes "How!": Representations of American Indian English in White Public Space'. *Language in Society* 35, no. 10 (February 2006): 93–128.
Méliès, Georges. Letter to the editor. *Le Courrier cinématographique* 3, no. 2 (10 January 1913): 42.
Mellen, Joan. 'Wind from the East'. *Film Comment* 7, no. 3 (Fall 1971): 65–7.
Meune, Manuel. 'Quand Lucky Luke et les (Amér)Indiens parlent franco-provençal bressan: Traduction et transposition, entre inaudibilité linguistique et visibilité culturelle'. *TranscUlturAl* 10 (2018): 45–62.
Metz, Christian. *Language and Cinema*. Translated by Donna Jean Umiker-Sebeok. The Hague: Mouton, 1974.
Michael, Charles. *French Blockbusters: Cultural Politics of a Transnational Cinema*. Edinburgh: Edinburgh University Press, 2019.
Miller, Cynthia, and A. Bowdoin Van Riper, eds. *International Westerns: Re-locating the Frontier*. Lanham, MD: Scarecrow Press, 2014.
Miller, Cynthia. 'Performing the Iconic West: Wild West Shows'. In *A Fistful of Icons: Essays on Frontier Fixtures of the American Western*, edited by Sue Matheson. Jefferson, NC: McFarland, 2017: 9–22.
Miss Cow-boy. Dossier. Fonds Crédit National. Archives of the *Cinémathèque Française*. Référence: CN422-B293.
Mitchell, Lee Clark. *Late Westerns: The Persistence of a Genre*. Lincoln: University of Nebraska Press, 2018.
Mitchell, Lee Clark. *Westerns: Making the Man in Fiction and Film*. Chicago: University of Chicago Press, 1996.
Mohr, Gregory. 'The French Camargue Western'. In *Crossing Frontiers: Intercultural Perspectives on the Western*, edited by Peter W. Schulze, Thomas Klein and Ivo Ritzer, 87–95. Marburg: Schüren Verlag, 2015.
Moine, Raphaëlle. *Cinéma Genre*. Translated by Alistair Fox and Hilary Radner. Malden, MA and Oxford: Wiley-Blackwell, 2008.
Musser, Charles. 'The Travel Genre in 1903–1904: Moving toward Fictional Narratives'. In *Early Cinema: Space Frame Narrative*, edited by Thomas Elsaesser and Adam Barker, 123–32. London: BFI, 1990.
Naficy, Hamid. *An Accented Cinema: Exilic and Diasporic Filmmaking*. Princeton: Princeton University Press, 2001.
Neale, Steve. *Genre and Hollywood*. London & New York: Routledge, 2000.
Neupert, Richard. *A History of the French New Wave Cinema*. Second edition. Madison: University of Wisconsin Press, 2007.
Nornes, Abé Mark. *Cinema Babel: Translating Global Cinema*. Minneapolis: University of Minnesota Press, 2007.
Paryz, Marek, and John R. Leo. *The Post-2000 Film Western*. New York: Palgrave Macmillan, 2015.
Perkins, V. F. 'Johnny Guitar'. In *The Book of Westerns*, edited by Ian Cameron and Douglas Pye, 221–8. New York: Continuum, 1996.

Pillard, Thomas. 'Une "curieuse rencontre": la "francization" du musical hollywoodien'. In *Voyez comme on chante: films musicaux et cinéphilies populaires en France (1945–1958)*, edited by Sébastien Layerle and Raphaëlle Moine, 97–104. *Théorème* 20. Paris: Presses Sorbonne Nouvelle, 2014.

Pillard, Thomas. 'Une voix de star française sur des images américaines: Fernandel dans *L'Ennemi public no 1* (Verneuil, 1953)'. *Studies in French Cinema* 14, no. 2 (2014): 63–75.

Pitman, Joanna. 'Brigitte Bardot as a Gunslinger'. *The Times of London Magazine* 18 June 2005, 6.

Planchenault, Gaëlle. 'Accented French in Films: Performing and Evaluating In-Group Stylisations'. *Multilingua: Journal of Cross-Cultural and Interlanguage Communication* 31, no. 2 (May 2012): 253–75.

Powrie, Phil, and Marie Cadalanu. *The French Film Musical*. London: Bloomsbury, 2020.

Powrie, Phil. 'The French Musical: Swing and Big Bands in the Cinema of the 1940s and 1950s'. *Screen* 54, no. 2 (2013): 152–73.

Powrie, Phil. 'Luis Mariano et l'exotisme ordinaire'. In *Voyez comme on chante! Films musicaux et cinéphilies populaires en France (1945–1958)*, edited by Sébastien Layerle and Raphaëlle Moine, 19–29. *Théorème* 20. Paris: Presses Sorbonne Nouvelle, 2014.

Powrie, Phil. 'Thirty Years of Doctoral Theses on French Cinema'. *Studies in French Cinema* 3, no. 3 (2003): 199–203.

Regnier, Isabelle. 'Le Cow-boy restera seul'. *Le Monde*, 20 October 2009. Online edition. Available at <https://www.lemonde.fr/cinema/article/2009/10/20/lucky-luke-le-cowboy-restera-seul_1256116_3476.html> (accessed 25 July 2022).

Richardson, Kay. 'Multimodality and the Study of Popular Drama'. *Language and Literature* 19, no. 4 (2010): 378–95.

Rickman, Lance. 'Bande dessinée and the Cinematograph: Visual Narrative in 1895'. *European Comic Art* 1 (Spring 2008): 1–19.

Rieupeyrout, Jean-Louis. *La Grande Aventure du western: du Far-West à Hollywood, 1894–1963*. Paris: Éditions du Cerf, 1964.

Rieupeyrout, Jean-Louis. *Le Western, ou, le cinéma américain par excellence*. Paris: Éditions du Cerf, 1953.

Ritzer, Ivo, and Peter W. Schulze, eds. *Genre Hybridisation: Global Cinematic Flow*. Marburg: Schüren, 2013.

Rivette, Jacques. 'Notes sur une révolution'. *Cahiers du cinéma* 54 (December 1955): 17–21.

Robé, Christopher. 'When Cultures Collide: Third Cinema Meets the Spaghetti Western'. *Journal of Popular Film and Television* 42, no. 3 (2014): 163–74.

Rocha, Glauber. 'Godard's Latest Scandal', 'Diagonal Thoughts'. Translated by Stoffel Debuysere. Available at <https://www.diagonalthoughts.com/?p=2020> (accessed 10 August 2021).

Roger, Philippe. 'L'Étagement de la mise en scène dans le diptyque *Les Disparus de Saint-Agil* et *L'Enfer des anges*'. *1895* 28 (1999): 69–82.

Rohmer, Eric. 'Redécouvrir l'Amérique'. *Cahiers du cinéma* 54 (December 1955): 11–16.

Rosen, Philip. 'History, Textuality, Nation: Kracauer, Burch, and some Problems in the Study of National Cinemas'. *Theorising National Cinema*, edited by Valentina Vitali and Paul Willemen, 17–28. London: BFI, 2006.

Ross, Kristin. *Fast Cars, Clean Bodies: Decolonization and the Reordering of French Culture*. Cambridge, MA: MIT Press, 1995.

Ross, Kristin. *May '68 and its Afterlives*. Chicago: University of Chicago Press, 2002.
Rouhaud, Jacques, and Patchi. *Luis Mariano: Une vie*. Bordeaux: Editions Sud Ouest, 2006.
Rouquette, Estelle and Sam Stourdzé, eds. *Western Camarguais*. Arles: Actes Sud, 2016.
Rydell, Robert W. and Rob Kroes. *Buffalo Bill in Bologna: The Americanization of the World*. Chicago: University of Chicago Press, 1994.
Saunders, Rebecca, ed. *The Concept of the Foreign: An Interdisciplinary Dialogue*. Lanham, MD: Lexington Books, 2003.
Scheie, Timothy. 'Cowboy and Alien: the Bardot Western'. *Studies in French Cinema* 19, no. 2 (2019): 103–21.
Scheie, Timothy. '*Chez nous* on the Range: Language, Genre, and the Vernacular French Western (1956–1961)'. *Screen* 57, no. 3 (Autumn 2016): 316–35.
Scheie, Timothy. 'Genre in Transitional Cinema: Arizona Bill and the Silent French Western 1912–1914'. *French Forum* 36, nos. 2–3 (January 2012): 201–19.
Schneider, Tassilo. 'Finding a New *Heimat* in the Wild West: Karl May and the German Western of the 1960s'. In *Back in the Saddle Again: New Essays on the Western*, edited by Edward Buscombe and Roberta E. Pearson, 141–59. London: BFI, 1998.
Schwartz, Vanessa. *It's so French!: Hollywood, Paris, and the Making of the Cosmopolitan Film Culture*. Chicago and London: University of Chicago Press, 2007.
Sellier, Genevieve. '"Le Chéri des midinettes": Luis Mariano dans le courrier des lecteurs de *Cinémonde* (1949–1956)'. In *Voyez comme on chante! Films musicaux et cinéphilies populaires en France (1945–1958)*, edited by Sébastien Layerle and Raphaëlle Moine, 31–42. *Théorème*, no. 20 (Paris: Presses Sorbonne Nouvelle, 2014).
Selznick, David. *Memo from David O. Selznick*. Edited by Rudy Behlmer. New York: Modern Library, 2000.
Senghor, Léopold Sédar. *Œuvres poétiques*. Paris: Seuil, 1964.
Servat, Henry-Jean. *Luis Mariano: Les Mélodies du bonheur*. Paris: Hors-Collection, 2013.
Shohat, Ella, and Robert Stam. 'The Cinema After Babel'. *Taboo Memories, Diasporic Voices*, Durham, NC: Duke University Press, 2006, 106–38.
Shohat, Ella and Robert Stam. *Race in Translation: Culture Wars around the Postcolonial Atlantic*. New York and London: New York University Press, 2012.
Siegfried, Detlef. *Time is on my Side: Konsum und Politik in der westdeutschen Jugendkultur der 60er Jahre*. Göttingen: Wallstein Verlag, 2006.
Simsi, Simon. *Ciné-passions: le guide chiffré du cinéma en France*. Paris: Dixit, 2012.
Slotkin, Richard. *Gunfighter Nation: The Myth of the Frontier in Twentieth-Century America*. Norman: University of Oklahoma Press, 1998.
'A Smashing Kleine-Eclipse You Should Have!' *Moving Picture World* 17, no. 2 (2 August 1913).
Smith, Andrew Brodie. *Shooting Cowboys and Indians: Silent Western Films, American Culture, and the Birth of Hollywood*. Boulder: University Press of Colorado, 2003.
Smith, Gavin. 'Interview: Jean-Luc Godard'. *Film Comment* (March–April 1996). Available at <https://www.filmcomment.com/article/jean-luc-godard-interview-nouvelle-vague-histoires-du-cinema-helas-pour-moi> (accessed 16 October 2021).
Smith, Henry Nash. *Virgin Land: The American West as Symbol and Myth*. Cambridge, MA: Harvard University Press, 1950.
Sorin, Cécile. 'The Art of Borrowing: French Popular Cinema before the New Wave'. *Studies in French Cinema* 4, no. 1 (2004): 53–64.
Staig, Laurence, and Tony Williams. *Italian Westerns: The Opera of Violence*. London: Lorimer, 1975.

Stam, Robert. *Subversive Pleasures: Bakhtin, Cultural Criticism, and Film*. Baltimore: Johns Hopkins University Press, 1989.
Stanfield, Peter. *Horse Opera: The Strange History of the 1930's Singing Cowboy*. Urbana: University of Illinois Press, 2002.
Stang, Joanne. 'Vive "Les Marias" From Paris Down Mexico Way'. *New York Times*, 21 February 1965).
Stark, Trevor. 'Cinema in the Hands of the People: Chris Marker, the Medvedkin Group, and the Potential of Militant Film'. *October* 139 (Winter 2021): 117–50.
Tasker, Yvonne, ed. *Action and Adventure Cinema*. New York and London: Routledge, 2004.
Taylor, Trey. 'The Rise and Fall of Katherine Hepburn's Fake Accent'. *Atlantic Monthly* online (8 August 2013). Available at <https://www.theatlantic.com/entertainment/archive/2013/08/the-rise-and-fall-of-katharine-hepburns-fake-accent/278505> (accessed 8 January 2019).
Teo, Stephen. *Eastern Westerns*. New York and London: Routledge, 2016.
Thomas, Kevin. 'Godard's "Wind" Opens Run'. *The Los Angeles Times* (25 February 1972): H 13.
Tompkins, Jane. *West of Everything*. Oxford: Oxford University Press, 1994.
Tudor, Andrew. 'Genre'. In *The Film Genre Reader* III. Edited by Barry Keith Grant, 3–11. Austin: University of Texas Press, 2003.
Turner, Frederick Jackson. *The Frontier in American History*. New York: Henry Holt and Company, 1921.
Venture, Rémi. 'L'Aventure en Camargue'. In *Western Camarguais*, edited by Estelle Rouquette and Sam Stourdzé, 111. Arles: Actes Sud, 2016.
Verhoeff, Nanna. *The West in Early Cinema: After the Beginning*. Amsterdam: Amsterdam University Press, 2006.
Villerbu, Tangi. *BD Western: Histoire d'un genre*. Paris: Karthala, 2015.
Vincendeau, Ginette. 'Acteurs européens et cinéma classique hollywoodien – *Casablanca*, accents et authenticité'. In *Le Classicisme hollywoodien*, edited by Jean-Loup Bourget and Jacqueline Nacache, 189–202. Presses universitaires de Rennes, 2009.
Vincendeau, Ginette. *Brigitte Bardot*. London: BFI, 2013.
Vincendeau, Ginette. 'Brigitte Bardot, ou le problème de la comédie au féminin'. *Cinémas: revue d'études cinématographiques / Cinémas: Journal of Film Studies* 22, nos. 2–3 (Spring 2012): 13–34.
Vincenedeau, Ginette. 'Fernandel: de l'innocent du village à "Monsieur tout le monde"'. In *Genres et acteurs du cinéma français*, edited by Gwénaëlle Le Gras et Delphine Chedaleux, 206–33. Kindle edition. Rennes: Presses universitaires de Rennes, 2012.
Vincendeau, Ginette. 'The Frenchness of French Cinema: The Language of National Identity, from the Regional to the Trans-national'. *Studies in French Cinema: UK Perspectives 1985–2010*, edited by Will Higbee and Sarah Leahy, 337–52. Bristol and Chicago: Intellect, 2011.
Vincendeau, Ginette. 'The Old and the New: Brigitte Bardot in 1950s France'. *Paragraph* 15, no. 1 (March 1992): 73–96.
Vincendeau, Ginette. *Stars and Stardom in French Cinema*. London and New York: Continuum, 2000.
Vincendeau, Ginette. 'Western Without Americans'. Liner notes for *Cemetery Without Crosses* (restored edition), dir. Robert Hossein. Arrow Films, 2015: 6–15.

Vincendeau, Ginette, and Catherine Wheatley, eds. *Je t'aime. . .moi non plus: Franco-British Cinematic Relations*. Oxford and New York: Berghahn Books, 2010.
Vitali, Valentina, and Paul Willemen, eds. *Theorising National Cinema*. London: BFI, 2006.
Walker, Janet, ed. *Westerns: Films Through History*. New York: Routledge, 2001.
Warshow, Robert. 'Movie Chronicle: The Westerner'. In *The Western Reader*, edited by Jim Kitses and Gregg Rickman, 35–7. New York: Limelight, 1998.
Wessels, Chelsea. 'A Third Western(?): Genre and the Popular/Political in Latin America'. *Frames* 4 (January 2013). Available at <https://framescinemajournal.com/article/a-third-western-genre-and-the-popularpolitical-in-latin-america> (accessed 20 March 2022).
Wessels, Chelsea. '"Do I look Mexican?": Translating the Western Beyond National Borders'. *Transformations* 24 (2014). Available at <https://www.transformationsjournal.org/wp-content/uploads/2016/12/Wessels_Transformations24.pdf> (accessed 10 July 2022).
Williams, Linda. 'Film Bodies: Gender, Genre, and Excess'. *Film Quarterly* 44, no. 4 (Summer 1991): 2–13.
Winkler, Martin M. 'Classical Mythology and the Western Film'. *Comparative Literature Studies* 22, no. 4 (Winter 1985): 516–40.
Winkler, Martin M. 'Clytemnestra and Electra Under Western Skies'. In *Women in the Western*, edited by Sue Matheson. Edinburgh: Edinburgh University Press, 2020.
Wolff, Mark. 'Western Novels as Children's Literature in Nineteenth-Century France'. *Mosaic: A Journal for the Interdisciplinary Study of Literature* 34, no. 2 (June 2001): 87–102.
Wollen, Peter. 'Godard and Counter-Cinema: Vent d'Est'. *AfterImage* 4 (Autumn 1972): 6–17.
'Wrecked in Mid-Air' (Manufacturers' Advance Notes). *Moving Picture World* 3, no. 19 (17 January 1914).
Wright, Will. *Sixguns and Society: A Structural Study of the Western*. Berkeley: University of California Press, 1975.
Zaretsky, Robert. *Cock and Bull Stories: Folco de Baroncelli and the Invention of the Camargue*. Lincoln: University of Nebraska Press: 2004.

Filmography

Annie Oakley (Edison Company, 1894)
Bucking Broncho (Edison company, 1894)
Ghost Dance (Edison Company, 1894)
Buffalo Bill: Peaux-rouges (Lumière Company, 1896 or 1897)
Cripple Creek Barroom (James H. White, 1899)

The Great Train Robbery (Edwin S. Porter, 1903)
Indiens et cowboys (Pathé Company, 1904)
Life of an American Cowboy (Edwin S. Porter, 1906)
Mireille (Alice Guy, 1906)
Le Cowboy (Joë Hamman, ca. 1907)
Le Desperado (Joë Hamman, ca. 1910)
Le Gardian de Camargue (Léonce Perret, 1910)

The Immortal Alamo (William F. Haddock, 1911)
The Lonedale Operator (D. W. Griffith, 1911)
The Redemption of Rawhide (William F. Haddock, 1911)
The Spring Round-Up (William F. Haddock, 1911)
Coeur ardent (Jean Durand, 1912)
The Red Man's Honor / La Conscience de Cheval Rouge (Gaston Roudès, 1912)
Their Lives for Gold / Le Railway de la mort (Jean Durand, 1912)
The Battle of Elderbush Gulch (D. W. Griffith, 1913)
Course de taureaux provençale (Jean Durand, 1913)
En Camargue (Jean Durand, 1913)
La Dernière Minute / The Last Minute (possibly Gaston Roudès, 1913)
Ferrade en Camargue (Jean Durand, 1913)
Le Mystère de la banque d'Elk City / The Mong Fu Tong (possibly Gaston Roudès, 1913)
La Ville souterraine / The Subterranean City, or, Trailing the Jewel Thieves (possibly Gaston Roudès, 1913)
Wrecked in Mid-Air (French title unknown; possibly Gaston Roudès, 1913)
Face au taureau / Dem Stier gegenüber / The Bull Trainer's Revenge (possibly Joë Hamman, 1914)
Birth of a Nation (D. W. Griffith, 1915)

The Cabinet of Dr Cagliari (Robert Wiene, 1920)
Le Gardian (Joë Hamman, 1921)
L'Arlésienne (André Antoine, 1922)
Mireille (Ernest Servaes, 1922)
Le Roi de Camargue (André Hugon, 1922)
Notre Dame d'amour (André Hugon, 1923)
Battleship Potemkin (Sergei Eisenstein, 1925)
Napoléon (Abel Gance, 1927)

L'Arlésienne (Jacques de Baroncelli, 1930)
Gitanes (Jacques de Baroncelli, 1932)
La Terreur de la Pampa (Maurice Cammage, 1932)
Mireille (René Gaveau, Ernest Servaès, 1933)
Paris-Camargue (Jack Forrester, 1935)
Le Roi de Camargue (Jacques de Baroncelli, 1935)
Le Crime de Monsieur Lange (Jean Renoir, 1936)
Notre Dame d'amour (Pierre Caron, 1936)
Old Corral / Texas Serenade (Joseph Kane, 1936)
Destry Rides Again (George Marshall, 1939)
Gone with the Wind (Victor Fleming, 1939)
Stagecoach (John Ford, 1939)

Casablanca (Michael Curtiz, 1943)
Frontier Gal (Charles Lamont, 1945)
Duel in the Sun (King Vidor, 1946)
The Harvey Girls (George Sidney, 1946)
My Darling Clementine (John Ford, 1946)
Ladri di bicicletti / Bicycle Thieves (Vittorio de Sica, 1948)
Red River (Howard Hawks, 1948)
Silver River (Raoul Walsh, 1948)
She Wore a Yellow Ribbon (John Ford, 1949)
Tulsa (Stuart Heisler, 1949)
Vendetta en Camargue / Miss Cow-boy (Jean Devaivre, 1949)

Annie Get Your Gun (George Sidney, 1950)
Cinderella (Walt Disney, 1950)
The Gunfighter (Henry King, 1950)
Winchester '73 (Anthony Mann, 1950)
An American in Paris (Vincente Minnelli, 1951)
Andalousie / Andalusia (Robert Vernay, 1951)
High Noon (Fred Zinnemann, 1952)
Monkey Business (Howard Hawks, 1952)
Moulin Rouge (John Huston, 1952)
Le Petit Monde de Don Camillo / The Little World of Don Camillo (Julien Duvivier, 1952)
Rancho Notorious (Fritz Lang, 1952)
Violettes impériales / Imperial Violets (Richard Pottier, 1952)
Crin-Blanc / White Mane (Albert Lamorisse, 1953)
L'Ennemi public no 1 / The Most Wanted Man (Henri Verneuil, 1953)
Escape from Fort Bravo (John Sturges, 1953)

Hondo (John Farrow, 1953)
Shane (George Stevens, 1953)
The Wild One (Laslo Benedek, 1953)
Broken Lance (Edward Dmytryk, 1954)
Bronco Apache (Robert Aldrich, 1954)
French Cancan (Jean Renoir, 1954)
Johnny Guitar (Nicolas Ray, 1954)
On the Waterfront (Elia Kazan, 1954)
Pushover (Richard Quine, 1954)
Seven Brides for Seven Brothers (Stanley Donen, 1954)
Vera Cruz (Robert Aldrich, 1954)
Doctor at Sea (Ralph Thomas, 1955)
Kiss Me Deadly (Robert Aldrich, 1955)
The Man from Laramie (Anthony Mann, 1955)
Oklahoma! (Fred Zinnemann, 1955)
Rebel Without a Cause (Nicholas Ray, 1955)
To Catch a Thief (Alfred Hitchcock, 1955)
Around the World in Eighty Days (Michael Anderson, 1956)
Le Chanteur de Mexico / The Singer of Mexico (Richard Pottier, 1956)
Et Dieu... créa la femme / And God Created Woman (Roger Vadim, 1956)
Fernand Cow-boy (Guy LeFranc, 1956)
Folies-Bergère (Henri Decoin, 1956)
Giant (George Stevens, 1956)
Helen of Troy (Robert Wise, 1956)
Love Me Tender (Robert Webb, 1956)
The Searchers (John Ford, 1956)
Casino de Paris (André Hunebelle, 1957)
Forty Guns (Samuel Fuller, 1957)
Funny Face (Stanley Donen, 1957)
Jailhouse Rock (Richard Thorpe, 1957)
Une nuit au Moulin Rouge / A Night at the Moulin Rouge (Jean-Claude Roy, 1957)
The True Story of Jesse James (Nicolas Ray, 1957)
Gigi (Vincente Minnelli, 1958)
Man of the West (Anthony Mann, 1958)
Mon oncle (Jacques Tati, 1958)
Sérénade au Texas / Texas Serenade (Richard Pottier, 1958)
Babette s'en va-t-en guerre / Babette Goes to War (Christian-Jaque, 1959)
Rio Bravo (Howard Hawks, 1959)
Warlock (Edward Dmytryk, 1959)

A bout de souffle / Breathless (Jean-Luc Godard, 1960)
Chien de pique / Jack of Spades (Yves Allégret, 1960)
Flaming Star (Don Siegel, 1960)
La Loi de la poudre (Paul Ricard, 1960)
Sergeant Rutledge (John Ford, 1960)
La Vérité / The Truth (Henri-Georges Clouzot, 1960)
Zazie dans le métro (Louis Malle, 1960)
La Belle Américaine / The American Beauty (Robert Dhéry, 1961)
Lola (Jacques Demy, 1961)

One-Eyed Jacks (Marlon Brando, 1961)
Cléo de 5 à 7 / Cleo from 5 to 7 (Agnès Varda, 1962)
L'Eclisse / The Eclipse (Michelangelo Antonioni, 1962)
The Man Who Shot Liberty Valance (John Ford, 1962)
Vie privée / A Very Private Affair (Louis Malle, 1962)
D'où viens-tu, Johnny? / Where Are You From, Johnny? (Noël Howard, 1963)
Le Mépris / Contempt (Jean-Luc Godard, 1963)
Angélique, marquise des Anges (Bernard Borderie, 1964)
Bande à part / Band of Outsiders (Jean-Luc Godard, 1964)
Goldfinger (Guy Hamilton, 1964)
Limonádový Joe aneb Konská opera / Lemonade Joe (Oldrich Lipsky, 1964)
Per un pugno di dollari / A Fistful of Dollars (Sergio Leone, 1964)
Cat Ballou (Elliott Silverstein, 1965)
Dear Brigitte (Henry Koster, 1965)
Per qualche dollaro in più / For a Few Dollars More (Sergio Leone, 1965)
Pierrot le fou (Jean-Luc Godard, 1965)
Viva Maria! (Louis Malle, 1965)
La Bataille d'Algers / The Battle of Algiers (Gillo Pontecorvo, 1966)
Il buono, il brutto, il cattivo / The Good the Bad and the Ugly (Sergio Leone, 1966)
El Dorado (Howard Hawks, 1966)
La resa dei conti / The Big Gundown (Sergio Sollima, 1966)
Die Söhne der grossen Bärin / The Sons of Great Bear (Josef Mach, 1966)
Stagecoach (Gordon Douglas, 1966)

La Chinoise (Jean-Luc Godard, 1967)
Les Demoiselles de Rochefort / The Young Girls of Rochefort (Jacques Demy, 1967)
Faccia a faccia / Face to Face (Sergio Sollima, 1967)
L'Indomptable Angélique / Untamable Angélique (Bernard Borderie, 1967)
Playtime (Jacques Tati, 1967)
Quién sabe? / A Bullet for the General (Damiano Damiani, 1967)
The War Wagon (Burt Kennedy, 1967)
The Way West (Andrew V. McLaglen, 1967)
Weekend (Jean-Luc Godard, 1967)
Angélique et le Sultan / Angélique and the Sultan (Bernard Borderie, 1968)
C'era una volta il West / Once Upon a Time in the West (Sergio Leone, 1968)
Corri uomo corri / Run Man Run (Sergio Sollima, 1968)
Il grande silenzio / The Great Silence (Sergio Corbucci, 1968)
Il mio corpo per un poker / The Belle Starr Story (Piero Cristofani and Lina Wertmüller, 1968)
One + One / The Rolling Stones: Sympathy for the Devil (Jean-Luc Godard, 1968)
Shalako (Edward Dmytryk, 1968)
Antonio das mortes (Glauber Rocha, 1969)
Butch Cassidy and the Sundance Kid (Richard Lester, 1969)
Une corde, un colt / Cemetery Without Crosses (Robert Hossein, 1969)
Le Gai Savoir / Joy of Learning (Dziga-Vertov Group, 1969)
Gli specialisti / The Specialists (Sergio Corbucci, 1969)
Luttes en Italie / Lotte in Italia ((Dziga-Vertov Group, 1969)
Il pistolero dell'Ave Maria / Forgotten Pistolero (Ferdinando Baldi, 1969)
Pravda (Dziga-Vertov Group, 1969)
Tepepa (Giulio Petroni, 1969)

Le Vent d'est / Wind from the East (Dziga Vertov Group, 1969)
The Wild Bunch (Sam Peckinpah, 1969)

Little Big Man (Arthur Penn, 1970)
Soldier Blue (Ralph Nelson, 1970)
Une aventure de Billy le Kid / A Girl is a Gun (Luc Moullet, 1971)
Les Pétroleuses / The Legend of Frenchie King (Christian-Jaque, 1971)
Soleil rouge / Red Sun (Terence Young, 1971)
Vladimir et Rosa (Dziga-Vertov Group, 1971)
Tout va bien (Dziga-Vertov Group, 1972)
Ulzana's Raid (Robert Aldrich, 1972)
Blazing Saddles (Mel Brooks, 1974)
Touche pas la femme blanche! / Don't Touch the White Woman! (Marco Ferreri, 1974)

Heaven's Gate (Michael Cimino, 1980)
Au revoir les enfants (Louis Malle, 1987)

Dances With Wolves (Kevin Costner, 1990)
City Slickers (Ron Underwood, 1991)
Thelma & Louise (Ridley Scott, 1991)
Unforgiven (Clint Eastwood, 1992)
The Ballad of Little Jo (Maggie Greenwald, 1993)
Posse (Mario Van Peebles, 1993)
Dead Man (Jim Jarmusch, 1995)
Western (Manuel Poirier, 1997)

Blueberry / Renegade (Jan Kounen, 2004)
Les Dalton / The Daltons (Phillipe Haïm, 2004)
Brokeback Mountain (Ang Lee, 2005)
Bandidas (Joachim Roenning and Espen Sandburg, 2006)
3:10 to Yuma (Kames Mangold, 2007)
The Assassination of Jesse James by the Coward Robert Ford (Andrew Dominik, 2007)
Big City (Djamel Bensalah, 2007)
No Country for Old Men (Ethan and Joel Coen, 2007)
Les Colts de l'or noir (Pierre Romanello, 2008)
Lucky Luke (James Huth, 2009)

True Grit (Ethan and Joel Coen, 2010)
Cowboys and Aliens (Jon Favreau, 2011)
Django Unchained (Quentin Tarantino, 2012)
La Loi des maudits (Pierre Romanello, 2013)
The Lone Ranger (Gore Verbinski, 2013)
The Revenant (Alejandro Iñárritu, 2015)
Les Frères Sisters / The Sisters Brothers (Jacques Audiard, 2018)
L'État sauvage / Savage State (David Perrault, 2019)

The Power of the Dog (Jane Campion, 2021)

Index

Note: Page numbers in italics are illustrations and those followed by n are notes. Film titles are given in the form given in the Filmography.

A bout de souffle/Breathless (Jean-Luc Godard, 1960), 193
Academy Awards, 122
'accented cinema', 118n
African American speech, 114
Aicard, Jean
   Le Roi de Camargue, 72
   Notre-Dame d'amour, 72
Aimard, Gustave, 2
L'Aïoli, 68
Algerian redubbing, 136n
alienation, 108–9
   Bardot, Brigitte, 137–61
Altman, Rick, 13–14, 29–30, 37n
American capitalism, 191–2, *191*
American culture industry, 95–6
American exceptionalism, 106
An American in Paris (Vincente Minnelli, 1951), 102, 125–7
American Production Code, 139, 165
Americanisation, 101, 134
Americanness, 1–2, 94, 134
   musicals, 123–9
Andalousie/Andalusia (Robert Vernay, 1951), 128
Anderson, Benedict, 33, 105, 138

Angélique marquise des Anges (Bernard Borderie, 1964), 174–5, *174*
anti-cinema, 183–9
Antonio das mortes (Glauber Rocha, 1969), 202n
Apaches, 137, 146
Arcueil quarries, 42
Arizona, 42
Arizona Bill films, 41–61, 58n, 64–7, 76n
L'Arlésienne (Jacques de Baroncelli, 1930), 75
'art and foreign' films, 139–40
'art cinema', 2
Au revoir les enfants (Louis Malle, 1987), 144
Audiard, Jacques, 208–9
Audiard, Michel, 139
Audouard, Yvan, 90
auteurs, 2, 17, 20, 24n, 138, 180–3
automobiles, 91–4, 96, 98n
Une aventure de Billy le Kid/A Girl is a Gun (Luc Moullet, 1971), 202n
awards, 122, 123, 163–4, 209, 213n

Babette s'en va-t-en guerre/Babette Goes to War (Christian-Jacque, 1959), 139
baguette westerns, 5, 162–204
bande dessinée (BD) albums, 2–3, 25n, 119n, 207–8, 213n
  Festival International de la Bande Dessinée, 207
Bandidas (Joachim Roenning and Espen Sandburg, 2006), 25n
Bardomania, 140–1
Bardot, Brigitte, 2, 103, 137–61, *142, 144, 151*
  in English, 117n, 149–50, *150*, 157
  'man's role', 141–4, 150–7
Baroncelli, Jacques de, 72–3
Baroncelli, Jean de, 156
  Le Monde, 149
Baroncelli-Javon, Folco de, 62, 64, 67–9, 73–4, 76–8n, 96
Barthes, Roland, 129, 178n, 199, 202–3n
Bastide, Bernard, 58n, 76n
La Bataille d'Algers/The Battle of Algiers (Gillo Pontecorvo, 1966), 201n
The Battle of Elderbush Gulch (D. W. Griffith, 1913), 48, 83
Battleship Potemkin (Sergei Eisenstein, 1925), 187
Bazin, André, 18, 19
Bellour, Raymond, 19, 26n
Bergfelder, Tim, 25n
Bergman, Ingrid, 122, 135n
Big City (Djamel Bensalah, 2007), 206
Bilhau, Emile, 85
Birth of a Nation (D. W. Griffith, 1915), 47
Blackman, Honor, 148
Bleton, Paul, 58n
Blueberry series, 3, 25n
  L'expérience secrète, 207–8
Boetticher, Budd, 203–4n
Bourdieu, Pierre, 133

Bourvil, André, 102, 127
Bowser, Eileen, 60n
box-office receipts, 122, 133, 139, 143–4, 156, 164, 176, 202n
Brando, Marlon, 94
Brazilian cinema, 187
Brecht, Bertolt, 181–2, 185, 189, 199, 202–3n
Brooks, Peter, 213n
Buffalo Bill, 145–6
Buffalo Bill's *Wild West*, 2, 64, 69–75, *70*, 77n, 86, 93, 96
Burch, Noël, 30, 36n
Burns, Emily, 58n, 79n

Cahiers du cinéma, 18, 25n, 93, 180–1, 189, 190, 193, 203n
California, 1–2, 42
Camarguais tradition, 67–74, 77n, 81–8
Camargue films, 57, 62–79, 81–8, 206
  de-westernised, 72–5
  re-westernised, 81–8
Camargue region, 2–3, 42, 53–4, 56–7, 58n, 61n, 69, 88–96
camembert westerns, 162–78
Campbell, Neil, 34–5
Canby, Vincent, 188
can-can dance, 126
Cannes Film Festival, 31–2, 123
Cardin, Pierre, 142
Cardinale, Claudia, 137, 150–7, 173
Caron, Leslie, 103
Caron, Pierre, 72
Casablanca (Michael Curtiz, 1943), 122
Cassel, Vincent, 3, 207
Cat Ballou (Elliott Silverstein, 1965), 151
Cawelti, John, 24n
  Six-Gun Mystique, 15
censorship, 144
Centre National Cinématographique, 139

C'era una volta il West/Once Upon a Time in the West (Sergio Leone, 1968), 151, 173, 176
Cerisuelo, Marc, 189, 201n, 203n
César awards, 123, 209
Chabrol, Claude, 25n
Le Chanteur de Mexico/The Singer of Mexico (Richard Pottier, 1956), 128–9
Chapier, Henri, 143, 149, 152
Chateaubriand, René de, *Atala*, 2
Chien de pique/Jack of Spades (Yves Allégret, 1960), 5–6
China, 188
Chinese criminals, 48–9
La Chinoise (Jean-Luc Godard, 1967), 181
Chion, Michel, 118n, 135n
Christian-Jaque, 2, 139, 150–7
Cimino, Michael, 163
cinéaste militant, 186
Cinecittà studio, 16, 166
Cinémathèque française, 31–2
cinéma-vérité, 187
Cinémonde, 128
Cineriz distribution company, 179
Cirque Pinder, 128–9
Clouzot, Henri-Georges, 139
Coca-Cola, 95–6
Cohn-Bendit, Daniel, 144, 179–80, 195–7, 197, 202n, 204n
colonial settings, 4–5, 101–20
Colorado, 42
'Les Colorados', 85–6
Les Colts de l'or noir (Pierre Romanello, 2008), 206–7
Connery, Sean, 137, 144–50
Constantine, Eddie, 5–6, 22, 27n
consumer culture, 91–4
Cooper, James Fenimore, *The Leatherstocking Tales*, 2
Copland, Aaron, 127
Une corde, un colt/Cemetery Without Crosses (Robert Hossein, 1969), 21, 168–77, 176, 199–200

Le Courrier cinématographique, 1, 9n, 46–8, 58–9n
Course de taureaux provençale (Jean Durand, 1913), 91
Le Cowboy (Joë Hamman, ca. 1907), 41, 44
Crawford, Joan, 140
Crépeau, Michel, 58n
Le Crime de Monsieur Lange (Jean Renoir, 1936), 4
Crin-Blanc/White Mane (Albert Lamorisse, 1953), 75
Crisp, Colin, 14, 19–20, 122
Crowther, Bosley, 165
'culinary epithets', 25n, 164
  baguette westerns, 5, 162–204
  camembert westerns, 162–78
  spaghetti westerns, 162–78

Dances with Wolves (Kevin Costner, 1990), 108, 163–4
Daney, Serge, 202n
Daudet, Alphonse, *L'Arlésienne*, 72
de Beauvoir, Simone, 140–1
De la Bretèque, François Amy, 77n, 97n, 98n
Dear Brigitte (Henry Koster, 1965), 149
Delafosse, Maurice, 113–14
DeMille, Agnes, 127
La Dernière Minute/The Last Minute (possibly Gaston Roudès, 1913), 52–7, 55, 65
Derrida, Jacques, 35
Destry Rides Again (George Marshall, 1939), 140
Devaivre, Jean, 81–8
de-westernisation, 64, 72–5
Dietrich, Marlene, 140
Disney, 112
Dmytryk, Edward, 146, 147, 152, 157
'Dollars Trilogy', 165–6
Dorsday, Michel, 152
D'où viens-tu Johnny?/Where Are You From, Johnny? (Noël Howard, 1963), 88–96, 89, 90, 93

dubbing, 103, 105, 108–9, 114, 171
  redubbing, 136n
Duel in the Sun (King Vidor, 1946), 83
Dujardin, Jean, 3, 208
Durand, Jean, 66
Dyer, Richard, 121–2, 137–8
Dynamite Jack (1961), 102, 129–34, *132*
  language, 129–34
  redubbing, 136n
Dziga Vertov Group, 168, 183, 187, 190, 201n, 202n

East Germany, *Indianerfilme*, 108
Eastwood, Clint, 163–4, 166, 179
Eclair studio, 2, 42, 56
Eclipse studio, 6, 42, 45, 48
Edison Kinetoscope device, 42, 84, 86
Eisenstein, Sergei, 187
El Dorado (Howard Hawks, 1966), 163
Eleftheriotis, Dimitris, 23n, 167
Eleventh Year (Dziga-Vertov Group, 1928), 187
English language
  in America, 106–7
  Bardot, Brigitte in, 117n, 149–50, *150*, 157
  in French film, 115, 208–9
  and French language, 210
  signs, 109–10, *110*, 124, 127, 130
L'Ennemi public no 1/The Most Wanted Man (Henri Verneuil, 1953), 133
Escape from Fort Bravo (John Sturges, 1953), 213n
Et Dieu ... créa la femme/And God Created Woman (Roger Vadim, 1956), 103, 137, 139
L'État sauvage/Savage State (David Perrault, 2019), 209–13
European cinema, 34
European pessimism, 173
European Union, 34
European westerns, 19–21

Face au taureau/Dem Stier gegenüber/ The Bull Trainer's Revenge (possibly Joë Hamman, 1914), 64–7, 69, 73, 76n
Falconer, Pete, 177n
Fanon, Franz, *Black Skin, White Masks*, 114
Far-West, 43–5, 57, 73, 82, 108 – *le Far-West*, Far West, Far-West
faux-westerns et curiosités, 20–1, 33, 206
Félibrige, 67–8, 77–8n
female characters, 113, 140, 150, 173
  'man's role', 141–4
female voice, 198–9
Fernand Cow-boy (Guy LeFranc, 1956), 22, 102, 109–16, *110*, 123–4, 130
Fernandel, 2, 102, 123, 130–3, 136n, 152
ferrade sequence, 66–8, 85–6, 88–90
Ferreri, Marco, 202n
Ferry, Gabriel, *Le Coureur des bois*, 2
Festival International de la Bande Dessinée, 207
film noir, 89, 91
filmed versions of stage shows, 128
Films Joë Hamman, 62–3
filone, 16, 164–71
fin du cinéma, 188
fin-de-siècle, 2, 126
Fisher, Austin, 171, 177n, 194
  Radical Frontiers in the Spaghetti Westerns: Politics, Violence, and Popular Italian Cinema, 166–7
Fonda, Jane, 121, 151
Fontainebleau forest, 2, 42
Ford, John, 83, *84*, 90, 107, 111, 146, 209–10
Forty Guns (Samuel Fuller, 1957), 140, 193
Franco-Belgian *BD*, 207
Franco-Italian co-production, 142–3, 151, 168–77

Frayling, Christopher, 24n, 170–1, 177n, 190, 194
  Spaghetti Westerns: Cowboys and Europeans from Karl May to Sergio Leone, 166–7
French cinema, 31–5
French Film Office, 139
French musical films, 128, 135n
French politics, 167–8
French westerns, 55–7
Frenchness, 4–9, 50, 101–4, 133, 134, 140
  musicals, 102–3, 125–7
  transnational, 101–2, 127, 129
Les Frères Sisters/The Sisters Brothers (Jacques Audiard, 2018), 208–9
Fuller, Samuel, 140, 193

Le Gai savoir/Joy of Learning (Dziga-Vertov Group, 1969), 181–2
Gainsbourg, Serge, 148
Gance, Abel, 4
Garbo, Greta, 121
Le Gardian (Joë Hamman, 1921), 63, 72, 73, 78n
gardians, 63–6, 70, 73, 75, 78n, 82–5, 90
  Nacioun gardiano ('Gardian Nation'), 68–9
Gaumont company, 6, 41–2, 59n, 61n, 76n
  actualités, 66
George Eastman Museum, 206
George Kleine Company, 46
German cinema, 30
German westerns, 108, 166, 177n
Gigi (Vincente Minnelli, 1958), 101–103
Gilbert, John, 121
Giré, Jean François, 20–1
Gitanes (Jacques de Baroncelli, 1932), 72–3
Godard, Jean-Luc, 2, 26n, 137, 179–204, 201–4n

Goldfinger (Guy Hamilton, 1964), 148
Gorin, Jean-Pierre, 183, 186–94, 198
The Great Train Robbery (Edwin S. Porter, 1903), 29, 42, 47, 59n, 151
Grey, Zane, 147
  Riders of the Purple Sage, 147
Griffith, D. W., 46–50, 83, 146, 187
Gunning, Tom, 43, 59n
Guy, Alice, 67

Hallyday, Johnny, 2, 88–96
Hamman, Joë (Jean), 21, 41–6, 49, 54–7, 58–61n, 62–71, 73–5, 76n, 78n, 87, 177n
Hansen, Miriam Bratu, 38n, 80, 116
Hayward, Susan, 58n
  French National Cinema, 23, 31–3
Heaven's Gate (Michael Cimino, 1980), 163
Hindi popular cinema, 23n
Holden, William, 213n
'Hollywood Injun English', 112–14, 120n
'Hollywood-Mosfilm', 189–90, 192–3
Hossein, Robert, 21, 168–77
Howard, Noël, 98n
humanism, 173

Il buono, il brutto, il cattivo/The Good, the Bad and the Ugly (Sergio Leone, 1966), 16
Il grande silenzio/The Great Silence (Sergio Corbucci, 1968), 147
Il mio corpo per un poker/The Belle Starr Story (Piero Cristofani and Lina Wertmuller, 1968), 173
Il pistolero dell'Ave Maria/Forgotten Pistolero (Ferdinando Baldi, 1969), 173
image juste, 186, 189, 191, 198–200
Indianerfilme, East German, 108

'Indians', 62, 66, 74, 77n, 82–3, 97n, 108, 115, 194, 198, 206; *see also* Native Americans
Indiens et cowboys (Pathe Company, 1904), 43
international westerns, 108, 164, 167
'Italian plot', 170–1
Italian westerns, 16, 177n, 193–4
    American stars in, 16
Italian-ness, 167

Jacob Ištá Ská (Jacob White Eyes), 71, 74, 79n
Japanese film, 30
'Jersey scenery', 46, 51–2, 54
Johnny Guitar (Nicolas Ray, 1954), 90, 140, 205
Jourdan, Louis, 103
just an image, 194–200, *197*

Kael, Pauline, 138–9, 149, 163–5
Keil, Charlie, 46
Kelly, Gene, 102, 125–7
Kitses, Jim, 24n
Kleine, George, 48, 56, 58n, 60n
Kommune I, 144
Kounen, Jean, 207
Kracauer, Siegfried, 30, 36n
Kuisel, Richard, 132–3

L.A. Times, 188
L'Abbé Prévost, *Manon Lescaut*, 2
Ladd, Alan, 146
Lagayette, Pierre, 213n
L'Amour, Louis, 146
Langford, Barry, 16
language
    'accented cinema', 118n
    African American speech, 114
    bilingualism, 155
    coach, 122
    Creole, 211–12
    Czech, 108–9
    Dynamite Jack (1961), 129–34

    'flattening' of linguistic identity, 112–13
    French and English language, 130–2, 210
    French speech, English writing, *131*
    'Hollywood Injun English', 112–14, 120n
    inconsistencies in, 130–2
    linguistic diegesis, 111
    linguistic stereotype, 113–14, 120n
    'Mainstream United States English', 112
    Mexican characters, 107
    'Middle-Atlantic' pronunciation, 122
    monolingualism, 106–7
    and the mythic West, 104–9
    native, 107–8
    pidgin dialect, 113–14
    Provençal, 66–74, 78n
    as signifier of ethnicity, 111–13
    Spanish, 107, 135n
    and star persona, 155
    of stars on the Francophone frontier, 121–36
    as uncinematic, 106
    'us' and 'them', 105
    see also English language
Lefrançois, Thierry, 58n
Leguèbe, Eric, 58n
Leone, Sergio, 16, 24n, 147, 151, 164–6, 169–70, 173, 175–6, 179
Lesage, Julia, 198–9, 202n
Limonádový Joe aneb Konská opera/ Lemonade Joe (Oldrich Lipsky, 1964), 108–9
Lippi-Green, Rosina, 112
Lloyd, Euan, 144–50, 157
La Loi des maudits (Pierre Romanello, 2013), 207
The Lonedale Operator (D. W. Griffith, 1911), 49–50
Loosely, David, 94
Lucky Luke (James Huth, 2009), 208

Lucky Luke series, 3, 119n, 207, 213n
Lumière awards, 209
Lumières, *actualités*, 42
Lux company, 41

Maison Méliès, 1–2
Malle, Louis, 2, 141–4, 179
Man of the West (Anthony Mann, 1958), 193
The Man Who Shot Liberty Valance (John Ford, 1962), 107
Mann, Anthony, 84–5, 193, 205
Maoism, 181, 188, 201n
Mariano, Luis, 2, 22, 27n, 102, 123, 125–9, *125*, 133, 135n
Marker, Chris, 201n
Marxism, 143–4, 167, 181–3
Marxist-Leninist critique, 181, 185, 198–9
mas du l'Amarée, 81–5, 89, 91
masculinity, 87, 115, 140, 157, 163, 173–4
Matheson, Sue, 173
May, Karl, 108, 166
May 1968, 167–8, 176, 179, 182, 184, 186, 195–8, 201n
McBean, James, 184
McClain, William, 165
McQuade, James, 60n
Meek, Barbra, 112–13, 120n
Méliès, Gaston, 1–2
Méliès, Georges, 1–2, 3, 9n
Méliès Company, 1–2, 42
Mellen, Joan, 188
melodrama, 36n, 126, 213n
Le Mépris/Contempt (Jean-Luc Godard, 1963), 137, 138
Mercier, Michèle, 174–5, 178n
Mexican characters, 171
   language, 107
Midi, 40–99, 71, 72, 88, 97n
Miller and Van Riper, *International Westerns: Re-locating the Frontier*, 25n
Mireille (Alice Guy, 1906), 67, 73, 75
Mireille (René Gaveau, Ernest Servaës, 1933), 73
mise-en-scène, 53, 65, 72, 80–1, 83, 85, 89–90, 185, 191, 192
misogyny, 173–4
Mistral, Frédéric, 67–8, 72–3
Mitchell, Lee Clark, 15
Mix, Tom, 83–4, *86*
Mohr, Gregory, 61n
Moine, Raphaëlle, 14, 20
   Cinema Genre, 26–7n
Monogram studios, 203–4n
montage, 85, 88, 148
'moral occult', 213n
Moreau, Jeanne, 2, 137, 141–4, *144*
Morricone, Ennio, 170
Motion Pictures Patent Company (Thomas Edison's 'Trust'), 1, 45–6
Moullet, Luc, 202n
movie magazines, 122–3, 128
Moving Picture World, 54, 59n, 60n, 61n
music
   D'où viens-tu Johnny?/Where Are You From, Johnny? (Noël Howard, 1963), 88–91, 94–5
   Une corde, un colt/Cemetery Without Crosses (Robert Hossein, 1969), 170
   Les Pétroleuses/The Legend of Frenchie King (Christian-Jacque, 1971), 150, 152
   Shalako (Edward Dmytryk, 1968), 144–6
   star persona, 123
   Le Vent d'est/Wind from the East (Dziga-Vertov Group, 1969), 184, 190
musicals
   "Americanness", 123–9
   D'où viens-tu Johnny?/Where Are You From, Johnny? (Noël Howard, 1963), 93
   French, 128, 135n

French language, 134
Frenchness, 102–4, 125–7
genre, 26, 29
Hollywood, 101
lavish production numbers, 126–7
Viva Maria! (Louis Malle, 1965), 143
Musser, Charles, 59n
Le Mystère de la banque d'Elk City/The Mong-Fu Tong (possibly Gaston Roudès, 1913), 48–52, 49, 51

Nacioun gardiano ('Gardian Nation'), 68–9
Naficy, Hamid, 118n
Nanterre student movement, 180, 196
Napoléon (Abel Gance, 1927), 4
national cinema, 28–39, 37n
Native Americans, 70–5, 78n, 107–14, 210
 language, 107–8
 silence, 130
 see also 'Indians'
Nazism, 30
Neale, Steve, 30
 Genre and Hollywood, 13
New Jersey, 42
New Wave films, 26n, 31–3, 133, 138, 148, 152, 179, 181
New York Times, 165, 188
Nickelodeon boom, 43, 71
'Nixon-Paramount', 187, 190, 193, 197
Notre-Dame d'amour (Pierre Caron, 1936), 72
Nouvel Observateur, 132

Oakley, Annie, 42, 84–5
Oklahoma! (Fred Zinnemann, 1955), 125, 127
On the Waterfront (Elia Kazan, 1954), 94
O'Neill, Terry, 154
Oscars, 163–4

panoramic landscape films, 46–7
panoramic views, 53–4
Paris, 41, 68–70, 88–96, 101–3, *126*, 128–9, 173–4, 183, 195–6, 201n, 205–6
Paryz, Marek, 25n
Pathé, 2, 9n, 42
Per un pugno di dollari/A Fistful of Dollars (Sergio Leone, 1964), 164, 179
Le Petit Monde de Don Camillo/ The Little World of Don Camillo (Julien Duvivier, 1952), 132
Les Pétroleuses/The Legend of Frenchie King (Christian-Jacque, 1971), 137, 141, 150–7, *151*
Pillard, Thomas, 133
Pixérécourt style, 126
Poirier, Manuel, 206
political 'spaghettis', 167
political westerns, 186
Pollard, Michael J., 153, 155
Pontecorvo, Gillo, 201n
pornographic films, 3
Porter, Edwin S., 42, 151
Pottier, Richard, 2
Pravda (Dziga-Vertov Group, 1969), 201n
Provençal identity, 67–8, 73–4, 77–8n, 93, 98n
Provençal language, 66–74, 78n
publicity campaigns, 122–3

radio shows, 122, 123, 128–9
Rancho Notorious (Fritz Lang, 1952), 140
Ray, Nicholas, 90, 193, 205
Raynaud, Fernand, 102, 109–16
The Red Man's Honor/La Conscience de Cheval Rouge (Gaston Roudès, 1912), 59n, 60n
Reilly, John C., 213n
Renan, Ernst, 73
Renoir, Jean, 4

return of the western repressed, 80–99
Rieupeyrout, Jean-Louis, 21–2
   Le Western, ou le cinéma américain par excellence, 19
Robé, Christopher, 177n
Rocha, Glauber, 187, 188, 189, 201n, 202n
Rodeo, 127
Le Roi de Camargue (Jacques de Baroncelli, 1935), 75
Roma, 71, 73, 81–91
Romanian shooting location, 208–9
Ross, Kristin, 91–4, 98n, 201n
Rousseau, Jean-Jacques, 2
RSA plot (repressive state apparatus), 171

Saintes-Maries-de-la-Mer, 91, 95
'Scènes de la vie l'ouest Américain' series of films, 41–2, 59n
Schwartz, Vanessa, 37, 103, 117n
   It's So French!: Hollywood, Paris and the Making of the Cosmopolitan Film Culture, 101
The Searchers (John Ford, 1956), 90, 209
Selig Company, western 'panoramas', 42
Selznick, David O., 122
Senghor, Léopold Sédar, 120n
Sérénade au Texas/Texas Serenade (Richard Pottier, 1958), 22, 102, 123–9, *126*, 133, 135n
Service de lancement des oeuvres nouvelles (SLON), 201n
Shalako (Edward Dmytryk, 1968), 137, 144–6, 155, 157
Shane (George Stevens, 1953), 89, *145*, 146
sharpshooting, 84–5
Shohat, Ella, 115
silent films, 2–6
   Camargue region, 57, 58n, 87, 206
   Christian-Jaque, 151
   exclusion of, 47
   French westerns, 19–20, 198
   Hamman, Joe (Jean), 42–3
   star persona, 121
   westerns, 16, 24n, 75
singing cowboy, 16, 24n, 90, 96, 125, *125*, 135n
Sioux Ghost Dance, 71
Slotkin, Richard, 47
   Gunfighter Nation: The Myth of the Frontier in Twentieth-Century America, 15–16
La société des films Neptune, 82, 88
Die Söhne der grossen Bärin/The Sons of Great Bear (Josef Mach, 1966), 108
Solanas, Fernando, 182
Sorin, Cécile, 21–2, 120, 133
South America setting, 4–5
Soviet socialist realism, 187
spaghetti-style westerns, 162–78, *170*, 179–80
Spanish language, 107, 135n
Spanish shooting location, 147, 151, 170, 208–9
spectacle, 68–9, 82, 85–8, 93
Stagecoach (Gordon Douglas, 1966), 163
Stagecoach (John Ford, 1939), 28–9, 36n, 83, 111, 146
Stalin, Joseph, 186–7, 196
Stam, Robert, 115
Stanwyck, Barbara, 140
Star Film Company, 3
Star Film Ranch, San Antonio, 1–2
'star image', 121, 123, 137–8, 140–1
star persona
   accent as, 121
   and language, 155
Stevens, George, 146
Strode, Woody, 146
stunts, 54–5, *55*, 61n, 73, 85–6
subtitles, 103, 105

Technicolor, 101, 146
technology, 69–71, 74–5, 78n, 80
television, 128–9
Texas, 42
'third cinema', 187
Tompkins, Jane, 15, 47, 107, 173
Touche pas la femme blanche (Marco Ferreri, 1974), 202n
tourism, 96, 98n
tragedy, 172–3, 178n, 199
transnational 'Frenchness', 101–2, 127, 129
transnational frontier, 33–6
trente glorieuses, 81, 91–2
The True Story of Jesse James (Nicolas Ray, 1957), 193
Tudor, Andrew, 28–9
Turner, Frederick Jackson, 106–8

underground cinema, 187
Unforgiven (Clint Eastwood, 1992), 163–4

Vadim, Roger, 137, 151
Vanel, Charles, 73
Vartan, Sylvie, 89, 94
Vendetta en Camargue/Miss Cow-boy (Jean Devaivre, 1949), 81–8, *86*, *87*
Le Vent d'est/Wind from the East (Dziga-Vertov Group, 1969), 168, 179–204, *191*
Vera Cruz (Robert Aldrich, 1954), 143
Verhoeff, Nanna, 59n, 60n
La Vérité/The Truth (Henri-Georges Clouzot, 1960), 139
'vernacular modernism', 80
Vie privée/A Very Private Affair (Louis Malle, 1962), 142
La Ville souterraine/The Subterranean City, or, Trailing the Jewel Thieves (possibly Gaston Roudès, 1913), 56
Vincendeau, Ginette, 117n, 118n, 128, 135n, 142, 157n, 168–77

Violettes impériales/Imperial Violets (Richard Pottier, 1952), 128
Viva Maria Gruppe, 144
Viva Maria! (Louis Malle, 1965), 137, 141–4, *142*, *144*, 156, 179
voiceover, 191–2, 195–8
Volonté, Gian Maria, 179, 183–4, 190, 192–4

The War Wagon (Burt Kennedy, 1967), 163
Warner Brothers, 122
Warshow, Robert, 24n, 35n
  'Movie Chronicle: the Westerner', 15
The Way West (Andrew V. McLaglen, 1967), 163
Weekend (Jean-Luc Godard, 1967), 181
Wessels, Chelsea, 24–5n
West Germany, *Winnetou* films, 108, 166
Westbound (Budd Boetticher, 1959), 203–4n
Western (Manuel Poirier, 1997), 206
'western melodramas', 29
westernness, 4–9, 28–9, 45, 48, 50–2, 66
western's demise, predictions of, 163–4
Wiezamsky, Anne, 195
Williams, Linda, 36n
Winchester '73 (Anthony Mann, 1950), 84–5, 205
Winnetou films, West German, 108, 166
Wollen, Peter, 189, 198
Wrecked in Mid-air (French title unknown; possibly Gaston Roudès, 1913), 56, 61n
Wright, Will, 35n
  Sixguns and Society: A Structural Study of the Western, 15, 47

'Zapata-Spaghettis', 171
Zaretsky, Robert, 68, 70, 78n
'zero degree', 182, 188–9, 199, 202–3n

EU representative:
Easy Access System Europe
Mustamäe tee 50, 10621 Tallinn, Estonia
Gpsr.requests@easproject.com

www.ingramcontent.com/pod-product-compliance
Lightning Source LLC
Chambersburg PA
CBHW051120160426
43195CB00014B/2277